Dangerous and Severe – Process, Programme and Person

Community, Culture and Change
(formely Therapeutic Communities)

Series editors: Rex Haigh and Jan Lees

Community, Culture and Change encompasses a wide range of ideas and theoretical models related to communities and cultures as a whole, embracing key Therapeutic Community concepts such as collective responsibility, citizenship and empowerment, as well as multidisciplinary ways of working and the social origins of distress. The ways in which our social and therapeutic worlds are changing is illustrated by the innovative and creative work described in these books.

other books in the series

A Life Well Lived
Maxwell Jones – A Memoir
Therapeutic Communities 11
Dennie Briggs
ISBN 1 84310 740 6

Thinking About Institutions
Milieux and Madness
Therapeutic Communities 8
R.D. Hinshelwood
Foreword by Nick Manning
ISBN 1 85302 954 8

Beyond Madness
Psychosocial Interventions in Psychosis
Therapeutic Communities 7
Edited by Joseph H. Berke, Margaret Fagan, George Mak-Pearce and Stella Pierides-Müller
Foreword by Robert D. Hinshelwood
Epilogue by Brian Martindale
ISBN 1 85302 889 4

Therapeutic Communities
Past, Present and Future
Therapeutic Communities 2
Edited by Penelope Campling and Rex Haigh
Foreword by John Cox
ISBN 1 85302 614 X

Introduction to Therapeutic Communities
Therapeutic Communities 1
David Kennard
ISBN 1 85302 603 4

Dangerous and Severe – Process, Programme and Person

Grendon's Work

Mark Morris

Community, Culture and Change 15

Jessica Kingsley Publishers
London and Philadelphia

The right of Mark Morris to be identified as author of this work has been asserted by him in accordance with the Copyright, Designs and Patents Act 1988.

First published in 2004
by Jessica Kingsley Publishers
116 Pentonville Road
London N1 9JB, UK
and
400 Market Street, Suite 400
Philadelhpia, PA 19106, USA
www.jkp.com

Copyright © Mark Morris 2004

Library of Congress Cataloging in Publication Data
Morris, Mark.
Dangerous and severe : process, programme, and person : Grendon's work / Mark Morris.
p. cm. -- (Community, culture, and change ; 15)
Includes bibliographical references and index.
ISBN 1-84310-226-9 (pbk.)
1. HM Prison Grendon. 2. Mentally ill prisoners--Rehabilitation--Great Britain. 3. Prisoners--Mental health services--Great Britain. 4. Dangerously mentally ill--Treatment--Great Britain. 5. Antisocial personality disorders--Treatment--Great Britain. 6. Psychopaths--Rehabilitation--Great Britain. I. Title. II. Series.
HV8742.G72G74 2004
365'.46'094259--dc22

2004010973

British Library Cataloguing in Publication Data
A CIP catalogue record for this book is available from the British Library

ISBN 1 84310 226 9

Printed and Bound in Great Britain by
Athenaeum Press, Gateshead, Tyne and Wear

Contents

Preface

This book has two aims. The first is to describe in an accessible way the work of Grendon Prison, a brave but successful 1960s experiment whose work has been reassessed in the light of the Dangerous and Severe Personality Disorder (DSPD) developments in the UK. The second aim is to examine more implicitly the nature of 'danger and severity' when referring to the sorts of people and issues that are dealt with in an institution like Grendon. The popular conception would be that many Grendon residents are both dangerous and severely personality disordered. Much less popular is the idea that their developmental experiences, society's reaction and the treatment processes offered by Grendon and other programmes may also be 'dangerous and severe'.

Several years ago there was a debate about a book published about Mary Bell, who was convicted of manslaughter for killing two young boys when she herself was but a child (Sereny 1999). To the popular imagination, she is a monster, referred to in the same breath as the Moors Murderers and Jamie Bulger's killers. The unease that this book stirred up was a result of the author telling Ms Bell's own story – a difficult and unpleasant story of an abusive home environment: *Cries Unheard* as the book is entitled. This was uncomfortable because it challenged a stereotype, and on reading it one's attitude to Ms Bell shifted somehow. The stereotype is of an evil woman deserving of punishment, something like a straight-to-video violent psycho movie, where the evil character gets its comeuppance in the end. The fuller Ms Bell story was more like a Greek tragedy – where the problem could be seen to be inexorably unfolding from the moment of Ms Bell's birth. From this perspective, the killings were part of an inevitable continuity of cruelty and hatred of which Ms Bell was the originator only in part.

At the time, in Grendon, we wondered about our own work, and a book that was being written, *Grendon Tales – Stories from a Therapeutic Community* (Smartt 2000). Inspired by the more famous set of tales by Chaucer, it is a collection of stories of the residents in Grendon. Each of these stories is like a mini Mary Bell book. Each is a long, winding tragedy that inexorably leads down into the pit of the enactment of violence or perversion. In each case, the violence is not meaningless, it is all too meaningful – it is all too understandable. It shouts 'if it were you, you may well have done the same'. Maybe if you grew up in a 'dangerous and severe' environment with the same experiences of deprivation and cruelty, you also may have turned out 'dangerous and severe'.

Alongside the dangerousness and severity of some of the convicts, and the dangerousness and severity of their developmental experiences, this book explores society's reaction to these people and issues. Hearing about crime and the suffering of victims, we are not drawn to reflect on our own violence, but rather we rush to exclude and punish or treat those who are responsible. Punishment, exclusion and at times treatment (for example lobotomy in the 1950s) can themselves be a dangerous and severe process. This book describes the treatment in Grendon, which could itself be described as dangerous at times and certainly as severe. The process of therapeutic community and group analytic type work with Grendon men is severe in that it can be traumatising and challenging for residents, and dangerous in that staff and other clients struggle psychologically to bear the accounts that they hear and the realities that they face.

The work in Grendon not only excavates the stories of those who end up in prison serving long sentences. The work in Grendon excavates the human condition. Grendon explores the evil that men do – not just the evil that *these* men do. This is why the Mary Bell book was disturbing – with the full tragic picture, she becomes one of us.

CHAPTER 1

Grendon Prison – An Introduction

Physically, Grendon is an off-the-peg 1960s prison; a big concrete wall sitting incongruously in the Buckinghamshire countryside. Culturally, it represents a bold experiment in prison technology, as well as a brave experiment in the treatment of psychopaths. In the following chapters, I intend to illuminate some different aspects of the work that takes place there, in the hope that some comprehension of the nature of the treatment process can emerge, but also to illustrate some of the dilemmas that are presented by this client group. To put the succeeding chapters in context, this chapter will start with a brief and bald introduction to the prison, its client and staff groups, and its programme. This will be followed by an account of its historical and organisational evolutionary context as a prison. Third, Grendon's position as a provider of a psychological therapy service for psychopathic personality disorder will be raised, followed by positioning Grendon's treatment process as a therapeutic community.

Grendon is a 230-bedded medium security prison (B category). It consists of five relatively autonomous therapeutic community units – known as, and inhabiting, the different prison 'wings'. Each wing community has 40 or so residents, and in addition there is an assessment and preparation unit for 25, run on a modified therapeutic community regime. Residents will spend two to three months on the 'F Wing assessment community'; then, if accepted for treatment, they will be allocated a treatment wing, where they will stay for a minimum of 18 months.

The client group are all volunteers. They have to be in prison, but do not have to be in Grendon undergoing treatment. About half are serving a life sentence, and the remainder have a determinate sentence, with an average length of about eight years. Almost all have been convicted for crimes against the person; about half have killed, about a quarter have committed a primary sex offence or have significant history of this. Half are psychopaths, scoring 25 or above on the Hare Psychopathy Checklist (Hare 1991), a quarter are severely so – scoring 30 or above.

9

The staff group comprises twelve prison officers, two senior prison officers, a prison psychologist, a probation officer and a psychotherapist, who takes the clinical lead. This group covers the main disciplinary bases that mental health teams have, with the prison officers acting as the main day-to-day carers, with a shift rotation, and the psychotherapist acting in the role of psychiatrist. The multidisciplinary team on each wing manages the work of the therapeutic community, both clinical and administrative.

The programme is fairly uniform across the different wings, with the morning sessions devoted to psychotherapy groups and the afternoons to work, education and various staff clinical and management meetings. On two days per week (usually Tuesday and Thursday) there is a large group community meeting, which serves as the democratic core of the programme. To this meeting, all issues and requests of individuals are brought, from requests for room changes, through changes to rehabilitation plans, to changing jobs. The community meeting is chaired by an elected chairman, who is supported by a vice-chair, and a cabinet. Three days per week, the community syndicates into five small, 'slow open' groups, with eight or so men in each, and with a constant facilitator drawn from the staff group. Notionally, the five groups are facilitated by the psychologist, the probation officer, a part-time psychotherapist and two specialist prison officers who have special training and a particular aptitude. These small psychotherapy groups are like group analytic therapy groups in that they are intensive, of fixed (slow open) membership and unstructured. They are unlike group analytic groups in that, in the main, they are not staffed by group analysts, their content is not confidential within the group – it is fed back into a larger community – and the members live together and are not strangers otherwise. The community psychotherapist facilitates the large group/community meeting, and supervises the small group work.

There is an emphasis on porosity of information, with an expectation that secrets will be disclosed as far as possible. After each small group, the main content is fed back to the community, and this is followed by a staff group meeting where the content of the small groups is discussed. The centrality of these 'feedback' structures is illustrated by the daily staff meetings and the staff meetings after community meetings, in addition to sensitivity meetings and a programme of reviews and assessments of prisoners in treatment.

There is an expectation that people will spend at least 18 months in treatment as there is an evidence base that shorter treatments are less effective, and this determines to some extent the population, in that prisoners are long-termers. The end point of treatment is something to be discussed in the therapeutic process rather than being fixed and defined. The starting point is more structured, with a two- or three-month stay in as assessment unit, which serves to introduce people to both the therapeutic culture and process.

Grendon's origins

Grendon Prison opened its doors to its first residents in September 1962. It had been two years since the laying of the foundation stone in 1960 by Rab Butler, but the confluence of ideologies and priorities that led to the bold commissioning and building of an 'experimental prison' had been developing in the two decades previously. The first and perhaps most direct of these antecedents was the problem of psychopaths in prisons. A Home Office report commissioned between the wars explored this phenomenon and concluded, 'We believe that the most satisfactory way of dealing with abnormal and unusual types of criminal would be by the creation of a penal institution of a special kind' (East and Hubert 1939). The report struggles clearly to define who these 'abnormal and unusual types of criminal' were, as society has always argued over the classification of those on its fringe. The technical classification of this group changes because, as with all psychiatric diagnoses, it is culturally determined. In time of war, this group may comprise the ruthless but heroic freedom fighters; in Victorian nosology, they were genetic and moral degenerates. In the last few decades they have been the antisocial, dissocial personalities or psychopaths.

In the 1950s there was much thought about 'abnormal and unusual' people in general. The development of the 1959 Mental Health Act threw up the difficulties of clearly diagnosing insanity and putting together a fair, safe and legally coherent structure to detain mentally ill people for psychiatric treatment. The development of this legislation was the second influential factor in the establishing of Grendon. Pinel (cited in Foucault 1965) characterises psychopaths as having 'manie sans délire' – i.e. they are mad without being insane. The experience of having a perfectly normal chat with a perfectly sane man about football who has in the past held captive and tortured is common to those working in the criminal justice field. Yet, although he appeared sane, the man's behaviour was, in all normal understandings of the word, 'mad', hence 'manie sans délire' – madness without psychosis. In a less dramatic way, this sort of experience extends to all those who we would now say had a 'personality disorder': those whose behaviour is clearly crazy, but who are not technically insane.

In the 1980s, as HIV began to spread amongst intravenous drug users, normally sedate and quiet infectious diseases wards began to fill up with heroin addicts. As a trainee psychiatrist, I would frequently be called to a patient in the ward who somehow was managing to create havoc. The patient would do this with emotional outbursts and manipulation, having rowdy and disruptive visitors; by setting staff against each other and by being impossible to reason with and manage. Eventually realisation would dawn on the ward staff that the chaos that surrounded this individual must have something to do with that particular patient, rather than there being a jinx in the ward, and the psychiatrist was called. The psychiatrist would acknowledge the difficulties but confirm that there is 'no evidence of mental disorder'. Technically this is correct, in that there is no treatable mental disorder – the person is neither demented nor suffering from schizophrenia or manic depression. If he or she has a personality disorder, this is simply how she or he is as a person. If she or he has a personality disorder there is not much that can be done about it by using conventional psychiatric treatments such as anti-depressants, anti-psychotics or electro-convulsive treatment. So the diagnostic group 'personality disorder' becomes associated with disturbed and difficult people whose problems are somehow a structural part of their make-up rather than secondary to another psychiatric illness. It is from this group that the 'abnormal and unusual types of criminal' are drawn. This debate about the nature of madness was the second element that contributed to the development of an 'experimental prison'.

The third element contributing to the atmosphere out of which Grendon grew was the development of psychological approaches to mental health problems in general, and the enthusiasm for residential psychological therapies in particular. In Britain, the influence of Freud had been in large part adopted by medical practitioners, and in turn had influenced the practice of psychiatry. In the war years, with large numbers of troops with shell-shock to treat, psychoanalytically orientated psychiatrists had been drafted in to the army medical corps to contribute. Bion's seminal work *Experiences in Groups* describes a rather short-lived, but highly influential six-week period in Northfield Hospital (Bion 1961), where he transformed the dependant sick role culture of one large Nightingale ward. By democratising the regime and utilising the group dynamic, the soldiers, who were healthy apart from their psychological symptoms, were enabled to take responsibility for aspects of the running of the ward: keeping it clean and so on. Furthermore, they were able to engage with issues of their management and regime, as well as to contribute significantly to the therapeutic progress of their peers. Sadly, the robust, verging on the anarchic, culture that is created in such environments ran counter to the tradition of army discipline and the unit was closed down after only six weeks; but in Birmingham, in Springfield Hospital, a similar and more long-lived experiment was taking place. In Springfield, several psychiatrists with similar views were replicating the Northfield ward environments with the same aim. As a professional peer group, Foulkes, Maxwell Jones and their colleagues had the opportunity to debate the development of the technology as it unfolded (Harrison 1999). Not only was the concept of the therapeutic community being born, but it was being weaned on a psychopathology that was particularly susceptible to its effects, namely, a psychological trauma state (combat neurosis) that could be totally debilitating and mimic psychosis, but which could be resolved by the process of grieving, talking and coming to terms with the traumatic experiences of the battlefield. Discussion, reality confrontation, working through in the company of peers are the stuff of therapeutic communities, and with this patient group they were seen to be effective.

So the third element that may have contributed to the development of Grendon was the experience of an effective treatment for severely psychologically disturbed people. There is a current view that this hope that therapeutic communities could effectively treat psychopathic personality was over-optimistic, and this will be explored in more detail below. However, it is true that the two pathologies, psychopathy and combat neurosis – or PTSD (post-traumatic stress disorder) as it would now be known – are very different. PTSD in soldiers exposed to combat is a psychological effect of extreme stress on a normal personality. A fundamentally sound psychological self buckles under the pressure of unimaginable experiences. Psychopathy, on the other hand, is where the structure of the personality itself is the problem. This, of course, can be debated, in particular because of the extent to which it becomes clear that many of the men in Grendon have childhood experiences resembling those of a war zone; but the fact remains that the 1950s and 1960s were a period when the new psychological therapies were very strong and influential in psychiatry and in medicine. In psychiatry, in the United States, there were brave programmes of treating chronic psychotic schizophrenics with psychoanalysis; and the science of psychosomatics, i.e. the interpretation of psychological conflicts as the root cause of physical disease, developed apace. It was not until effective physical treatments for psychosis, asthma and so on had been developed in the 1960s that doctors could step back from the psychologisation of these diseases. The crucial mistake that was made in the 1950s was to confuse understanding with treatment. Using psychoanalytic techniques, it is possible to understand in some detail the inner life of a schizophrenic or asthmatic person; it remains an open question whether this understanding is therapeutic and helpful. Sadly, as effective treatments have developed, the importance of understanding patients has waned, but suffice to say that Grendon was born in the wave of optimism in the 1950s for the effectiveness of exploratory psychological treatments.

Grendon as a prison

In the therapeutic community literature, Manning (1989) has distinguished two phases or functions in the historical development of individual communities: the phase of the charismatic leader and the subsequent phase of routinisation of practice. In the first phase, because the culture of a therapeutic community is so antithetical to more standard, hierarchical organisational mores, the ability to argue for, carve out, and then to maintain the differentiated area of the therapeutic community requires a strong central leadership, with a clear vision and a potent focus and drive to achieve it. This charismatic leader acts as an umbrella or an exoskeleton for the fledgling community to allow it time to establish itself, time to establish a sense of identity and an internal coherence and solidity. In time these aspects are able to act as an endoskeleton, preserving integrity and internal strength when things get tough. Gradually, the internal processes of the community form a fairly tight bureaucracy that acts as a stabilising influence. By this time, the community requires something different from its leader. It requires not a charismatic visionary who will trample over routines and established process in pursuit of his or her vision but a bureaucrat who, sensitive to the culture and established political structures, will be able to maximise the potential and productivity of the community as it has developed. In Grendon, these two ages of 'charisma and routinisation' have been characterised by changes in the structure of the leadership. For its first two decades, Grendon was led by a physician superintendent – a prison service senior doctor who, as I shall argue, provided a charismatic exoskeletal presence to allow the community to develop. Subsequently, the executive leadership has passed to a prison governor, to facilitate the established bureaucracy internally and to oil the cogs of Grendon's presence within its larger organisational setting, the Prison Service.

At the time of writing, concern has been expressed by the Chief Inspector of Prisons at the variable quality of medicine practised in prison settings, and the independent prison medical service is effectively being dismantled and subsumed into the Department of Health and the National Health Service (NHS). It is interesting to reflect, however, that the British Prison Service Department of Healthcare has a longer history than the NHS as a public provider of medical services, having been established as a result of the Prisons Act of 1853. The Prisons Act is the legal frame on which the Prison Service is built, and it clearly states that it is a requirement to have a vicar and a doctor attached. While it is interesting to speculate that this requirement echoes the long debate about the origin of criminal behaviour as a moral activity requiring absolution and redemption or as a medical phenomenon, the practical upshot of this was the development of a charismatic and politically vocal lobby within each prison who centred round the doctor and the health care service.

Arguably, the presence of a doctor in each prison maintained a tension between the rights and interests of prisoners considered as individuals and their incarceration by the State, deprived of civil liberties. Anecdotally, prisoners seem to trust their solicitor first as the person with their interests at heart, and their medical officer second – which illustrates this human rights function. Indeed, this important protective function of health care in prison settings is structured in by the 'statutory duties' of the prison doctor. Before prisoners can be transferred, before they can be questioned about misdemeanours, before they can be secluded and after they have been physically restrained, they have to be seen by a doctor. While arguments can be made that this merely reflects best practice in a residential institution, it is also true that the doctor functions as an insurance against an abuse of power. The reason why such systems of checks and balances in prison settings are necessary is much more complicated than the simple idea that vulnerable prisoners are at risk at the hands of prison staff in power over them. Fundamentally, the central pathology of prisoners which leads them to offend is their own abuse of power over their victims: a dynamic that they subsequently bring into the prison setting, for example, when they make unfounded allegations of brutality. The significant point is that one of the roles of the prison doctor is that of neutral broker between two powerful groups, and he or she also acts as a humanitarian resistance to the abusive potential of both sides in a setting where resistance is seen as a dangerous challenge to security. A good prison doctor needs to be a strong, dedicated humanitarian warrior in a potentially adverse organisational culture contributed to by both sides.

For the first two or three decades of Grendon's existence, it was led by such figures. What they lacked in formal psychotherapeutic or even psychiatric qualifications, they made up for with prison political *savoir-faire*, and a strength and toughness born of prison medical practice. Grendon was a hospital in the prison service. In the same way as a prison doctor's health care centre, like a small community hospital, was his or her own domain, Grendon was the domain of the physician superintendent, conforming to the vision of its powerful and charismatic medical leader and resistant to external and internal deviating forces. With this doughty exoskeleton Grendon was able to develop and establish its own culture and mores. Grendon developed the 'Grendon Way'.

Over these first two decades, there were other factors that enabled Grendon to develop its practice relatively unhindered. One factor was that Grendon was somewhat idealised as the jewel in the crown of the British Prison Service. It achieved this in several ways, themes which will recur through the book. First, it provided a model of a different way of imprisoning people, and this appealed to the penal establishment. Like the development of the panopticon (the system of prison design where, by structuring buildings as radial arms from a central hub, the prison staff maximise their ability to see what is going on), Grendon's practice of facilitating the prison culture so that prisoners were instrumental in the maintenance of good order and discipline seemed revolutionary. The Grendon model of imprisonment was more humane for both prisoners and staff and was an inspiration to those in the field. Second, the culture in Grendon was pro-social and anti-criminal. The structure and focus of the work was to understand why people offended as a way of reducing their criminality. In this way, it was seen as an innovative re-habilitative package to tackle recidivism at a time where rehabilitative activity in penal policy was not the main aim. Third, it was seen as a therapeutic programme – i.e. one in which the prisoners were receiving a medico-psycho-logical treatment, and it was protected by the sort of hushed halo that can surround medical treatments carried out under 'doctor's orders'. As such, it was a unique institution to be supported and praised by a structure which wished that more of its prisons could be rehabilitative and more decent places for staff and prisoners to live and work.

The second factor that enabled Grendon to evolve its practice unhindered was the culture of management of the British Prison Service at the time. Recently, there has been some debate about whether it is legitimate for trainee prison officers to learn to march as part of their basic training. While in a modern prison the militaristic elements of prison culture may be diluted, historically this is an important cultural strand, partly derived from heavy recruitment from ex-forces in years gone by and partly by virtue of the operational necessity of a tight and clear command structure in times of crisis. At an extreme, the staff of a prison can be characterised as an army of occupation inside the prison wall, where there is a clear anti-hegemonic majority who plan and execute acts of resistance. More modern prison practice emphasises that which wise prison officers have known all along, that engagement and negotiation is more effective. A better metaphor, therefore, might be that of a UN peacekeeping force with clear rules of engagement, trying to maintain peace and order in a potentially extremely volatile environment. A more gentle metaphor still is that of the ship's company. The quasi-militaristic ethos that pertains on a seagoing vessel, with the captain and a structure of ranks below, is usually a purely bureaucratic[1] hierarchy until a time of crisis when orders may be given and will need to be obeyed. The structure of ranks of authority have functional significance in everyday life, but in times of crisis they revert to chains of command. The prison governor is like the captain, someone who has absolute authority who, one hopes, rarely has to use it, but who retains that absolute and relatively independent leadership role. The significance of the governor as the captain of a ship is that in the 1970s, the structure of prison management was to allow a relatively high level of self-governance on each vessel; only intervening when there were significant ship-to-shore communications of distress. In such waters, Grendon was allowed to follow its own idiosyncratic course, along with other prisons which were also more or less idiosyncratic in their outlook or approach.

This rather isolated ability of Grendon to chart its own course continued through the years of the 'collapse of the rehabilitative ideal' initiated by Martinson with his influential article arguing that 'Nothing Works' for recidivist criminals (Martinson 1974). This was a period when there was a large-scale dismantlement of rehabilitative activities in prisons because of a view that these activities did not have any effect in terms of reducing the rate at which offenders returned to their old ways following release. Grendon escaped this in part because it was a prison rather than a psychological programme within a prison, in part because of the isolationist managerial culture mentioned above and in part because the stuff of Grendon is about a culture of custody – about a way of being a prison officer or a prison governor (albeit, somewhat idealised), rather than a specialist import.

By the late 1980s, following the evolution of management in the health service, where the omnipotence of the physician superintendent was being deconstructed to make way for professional hospital managers, the medical leadership of Grendon passed over to a prison governor. Now that it was well established as a therapeutic community, this might have been seen as part of the move from charismatic leadership to a more routine bureaucratic one and, arguably, brought Grendon as an organisation more safely into the remit of being a prison along with many others. However, there were other changes developing that brought forward a different set of environmental constraints and dynamics. As part of the general growth of managerialism in the public

---

1   I am using the term in its political sense, meaning rule by the office or officials (Weber 1946).

sector in the 1990s (influenced in particular by the 'Total Quality Management' movement), quality of performance of a prison establishment was identified as a function of performance against centrally determined targets. These targets, in large part, were relatively common-sense things that one would hope that a prison would do, expressed as a number. For example, one might expect that a well-performing prison might have no (i.e. zero) escapes. The difficulty with this reasonable approach in a command structure organisation like a prison is that the targets become concrete. The function of a prison changes from 'trying to be a good prison', which can be demonstrated by measuring performance against these performance indicators, to its being to 'score highly on the performance indicators'.

At the same time, the 'What Works' approach to psychological interventions was gathering pace. In brief this approach involved four elements. The first was to carry out meta-analysis of the outcome studies that were available in the literature for cognitively orientated psychological treatment/rehabilitation programmes for offenders, and to demonstrate that which practitioners (and indeed Martinson himself) had known all along, namely that treatment *is* effective. The second element was to set up a split between those rehabilitative programmes that were effective and those that were not – identifying specifically more psychodynamic treatments as those less effective (McGuire and Priestley 1995). Third, the difference between effective programmes that were 'What Works' and others was characterised in terms of a rational and evidence-based model of the treatment and a rigorous system of quality control to ensure consistency of programme delivery. A distinction was made between bad programmes that were not rigorously controlled, whose aim and style of delivery drifted, and good programmes that were delivered in an identical manner. The manual was to be followed to the letter in the sessions by the facilitator, not interpreted or used as a starting point. It is interesting to note in passing how antithetical this is to a clinical approach where there is a notion of different individuals requiring tailored treatments flexible enough to change as they do. To some extent this difference is symptomatic of two alternative approaches to the profession and practice of psychology: on the one hand that which is empirically based and, on the other, one that which is rooted in more clinical traditions. Finally, in the British version at least, there was designed an equally rigorous managerial structure to ensure adequate resourcing.

The success and influence of this 'What Works' ideology cannot be over-emphasised; suffice to say that it has become a policy watchword being applied to everything from health care to transport. Its combination of applying centralist managerial performance target determination and setting with the mantra of a clear and unequivocal evidence base clearly captures a societal zeitgeist.

In the early 1990s it was clear that Grendon needed to establish its own evidence base to maintain its position. In the following decade a number of outcome studies were mounted, starting with Cullen (1994) who clarified that, whereas the earlier outcome study of Gunn and Robertson (1982) had been unable to establish a treatment using reconviction rate as a measure of treatment, if one distinguished those who stayed more than 18 months as treatment completers, then there was a reconviction effect for those who completed treatment. This finding was replicated by Marshall (1997) using a larger cohort, and the reception to this evidence that 'Grendon works' was such that Grendon lost its 'experimental prison' status.

This account of the change of the managerial environmental culture and the development of 'What Works' provides the backdrop to Grendon's history over the past decade. The firming up and centralisation of Prison Service management along with the leadership of a governor has undermined Grendon's ability to carry on its work in the penumbra of both the prison and health services. Grendon has had to take its place as a prison and have its performance measured and audited as a prison, to be compared with other prisons without a therapeutic task. Second, Grendon's therapy activity has had to establish a legitimate niche for itself within the current criminal justice rehabilitative structures, where 'What Works' is the lingua franca. So for the past decade, the story of Grendon has been about legitimising and mainstreaming its work via a process of accreditation of the treatment process by the committee set up to ensure the evidence base and consistency of programme delivery of the 'What Works' cognitive programmes. The difficulties of this project are explored in more detail below, but in summary one can argue that the 'What Works' ideology is built on the rejection of a more professionally autonomous case-working or clinical approach because this cannot ensure programme integrity and consistency of delivery. Some see the therapeutic community as the apogee of this pragmatic clinical case-work approach, where chaos and confusion are tolerated and flexibility is an essential aspect in order to allow the naturally chaotic and hidden parts of the client's personality to emerge. Grendon is about debate, and this particular one continues to be fascinating.

Prison and personality disorder

Much of the task of management in Grendon is about the strategy of steering a clinical service within a custodial environment: a clinical service with needs, values and assumptions that are not part of the lexicon of senior prison managers. However, even though Grendon is paradoxical in its prison service setting, in that it provides a clinical service, there is a way of construing the prison service's task as a clinical one in the treatment of antisocial personality disorder. Prior to exploring the relevance of personality disorder in the criminal justice frame, it is worth alighting on the whole issue of personality disorder itself.

The diagnosis and classification of personality disorders have been somewhat controversial among psychiatrists, with many arguing that the term is pejorative, stereotyped or simply unhelpful. There have always been ways to identify 'difficult people' using various forms of shorthand; for example, some talk of 'heart sink patients', or 'chronic neurotics'. This ambivalence is nicely illustrated by the title of a recent Department of Health strategy document entitled *Personality Disorder: No Longer a Diagnosis of Exclusion* (2003).

One way of conceptualising the group is to suggest that in medical practice there are three realms wherein pathology can be manifest. For the physically ill, the disease is manifested in the body – for example, an abscess, which is clearly a sore red lump present on or in the body of the patient. The second arena of pathology is that of the mind of the patient. The mentally ill patient gives an account of hallucinating a voice or of the experience of depression that is not present in external space, and so has a disorder of mind. Those with a personality disorder, on the other hand, locate their pathology in a third space. Their pathology is to be found in the relationship between two people. The personality disordered person may feel OK herself, but may make the doctor feel helpless – hence the 'heart sink' epithet; the borderline patient may be quite happy to cut his skin as a form of emotional release, but this may disturb his family or carers; the antisocial person may be easy with the trade of house burgling, but the victims are made to feel bad.

The lack of clarity about the nature of personality disorders is illustrated by the classificatory difficulties that there have been with the group. For example, it seemed odd that there was considerable similarity between obsessional neurosis – defined as a neurotic illness – and obsessional personality disorder – a personality disorder. When all was said and done, the difference seemed to be that a neurosis would get better, and therefore be a temporary phenomenon, and a personality disorder would not, being a structure of the person's psyche. A major step forward was taken by the American Psychiatric Association in DSM-IV (1994) with the model of different axes or dimensions. In this model, a person can have depression or psychosis or a panic disorder (panic attacks) in the setting of a particular personality disorder. The two different diagnoses exist side by side, rather than as either/or. While good, this model is still not the whole story; diagnostically there is supposed to be a clear difference between a personality disorder and a psychosis, but the problem is that a person with a paranoid personality will usually break down to have a paranoid psychosis. Also, the mainly antisocial or psychopathic personalities that end up with long prison sentences, and therefore in Grendon, are disturbed to a greater degree at some times and a lesser degree at others; this can be clearly observed. As for people suffering a classic neurotic illness, these people often experience a life event that can be identified as then leading to a period of more violent or risky behaviour that will wane in time. Personality disorder may not ever get better, but there are times when it gets worse.

A medical model of offending conceptualises the destructive behaviour as symptomatic of a personality disorder, which is defined in terms of the usual diagnostic parameters of ingrained patterns of behaviour causing harm to self or others, present since adolescence and so on (DSM-IV). As with other medical conditions, the personality disorder is the result of a particular combination of constitutional and environmental factors. Taking the argument to its extreme then, as with other medical conditions, the symptoms of the personality disorder are morally neutral. To say the personality disordered person is responsible for a particular symptom or piece of behaviour is as absurd as saying that a diabetic is responsible for his or her hypoglycaemic coma. As with other medical conditions, there will be a research effort to try to identify the pathology underlying the disorder, which will be linked to therapeutic work to alleviate it. This is an absurdly reductionistic conclusion, but one that underlies to some degree a therapeutic approach to this group. The pure medical model of offending as a symptom of a personality disorder absolves the perpetrator of a crime from moral responsibility. While this perspective may not be particularly helpful from a public policy perspective, and may not satisfy the moral philosophers, the provision of treatment to this group requires some similar sort of view. Faced with an individual who has committed a crime that is particularly difficult to bear hearing about, staff members need to have a way that enables them to approach that individual with some sympathy. A deterministic and medical model of crime as a symptom of antisocial personality disorder goes some way towards this. The question of 'Why did you kill your child, what a terrible, unforgivable thing to do' moves to 'Why did you kill your child: was it because you were nearly killed repeatedly as a child, or did you feel your child killed your marriage, or did being unable to meet your child's needs so it carried on crying threaten your own identity so it felt as if it were a choice of your child or you?' The moral perspective leads to a foreclosure of exploration that is limited to 'You killed your child because you are a terrible person'. A medical model allows a space in which explanation and understanding can grow, develop and emerge, which in the long run will have a more potent effect on future behaviour.

Having briefly explored the nature of personality disorders as a pathology requiring a clinical treatment, and in the process of positioning Grendon as a treatment unit for this personality disordered group, we now face the question: Why is this treatment facility placed in a prison? Until the publication of the Office of National Statistics study (1998) which showed that 70 per cent of sentenced prisoners had one or more personality disorders, the term 'personality disorder' was simply not part of the prison industry lexicon. In a prison environment, the management of inmates is understood in terms of security and intelligence, risk assessment and constructive regimes. Yet the core business of a prison service is managing and containing people with dangerous personality disorders; the core skills of those working on the landings is the management and containment of those with dangerous personality disorders; the core occupational strains of prison work derive from the task of working with those with dangerous personality disorders 'in your face all the time'. Things that go wrong can be understood as the occupational hazards of working with a personality disordered population.

By default, prison regimes, including Grendon's, address aspects of personality disorder, although not conceiving the activity as such. While in Grendon it is clear that the organisation can be conceived both as a prison and also as a clinical service, this is also true of other prison settings. One of the curiosities of prison culture is the way the men pay such attention to their physical health, their dental health, the health of their skin and scalp and so on. Health workers outside prison settings complain of the difficulties of bringing young men to services – young men visit their doctors and dentists rarely. This is reversed in prison settings, where use of these services rockets. Prisoners become connoisseurs of which hair preparation is most effective for reducing skin flakes, which skin moisturiser is best for dry sensitive skin and so on.

There are several reasons for this shift in attitude to health services, the main one being pure boredom. In a monotonous existence, a visit to the health care centre is a change from the routine, and may mean a rare and valuable visit to an outside hospital for a check-up. It may also mean a prescription of something that can be traded and sold to fellow prisoners. In a deprived environment like prison, everything out of the ordinary becomes currency, including special soaps and shampoos. This interest of prisoners in their health in prisons contributes to the often hypothesised phenomenon of 'prisoner servicing' – every two or three years a Brixton crack dealer gets a two- or three-year sentence. During the time inside, he detoxifies from his addiction, is regularly fed a balanced diet, gets regular sleep and passes his time visiting a health care centre, receiving a full dental and health check-up and working out in the gym. He is released 18 months later, very much fitter and healthier than when he went in. He re-connects with his former lifestyle, becomes re-addicted to cocaine, lives riskily, runs down his health to such a point that he is once again caught, is prosecuted and sentenced and sent to prison where the cycle can re-start.

Some years ago, there was a vogue for personality disordered patients in secure mental health settings detained under the Mental Health Act to argue that they should be released because there was little or no active treatment of their condition in hospital. They complained that they were living in hospital rather than being treated in hospital. The debate turned around the nature of treatment for those with personality disorder and a conclusion emerged that, for this group, treatment included reducing the deterioration of the condition. The secure hospitals might not be carrying out active treatment for these people, but by housing them in a secure environment, they were preventing the condition deteriorating and thereby treating them. It has long been recog-nised that the survival rates for crack cocaine dealers and addicts in prisons is longer than on the street, so prison similarly prevents a deterioration for many of its personality disordered clients.

So, from both these perspectives, prison can be conceived as a treatment for personality disorder, by 'servicing' people during sentenced breaks from a risky and destructive lifestyle, and by taking them off the streets and thereby preventing a deterioration in their condition. But this concept of prison being a treatment for personality disorder can be taken much further, and it can be argued that elements of a prison system or environment are specifically psy-chologically therapeutic for antisocial personality disorder.

Prison as psychotherapy

A number of different aspects of prison life contain psychotherapeutic elements of the different approaches to psychological treatments, behavioural therapeutic aspects, cognitive and depth/psychodynamic approaches. Psychi-atry itself has always sat on the edge of an epistemological chasm in its wavering between psychological examination of the mind and physical treat-ments of the body – or the brain – such as psychotropic medication, elec-tro-convulsive therapy and psychosurgery. In prison, the two sides of the mind/body are contained in specific general physical health care which looks after the body as described above, and in more diffuse but specific beneficial psychotherapeutic aspects. Before illustrating how this is so, the nature of the difference between the complementary approaches to psychotherapy will be touched upon.

One way of conceiving the different types of psychological therapy is to examine the different mental levels at which they operate. At the topmost observable level is behavioural psychotherapy. A Skinnerian behavioural approach argued from a highly empiricist perspective that mental contents were purely conjecture, and that there was nothing to be gained by studying them or utilising them therapeutically. All that one could see and measure of mind was its physical manifestation, namely behaviour. Thus, the mind was conceived of as a 'black box' that was unknowable and largely irrelevant (Skinner 1938). This theoretical perspective is what underlies an extreme form of behaviourism, where the psychological problem is conceived as a form of behaviour – for example, spider phobia is a problem of running away from spiders. Therapy might involve presentation of a stimulus (one or more spiders in close proximity) and the prevention of the behaviour of running away. After a while the terror subsides, and the symptom of spider phobia might be successfully treated.

At this level of psychological therapy, psychopathy is treated by preventing the behaviour, thus the first therapeutic element of prison environments. At a behavioural level, the prison wall and physical containment physically limit the opportunities for offending behaviour. Staff and residents have clear roles enshrining clarity about the boundaries of their relationship. Transgressions of prison rules are punished after a hearing by a prison governor, enabling strict enforcement of rules by officers who while on duty are constables of the law.

Pavlov's experiments with dogs demonstrated that rewards for particular stimuli could lead to learning – a bell rung at the time of feeding could lead to the dog salivating at the sound without the food after a while. This finding was extended to a theory of learning which remained relatively true to the original 'black box' ideology. If particular activities are associated with a reward, the performance of these activities will be preferred and will occur more often. How or why this happens is less important than that it does. In a sense the whole criminal justice system can be conceived of as a behaviour modification programme, where psychopaths receive an unpleasant stimulus (punishment/imprisonment) for carrying out a particular piece of behaviour (robbing banks), and in time learn to desist. In passing, it is worth noting that a significant social problem is that psychopaths apparently do not learn to desist according to this model, and indeed a lack of such learning forms part of the syndrome.

The problem with this perspective is that it doesn't take into account the enormous positive stimuli that are involved with robbing the bank – the plea-surable intrigue of plotting and planning; the 'rush' of the robbery itself with the short-lived omnipotent control of the situation with a gun in hand and victims crouching on the floor obeying the robber's every wish, which is enor-mously satisfying and re-lived in fantasy over and over again. Then, if the robbery is successful, there is the high of having a large quantity of money that is often spent in a short space of time.

Nevertheless, the behavioural learning model is very powerful in more normal situations than extreme criminality, and a specific behavioural tech-nique emerged in the 1970s to capitalise on this learning theory in residential settings. In 'token economies', as these regimes were called, good or desirable behaviour was met by the giving of 'tokens' that could be exchanged for some sort of reward. A hierarchy of rewards for different levels of good behaviour was established – the 'token economy' itself. Prison settings have long had quite complex systems for the reward of desirable behaviour, where reliability and trustworthiness as a prisoner would result in being given the better insti-tutional jobs – for example, working in the kitchens. More recently, this has been more specifically structured into an 'incentives and earned privileges' scheme, where rewards can include having money in one's possession, having particular visiting arrangements, being allowed to have a TV in one's cell and so on; all of these comforts have to be earned by the maintenance of reason-able standards of behaviour and are removed if behaviour is poor.

From the behavioural perspective, one significant technique for the changing of behaviour is the provision of a different 'model' – allowing the patient to see a different way of behaving. For example, the spider phobic might watch a therapist sit with spiders crawling all over her. The therapist might model 'not running away' or ways of controlling the spiders if they crawl into places that are not welcome. The patient can then simply imitate the behaviour and learn to behave differently. For psychopaths, the environments in which they have grown up are often themselves psychopathic – unfair, ma-nipulative and exploitative. This experience is usually compounded by the social environments in which they have lived prior to prison, such as gangs and antisocial groups, which are usually similar. In a prison environment there is an attempt to behave fairly and decently so that residents can gain some ex-perience of what fair behaviour looks like, which they can then model. For example, fairness and decency can be modelled by reasonable and decent pro-fessional behaviour by staff and fairness in their dealing with residents' issues.

In prisons the need for those who are in a position of power – namely the staff – to be and to be seen to be fair and accountable for their behaviour and decisions is paramount, and is ensured by a strictly audited and enforced complaints procedure with clear protocols for the investigation of prisoners' complaints, and avenues for appeal if the complainant is unsatisfied.

So, one aspect of treatment for psychopaths in prison is behavioural modification, at its most frank with the prevention of freedom that limits the opportunities for offending behaviour, but also in more subtle ways through behavioural modification and modelling elements. The next therapeutic layer in this topographic model of psychotherapeutic interventions that are present in a prison is cognitive. The cognitive approach lifts the lid on the 'black box', but only to the degree that the mind is conceived of as a rational processor. The spider phobic in cognitive therapy would be challenged to provide a rational explanation about why he was afraid. The reasons that he gave would be tested for their rationality. For example, a fear that spiders might have a poisonous or painful bite could be discounted by rational argument that, at least in temperate climates such as Britain, there are no species of spider that bite or are poisonous. A fear that the spider might attack the individual in some other way, by crawling up to and over the phobic, could be challenged on the basis of first the spider being much more timid than the human and second, the spider being much smaller than the human. The aim of cognitive therapy is to challenge irrational beliefs about the symptom that maintain and exacerbate it, for example, the spider phobic who feels that he was 'constantly seeing spiders' might keep a diary and find that, actually, he only saw one twice a week – itself much more manageable than the fear of 'constantly' seeing them.

Much offending behaviour can be analysed according to this format. The bank robber mistakenly believes that the bank teller will quickly forget the experience of having a gun pointed at her, or that the security guard who was shot will get a big insurance pay-out, so it will be OK; or that the banks fleece their customers, so it is OK to steal from them. These sorts of beliefs are characterised as rationalisations, minimisations or cognitive distortions, and can one by one be challenged. Victim statements by those psychologically disabled by the experience of being robbed or physically disabled by such violent incidents can be brought forward as proof of the contrary to the offender's belief. The reality of bank customers having to make up for increased security spending or financial losses can challenge the offender's position.

Often, the offender's account will differ markedly from the victim's, attributable to the offender's airbrushing out less palatable or acceptable aspects of the event. Simply going through the two sets of recollections, victim's and perpetrator's, side by side, dismantles much of the offender's retrospective obfuscation of the events. One illustration of a cognitive intervention took place in a Grendon group, where a bank robber was clearly quite proud of the haul of twenty thousand pounds that he had made for a morning's work. A fellow bank robber, further into therapy, challenged him about this, clarifying the sum of money and the sentence that he had received when caught, the ten-year sentence received for a twenty-thousand pound haul. Then the fellow bank robber worked out that he had 'earned' two thousand pounds per year. 'That's about a fifth of what a dustman gets paid – well done; good move.' The cognitive distortion was that the offender had made some fast money – the reality was that it was in fact very slow and at considerable personal cost.

A second important element of a cognitive approach to psychological treatment is basically educative: teaching the spider phobic about what anxiety is, about how sweaty palms, a subjective sense of fear and palpitations are normal manifestations of anxiety, not preludes to instant death, for example. The phobic in this example is taught also about the different manifestations of anxiety and about how phobic anxiety focuses on a particular stimulus which is then avoided. In offending behaviour, a significant element is simply impressing on the offender that there is mentation at all, that there is a thought between impulse and action. That, when insulted, the offender's ear is not attached to his fist, and that there are intervening thoughts and decisions and choices are being made between hearing the insult and punching the speaker, and that at any of these 'choice points', an intervention or another thought might prevent the violence. Prison service offending behaviour programmes combine such general educative elements with the sort of challenging of cognitive distortions described above.

This cognitive approach to offending that forms part of the overall treatment package available in prison settings for psychopaths forms the highly successful and influential 'What Works' initiative, and the offending behaviour programme industry that has been built on the raft of legitimacy that it has provided. As mentioned above, these programmes explicitly tailor the combined approaches of challenging cognitive distortions with the educative process of explaining the cognitive models and mechanisms of offending. Although this represents a specifically structured form of cognitive intervention, such efforts have been around for a long period in an informal way, and in the form of local programmes attempting to structure this powerful therapeutic technique.

The third level of psychological treatment that forms part of a prison experience is the psychodynamic, or depth psychotherapy. Taking this perspective, in the example of the spider phobic one is looking for underlying reasons, understandings and meanings for the symptom. Spider phobic people sometimes associate the hairy insect with a frightening childhood sight of parental genitalia; the association might be to a cocooning and entrapping parent or to a frightening experience of 'spider coming to get you' where a child is tickled with a relatively big adult hand, owned by an adult who is not entirely trusted. For each person, the meaning and significance of the symptom will be different, and the task is to explore and begin to unlock this. The idea is that as the meaning emerges, the issue that the symptom represents can be worked through, reducing the need for the symptom. For example, the spider phobic who as a child was frightened of a rather inappropriate game of 'spider is coming to get you' by an abusive adult which would result in intimate tickling would be able to recognise this, and as he came to terms with the abusive experiences, so the irrational fear of spiders would subside.

Like cognitive interventions, there are formal and informal manifestations of this. At an informal level, those prison staff who get to know a prisoner well enough to have some knowledge of his offending and his background will begin to see psychodynamic links and patterns, and suggest these to the prisoner. The insight might be as simple as somebody convicted of robbery to support a heroin addiction talking to the prison doctor or nurse, and it becoming clear that there was an acceleration in the drug addiction when a loved grandparent died. The meaning of the addiction in part might be a way of healing the pain of the bereavement. Drug-taking and 'grafting' (criminal work such as theft to earn money for drugs) may have a crescendo pattern when, during a prisoner's teenage years, parents were fighting or abuse was taking place; this can be explored.

It must be borne in mind that psychodynamic therapeutic hypotheses are merely developments of common-sense psychology, and so are similar to the ideas that occur to each one of us every day about why things happen and why people behave the way they do. In a prison setting, psychopaths who have done particularly horrifying things prompt this sort of speculation in the staff that work with them. For example, a young man who rapes and kills a pensioner quite painfully prompts the question in staff who work with him, 'Why?' People who have survived traumatic experiences often become preoccupied with why the event happened, and this has been called an 'effort after meaning'. It seems that particularly horrific stories of offences are traumatising to the staff group in this same way, prompting hypotheses about 'Why?' Some of these will be fed back to the prisoner, possibly hitting the mark and stimulating further thinking by the offender himself.

A significant part of the court process seems to surround the issue of explaining and understanding why the offence has been committed – either to make it understandable and thus excusable so that the jury and the court are lenient, or in a more neutral way to put the offence in context to help the court in its work of deciding on an appropriate disposal. For example, if a woman stabs a man in his sleep twenty times, including through the eyes, it seems pretty unforgivable. If a common-sense psychological explanation is put forward that this is in a marriage where she is regularly raped and battered, it provides some understanding for the attack.

Often, the series of pre-court reports provided by psychiatrists, social workers or probation officers and so on are the first opportunity that a very disturbed and damaged individual will have had to recite his story to professionals who might make these sorts of links, and it is interesting how often the formulations made at this time remain with the prisoner as meaningful explanations of what has happened to him. Day-to-day interactions with staff and the process of assessment involved during conviction and in the assessments prior to release will all dig for understandings of and meanings for the violence that has brought the person to prison, which can be broadly understood as a psychodynamic input.

The last element of a prison sentence that can be construed specifically as a treatment for personality disorder is the structuring of the sentence in the form of reducing levels of security as the sentence progresses. The different levels of security, from the 'dispersal' maximum security to Category B high secure and on through Category C prisons to the Category D 'open prisons' or resettlement prisons, represent a sequence of rehabilitative stages which prisoners on long sentences gradually follow (Newell 1999). Release is managed nearly always with a period of supervision by the probation service during which the concerns of resettlement can be worked through, increasingly with multi-agency co-operation between police, the probation service and the prisons.

So, arguably, prison is a treatment for psychopathy, both by preventing a deterioration in the condition via further offending or self-destructive behaviour, and by having a 'servicing' function during periods of relative respite from a chaotic and destructive lifestyle. In addition, aspects of the prison environment – behavioural, cognitive, psychodynamic and via structured rehabilitation back into the community – can be conceived as specific treatment elements. Within these non-specific aspects of prison environments, the Grendon experiment represented a more targeted and specialist treatment programme, possibly for those who were not contained or did not respond to the interventions described above.

Grendon among therapeutic communities

Grendon is a specialist service for those with severe (usually antisocial) personality disorders which utilises a therapeutic community 'technology'. The task in this introductory chapter is to put into context the discussion of the various dimensions of Grendon's treatment that follow. So, having described some aspects of the external context by referring to currents in the criminal justice world and aspects of prison culture, it seems appropriate to contextualise the treatment process and the clinical treatment model on which it is based.

The vision of the founders of Grendon was that within the structure of a prison setting, which benefits from the structural integrity and clarity described above, within this prison structure, a more specialised therapeutic unit could be sited: East and Hubert's 1939 vision of a 'psychiatric hospital in a prison'. The hope was that the more structural and behavioural needs of the antisocial personality disordered might be taken care of by the routines and culture of the prison, while at the same time a more treatment-focused approach could be applied – the therapeutic community. It would bring together mind and body – the actions of the body would be managed by the secure setting while therapeutic activity could address the problems of mind that perpetuated the problems that the body perpetrated. It was a brave and a bold vision and one that has been and continues to be successful, although with continuing struggle.

The folk wisdom is that it takes about a year to get to understand what Grendon is all about, and that this is true for both staff and residents. One of the confusions for those new to therapeutic communities is between the chaos and order that is present. A first impression may be of things being completely chaotic, with decision-making and the structure of authority obscure and unclear; with no one person taking a lead or making decisions, and with a cacophony of different and divergent claims and counter-claims. At the same time, the work is highly regimented and structured. In a community meeting, everyone is there at exactly 9 a.m. with no exceptions. The meeting will finish at 10:30, irrespective of the issue or emotion being expressed. The structure of decision-making will be followed bureaucratically, with requests being taken to the small group, then to the large group and so on. This combination of structure and chaos is difficult to describe, but is characteristic of therapeutic communities.

The technology of the therapeutic community can be approached from several different perspectives. Broadly, therapeutic communities are residential environments that utilise the residential aspect for therapeutic gain, and they achieve this by introducing particular structures into the daily routine, namely group and community meetings where residents can discuss the process of living together. In essence they are residential settings where structures are put in place to facilitate communication between the residents in the environment. The classic research work on therapeutic communities in the 1960s was carried out by Rapoport (1960) who, following an observational project in the Henderson Hospital, proposed that the characteristic features of a therapeutic community were a flattened hierarchy of authority, communalism, tolerance of behaviour, and reality confrontation. Taken in turn, it is clear why each of these factors makes an important contribution to the process. The flattened hierarchy promotes a sense of licence, a feeling of freedom that one can challenge structures and say what one thinks without fear of being squashed by someone more senior. The communal element captures the 'living learning' aspect, that, by living together, people will rub, conflicts will develop, but the communal aspect will mean that these difficulties have to be worked with for the good of the community and to enable the community to survive and continue. It also reflects the importance of having an investment in the community, so that each individual has a sense of collective responsibility. Tolerance of behaviour captures the notion that people are in a therapeutic community because of difficult aspects of their behaviour, and that if as soon as they start to display these characteristics they are removed, not much progress can be made. However, this tolerance needs to be followed by reality confrontation, so that while difficult behaviour is tolerated, it is not unnoticed; and, after the event, the individual will be faced with the disapprobation of peers and with the effects that the behaviour has had on the different community members.

For many personality disordered people, the disturbed behaviour – for instance violence or self-harm – is a way out of unbearable psychological suffering. The behaviour evacuates the psychological pain, and both can then be forgotten. A classic example is the person who has suffered abuse for which he or she feels guilty. As the tide of feelings builds up, it can be stopped and forgotten about by self-cutting as either a recapitulation of the damage done by the abuser or self-punishment for perceived collusion with the abusive events. In this situation – unknown to the cutter – other people in the environment feel 'cut' and assaulted by the act of self-harm. In a therapeutic community context this trauma felt by those around the self-cutter can be fed back. If the behaviour is tolerated and subsequently challenged, both the meaning of the self-cutting and the causative trauma will emerge and can be explored.

Therapeutic communities became popular in the UK in the 1970s as part of the anti-psychiatry and anti-institutional movement. A series of writers had focused attention on various issues about institutional living, in particular Goffman (1961), in his book *Asylums*, which proposed a model of a 'total institution'. He described the ritual of admission to these institutions (which included hospitals, prisons and the armed forces) as a process of mortification, where the individuality of the new resident is dismantled by his or her being physically stripped of his or her own clothes, often actually washed, and forced to comply with the institution's set of rules and procedures. This is followed by a process of re-emergence of the person as a member of the institution, in the institution's garb, obeying the institution's rules and even adopting them as their own. The original person would seem to disappear and, instead, a member of the institution would emerge, happy to 'batch live' in the setting. Other writers went on to develop the idea of the damage that could be done to people in such institutions, in particular Barton (1959), who coined the term 'institutionalised' to describe those who are so used to the routine of the institution that they cannot look after themselves when released from it – or, at a more fundamental level, are unable to think or live for themselves out-with the frame that has been provided. This thinking was linked up with the anti-psychiatry movement and with Laing (1959), who argued that schizophrenia was nothing more than a socially induced phenomenon. Gradually, the dreadful 'negative symptoms' of schizophrenia, with apathy and poor self-care, were seen not as being a biological or post-psychotic burn-out state, but rather symptoms of institutionalisation. Using this model, the chronic shuffling masses that filled the mental hospitals were seen as products of the institution themselves. If liberated from the institutional strait-jacket they would be cured of their apathy and self-neglect.

One response to this growing criticism of institutions was to modify the internal culture so that it was challenging and promoting of the exploration of individuality, rather than of uniformity, and these experimental institutions became the therapeutic communities. The original therapeutic communities in this new wave were places like Kingsley Hall (Boyers, Orril and Specials 1972), where an environment was provided that respected and supported the experience of the individuals therein. The psychotic breakdown of one of its residents, Mary Barnes, described in startling detail, was thought to be containable by such a communal social structure but, anecdotally, was possible partly because of the high level of professional expertise that was living in the same environment. Nevertheless, it illustrated the way that a residential environment could hold and allow the disturbance of the individuals in its midst to be explored. By the late 1970s, many hospitals had a small therapeutic community unit which became colonised by local personality-disordered people who used the setting to get some handle on their own chaos.

In the meantime an effective drug that could treat psychosis was stumbled upon, namely, Chorpromazine, and large numbers of people in such asylums became well enough to be looked after in the community. Together, these factors led to the wholesale closing of the asylums, the embracing of community care and the illusion that symptomatic drug treatment and liberation from the asylum would lead to cure. While the development of community care and effective drug treatment of psychosis have undoubtedly improved the lot of people suffering from chronic psychotic illnesses, criminal justice and community workers know that too many now shuffle bewilderedly round prison cells or the streets in which they sleep, rather than being provided with asylum in the benevolent sense, and a hospital place they can go to where they will be looked after and protected. Without large residential treatment settings, the hospital therapeutic communities became unsustainable, and in the 1980s most were closed.

Among the therapeutic communities that had sprung up, two different models could be discerned. By and large, UK therapeutic community culture was heavily influenced by psychodynamic thinking, a legacy of the Bion, Maxwell Jones and Rickman work in the Second World War. This was to be distinguished from the 'concept' or 'hierarchical' therapeutic community movement that emerged in the US, which was similar in that it involved the utilisation of the residential environment structured to facilitate communication, but different in that its underlying ideology was derived from the twelve-step self-help movement. The twelve-step approach had become enormously popular initially in the US, spawning Alcoholics Anonymous, Narcotics Anonymous and the various other symptom clusters that have benefited from this approach, including binge eaters, sex addicts, the partners of alcoholics and so on.

The US twelve-step therapeutic communities have been termed 'hierarchical' or 'concept' therapeutic communities, whereas those based on a more British psychodynamic orientation have been termed 'democratic' therapeutic communities. The difference between the two is at the same time clear and subtle. Both have hierarchies, both are quite clearly concept driven, and both have a democratic element to their functioning. More commonly, addiction-focused therapeutic communities are in the US style, with a synergy between the AA concept of an allergy to the substance of addiction, and a quasi-religious exhortation to abstinence. The hierarchy begins at the point of achieving abstinence, and increasing wisdom is assumed with passing time 'on the wagon'. In contrast to this, the more British, psychodynamically-orientated therapeutic communities are more purely exploratory. There is no overriding symptom shared and owned by the whole group. In a sense, the nature of the individual's problem is not assumed to be alcohol or drugs. The nature of the individual's problem is itself the central dialectic, and the central issue to be explored.

Most crucially, a difference is that the psychodynamic frame has the potential to focus its deconstructive process upon itself. If the central tenet of a community is that abstinence from drugs is required, then this is an irreducible bedrock of ideology. If (as in the psychodynamic therapeutic communities) the central tenet is that things need to be thought about and explored to understand them better, if the central tenet is that one must strive to gain a greater insight – then this ideological bedrock can be used to interrogate itself. Are insight and understanding relevant? Is it an illusion to think that understanding and exploration will be beneficial? It may be this flexibility of the ideological underpinning that makes the UK type of psychodynamic community structure more flexible and 'democratic'.

Within the UK psychodynamic-type therapeutic communities, there are variable currents. On the one hand there is the Cassel Hospital type of approach, where patients receive individual psychotherapy sessions in addition to their therapeutic community groups and structures. The Cassel Hospital model is heavily influenced by psychoanalysts who have trained in the individual modality to such an extent that some would argue the environment is not a therapeutic community, but rather a psychoanalytic hospital along the lines of Chestnut Lodge in the US. A second model is that of the Henderson Hospital, where there is an explicit prevention of individual meetings or sessions; everything has to take place in the group setting, including the process of pre-admission assessment. A third perspective would critique both the Cassel and the Henderson as being over-reliant on the psychodynamic underpinning at the expense of the power of the social dimension. Maxwell Jones in his later years at Dingleton Hospital developed this latter orientation.

In Grendon the flavour is more Henderson than Cassel, with a heavy emphasis on groups and no resource to plough into more intensive individual work. However, some of the splits that emerge in a Cassel type of setting happen in Grendon because, unlike at the Henderson, individual consultations are not forbidden and indeed staff have to interview prisoners individually quite regularly to complete reports for the various statutory review and risk assessment processes that are taking place. Arguably, in Grendon, there has been a move from a more Dingleton-type social emphasis therapeutic community to a more group analytic orientation because of the importing of group analysts over the past decade, although since the staff group is largely analytically unqualified it probably retains a more social dimension.

One interesting debate is about the extent to which Grendon and the other prison therapeutic communities are democratic or more concept/hierarchical in nature. As Grendon has increasingly placed itself in the 'What Works' frame, arguing that it is an effective offending behaviour programme, the central concept of offending being bad – of one's having to become abstinent from breaking the law – seems to grow. The 'buzz' of the offence – the preparation, the exhibition of contempt for the victim, the excitement of the risk of apprehension and the pleasure from the haul or the act are all powerful stimulants, and an addiction model of understanding offending is never far below the surface at Grendon. Likewise, the hollowness of the recidivist resident's reassurance to staff that he has decided to make 'no more victims' mirrors the heroin addict's initial empty renunciation of opiates. With the focus of work in Grendon on reducing re-offending, an addiction/abstinence model becomes more powerful. If abstinence from offending becomes the goal, does a more concept/hierarchical/twelve-step flavour creep in to the therapeutic communities practice and discourse at Grendon?

Traditionally, clinical practice with offenders argues that if you treat the condition from which the offending derives – be it schizophrenia or a personality disorder – then the offending will reduce, that the aim is to treat the underlying cause rather than the symptom and that the underlying cause is a chaotic personality, its history and its way of being in the world. There is a concern that if Grendon residents spend their time trying not to offend, they will waste the opportunity to explore their personality, experiences and difficulties, and the Grendon treatment will be less effective overall. These are large and current issues debated in both staff and resident groups.

From a psychodynamic perspective, there are pitfalls in the individual treatment of psychopaths, one being the ease of the therapist being duped and conned, another, the difficulty that the therapist might easily be overwhelmed by the transference/counter-transference dynamics. For example, the therapist might realise that the patient's core object relation is concretely murderous in a treatment setting where the therapist attracts that object relation, or that the last person that a lifer felt passionate about, he killed – and he is passionately angry about an interpretation made by the therapist.

As a technique, the application of a psychodynamic treatment for psychopaths works better in a group setting, where there will be a flux of relational dynamics at any one time. While there might be one psychopath feeling murderous towards the therapist, it is likely that there will be at least three or four who are not, and who would physically protect the therapist in the event of a physical attack. In a group there is the added advantage of the members being other psychopaths; adroit at the duplicities that a psychopath might practise, they can challenge these as they are trotted out by other members. The problem, however, is that an hour per week or so can easily be forgotten or, more likely, the psychopaths can learn to 'talk the talk' but, at the end of the group, simply return to their normal ways. This is where notion of the living in therapeutic unit becomes pertinent. By establishing a whole residential culture with a therapeutic exploratory ethos, the effectiveness of the treatment is potentiated. It becomes a culture that is lived, rather than a group that is attended. It is more difficult to split off alternative ways of functioning if one is immersed in a therapeutic environment rather than visiting it. There is an argument, therefore, that this sort of therapeutic set-up is the most effective way of delivering a psychodynamic treatment to a severely personality disordered population. It is more effective because it increases the intensity and dose of the treatment. With the deeply ingrained maladaptive patterns that comprise this group's personality disorder, high intensity, high dose treatment is required.

In addition to looking at the nature of the therapeutic community technology from the perspectives of the underpinning ideology of mind, a therapeutic community can be conceived of as a small organisation, and therefore in terms of the management literature. Therapeutic communities seem to fit quite closely with a type of organisational structure loosely referred to as a 'learning organisation' (Dale 1994). In brief, the learning organisation is perceived as a way of unlocking the full potential of a staff group; the rather evangelical management literature rhetoric suggests that the cleaner might be able to tell the chief executive a thing or two about how to run the company or, more practically, about how to save money on cleaning products. It argues that in many organisations a hierarchical and closed communication culture prevents the cleaner from being heard, even if he or she has some great ideas. If this communicative constipation extends up and down the organisation, it is clear that the total staff resource becomes vastly under-utilised. The antidote to this situation is, as in the therapeutic community described by Rapoport to flatten the hierarchy of authority, to increase a sense of shared ownership of the task (like Rapoport's communalism), to find ways of facilitating communication – via suggestion boxes or larger meetings and consultations. Facilitating this communication will encourage a debate initially about operational details, but it may move on to discussing the organisation's functioning, vision and higher order issues, allowing the practice of managers to be challenged healthily.

The 'learning organisation' model of a therapeutic community sheds some light on a particularly puzzling issue that pervades Grendon as well as other settings, namely that it is questionable as to what extent the staff group is instrumental in helping the residents. Anecdotally, the most helpful things ex-therapeutic community residents have taken from their experience is an insight or a challenge or a shoulder to cry on from another resident, not the intervention of a member of staff. In Grendon, some career bank robber has gone through his whole life with nice middle-class people exhorting him to behave better. Teachers, probation officers, lawyers, judges and psychiatrists and then, in Grendon, psychotherapists have all had a go, and the advice will have been ignored. The person who might make him stop and think in Grendon will not be yet another middle-class person, it will be a fellow bank robber. Likewise, in a therapeutic community, when one borderline self-cutter has caused a community commotion by cutting her wrists with lots of blood, calm professionals saying that this is not a good idea is water off a duck's back. It takes the ferocity of a fellow borderline patient, disturbed by the incident, aggressively challenging the cutter's complacency to get the message through. The learning organisation captures this phenomenon by drawing a difference between standard residential settings, such as hospital wards or prison wings, and a therapeutic community. The difference is that in the latter, the therapeutic abilities of the client group are utilised. The environment is structured in such a way as to establish a sense of shared aim, and to facilitate the participation of the clients. So the clients do the bulk of the therapeutic work; after all, they know what it is like to feel the rush of a bank robbery in a way that the staff don't; after all, they know how useful but ultimately fruitless it is to evacuate mental pain by self-cutting, and how easily a blasé attitude to the consequences can be adopted.

Grendon in its contexts

The prime managerial task in Grendon is to straddle divides: the divide between the fact that Grendon is a prison in which security issues take primacy, and the equal and opposite fact that Grendon is a therapeutic unit and so clinical concerns come first; between the fact that perpetrators need to be punished, and the equal and opposite one that they are victims and need help and support. In subsequent chapters, I hope to provide a sense of Grendon and its work by illuminating a little of these different perspectives that together can provide a three-dimensional impression. An underpinning theme will be that to get to know and understand the structure of a personality requires multiple perspectives. So the complexity and different dimensions that comprise Grendon are not a weakness or a lack of clarity in its aim, mission or task. They are its strength. Out of the debate come insight and understanding. With personality, and criminal personalities in particular, premature clarity and certainty may simply mask a primitive judgementalism.

CHAPTER 2

Grendon's Men

When visitors come to Grendon, they are invited to participate in an unstructured meeting with a group of residents. The visitors and residents meet for an hour or so, and usually both groups get round to saying what they are doing there and discussing a bit what the place is about. What is interesting is that while visitors arrive wanting to know about the place, they leave having met some people. They come to see a programme and go away having met Eddie, John or whomever. Interest in the place or the treatment technology dissolves into a more pressing engagement with the stories of the people they meet. This phenomenon also seems to happen with film crews, who come to film the process and end up telling some of the stories of the residents, making them real as people rather than telling the story of the unit.

In many ways, it seems that the structure and therapeutic activity of Grendon is itself a lens through which the residents can be seen a little better. The residents can feel a little less paranoid about visitors and 'suits' when they visit, and can tell their stories. Outsiders engage with people, they don't come and look at criminals. As with a real lens, visitors become more interested in what can be seen through this metaphysical lens than the instrument itself; they become interested in the people rather than the prison. In treatment, the residents can talk a little more freely about themselves without paying for it later at the hands of fellow resident or staff persecutors, so that they can see themselves, each other and their histories more clearly.

In this chapter I hope to describe the client group, but trying to maintain the focus on the lens, the technology, rather than simply recounting people's stories. The problem is that it is difficult to describe a lens without demonstrating what it does. Likewise, Grendon is rather dry without some clinical material to illustrate it or demonstrate how it actually operates. To try to balance these differing demands I shall introduce three fictitious Grendon residents who illustrate some of the characteristics of the client group, and who, in later chapters, will be able to illustrate some of the issues that emerge.

EDDIE

Eddie is a 35-year-old man five years into a life sentence for murder. He stabbed his friend Dan in a fight outside a pub, then ran away as Dan bled to death. This is his fourth prison sentence. In the past he has had convictions for various episodes of violence in fights in which he has become involved, including a three-year sentence for grievous bodily harm for an attack on some football fans of an opposing team. Violence in the context of football is simply one of the avenues that Eddie has for articulating his violence; others include the ritual of going out at the weekend with the express purpose of getting drunk and engineering a fight. There had been a suggestion of affiliation with extreme right-wing organisations whose demonstrations often end in violence.

Eddie's father was an alcoholic and Eddie's first memory is of, at the age of six, cowering under the bed with his older sister while Father, drunk and swearing, enraged at some trivial misdemeanour, was searching for them. Frequently, Father's drunken return home would result in either Mother or the children being subjected to some form of violence. On one occasion, he remembers rushing next door to a neighbour to get help, leaving his sister by Mother's side as she lay bleeding and unconscious on the kitchen floor; on another, aged eight, he was forced to watch, sitting on the sofa, while Father 'taught Mother a thing or two', punching her repeatedly in the face.

In his early teenage years, Eddie increasingly stood up for himself against Father, such that he began to get himself in the middle of the violence between Father and Mother. Father's rage began to be directed towards him more directly. Of course, as he grew, he became more of a match for his father physically, and a distinct memory is from the age of 15, when he 'lost it' and hit back. Following this, Father's attitude changed, and it may have been at this time that Eddie's identity as a man of violence crystallised. By being violent he could have an effect. By being violent he could change things.

He was expelled from two schools; in one a fight with another pupil was the cause, in the other, punching a teacher. In his third school there seems to have been a stand-off, such that Eddie truanted and the school tolerated it. Physically strong, he would get casual work on construction sites, but this was usually short-lived because Eddie would get into a confrontation with a fellow worker or manager. He tried a spell in the army, lasting six months before being discharged for fighting, but remembers this as an achievement and a place where he fitted in.

He has had two serious relationships and several one-night stands. Julie was a girlfriend from the age of 13 or so until he was 20, when she became pregnant by and then married another man in their social circle. Dawn had been in the background before the separation and indeed her close friendship with Eddie may have contributed to the split with Julie. In spite of this, the ending of the relationship with Julie sent Eddie 'off the rails' a bit, and he remembers more fights and injuries at this time. The relationship with Dawn continued in this chaotic vein; they ended up having two children, with the couple living together at times and apart at times, their life punctuated by domestic violence and acrimony, but returning to each other after each break.

In terms of the number of crimes Eddie committed, his offending history was mainly for thefts and burglaries, but it seems that he was taken along for 'the buzz' rather than his having developed a trade in this activity. Likewise, his involvement in violent political demonstrations and football hooliganism seems not to have an anti-establishment flavour: it was simply an opportunity to be where some violence and some fun was to be had, and he went along with his mates. His first three prison sentences, however, were for violent incidents taking place in such settings.

His account of the index offence was around the time that relations with Dawn were particularly bad; the children had been taken into care, and Dawn felt she was faced with a choice of having either the children or Eddie. They both denied violence to the children, although the social services were suspicious of some of the children's injuries. They had gone into care when a social worker had visited in the middle of a row between Eddie and Dawn, and Dawn blamed Eddie for the situation.

Eddie called up some of his mates after a particularly acrimonious row, and they went on the town, clearly looking for a fight. At some point in the evening violence emerged between the friends and there was a fight involving a knife. Eddie can't remember what happened, but the next day the police visited and he learned that Dan was dead.

Eddie reacted badly to being imprisoned. Twice he became suicidal – when imprisoned initially, and again when sentenced. Initially, he tried to cut his wrists and later, when sentenced, took an overdose he had saved up. After several weeks on suicide watch, his articulation of his distress returned to its default mode, and he began to fight his imprisonment, getting involved in the politics of the prison wing he was on, and in the fights that took place. He was identified as something of a management problem by prison staff and he spent increasing amounts of time in segregation, where he would fight the prison staff directly.

In his pre-sentence reports, a psychologist had picked up on the link between his relationship difficulties at the time of the offence with Dawn and his offence itself, suggesting that he might benefit from the treatment programme at Grendon. Each time Eddie moved prison (as happened occasionally to share out between prisons the burden on staff that a fighting prisoner represents) a new group of staff would read this, and raise the possibility. On one occasion, during a fight, Eddie had boiling water and sugar poured on him, resulting in burns that required regular dressing. He began talking to the health care prison officer who dressed his wound and they talked about Grendon, as the officer was aware of the recommendation in his file. Eddie began to wonder about himself and his life, and about what he could learn about himself there. At any rate, it sounded like 'easy bird', so he decided to apply.

Grendon's admission criteria

Grendon's admissions policy enshrines four or five important values, which have effects throughout the work that is carried on there. The first is that treatment is voluntary. People have to be in prison, having been sentenced by the courts, but the issue of whether they wish to transfer to Grendon is entirely a voluntary one. The fact that the inmates are there of their own free will and can leave at any time alters quite significantly the organisational dynamic of the prison. Whereas, in most prisons, by and large the prisoners do not want to be there, to some degree they do want to be in Grendon. Whereas in many settings the threat of being expelled from a particular prison is not a particularly potent motivator, in Grendon it is. If one of the communities decides that a particular resident's 'commitment' is in doubt, because he has been caught breaking the rules, taking drugs, being threatening or violent and so on, he could be expelled; and this is a powerful motivator for him to change his behaviour and explore the antecedents of the incident.

Treatment is also voluntary because it represents a powerful psychological intervention for which residents need to give consent to undergo. The issue of consent in the psychotherapies is vexed, because the ways that the more exploratory or psychodynamic psychotherapies affect an individual are very difficult or impossible to describe, and because they affect different people very differently. The one certainty is that it is important for people to be able to remove themselves from the process if it becomes too intense, or if aspects of their personalities and lives are emerging that they cannot face.

The second value underlying the admissions policy is that of inclusivity. Much is written about assessment for psychotherapy; while in the more structured cognitive and psychological symptom-focused therapies one can assess suitability in terms of actuarial indices of particular symptom clusters, the assessment of personality is much more complicated. Arguably, the process and constraints are more similar to those involved in assessing somebody for a job. What you really want to know is what the person is like. At the turn of the last century, Freud's approach in the early days of psychoanalysis was to offer people a 'trial analysis' – to agree to meet for a few weeks to see how things went. This is the broad approach that is taken at Grendon. We try to offer anyone who wishes to engage the opportunity to do so, to see how they get on and whether they make any progress. We acknowledge that many will not be able to work with the therapeutic medium. The process of lifting off the oppression of externally imposed control to allow some freedom of expression will prove too tempting to these people and they will utilise their freedoms for nefarious activity such as drug running or bullying rather than for a process of self-exploration. For many, the task of self-exploration will be too frightening and they will take flight. Some (a very small number) may be driven mad by it. It is important that they have had the opportunity to have a taste of how an exploratory psychotherapy works; and it may be that in the future they will wish to have another go. However things turn out, the inclusive approach to admission seems an important plank. If somebody gets to a position of having a passing thought about the possibility of self-exploration helping him or her with his or her difficulties, this is an important step in the process of ownership of responsibility and self-actualisation and should be given an opportunity to grow, if it can.

These two broad values operate within some boundaries. Applicants have to have at least two years remaining to serve of their current sentence. The reason for this is partly that the evidence base demonstrates a treatment effect beyond this time and partly that there is a clinical sense that 18 months to 2 years is the absolute minimum at which people can be seen genuinely to change. In fact, the population profile consists of something like 50 per cent serving a life sentence and, of those with a determinate sentence, the average is 7 years. Most of the life sentence prisoners are longer-term lifers, and they need to have spent a few years of their sentence in prison before they are ready to be transferred. The aim of Grendon's treatment is to explore their personality, rather than the adjustment reaction to having received a life sentence that is worked through in the first few years of a newly imposed life sentence.

Applicants need to be free from psychotropic medication. This requirement is one that is repeatedly challenged by colleagues and potential residents. They rightly make the point that being prescribed anti-depressant, anti-psychotic or anti-anxiety medication may have no effect on their personality or personality disorder. Using the DSM-IV model of personality disorder mentioned in Chapter 1 (American Psychiatric Association 1994), they may be legitimately treated for a psychiatric Axis 1 disorder with medication and need treatment in addition for their Axis 2 personality disorder. It is this thinking that has paved the way for the notion of 'dual diagnosis', and the need for the different treatment of an individual's different dimensions. In spite of these protestations, the line is held that Grendon needs to be free of psychotropic drugs. There are three reasons for this. First, it is easier to hold a blanket ban as a policy than to allow flexibility. Many of the Grendon residents at some point during their treatment will feel depressed or anxious and even have short psychotic-type experiences, and they might legitimately demand medication. Many Grendon residents have been prescribed large quantities of psychotropic medication for long periods in the past, so prescription is a well-practised and comfortable response to difficult emotional states. All this medication can then become contraband, and the issue of whether to prescribe takes up large amounts of discussion time that might otherwise be spent trying to understand the individual himself.

The no psychotropics rule also means that the Grendon population is a more 'pure' Axis 2 personality disordered group. The ability to be clear about this may be behind the relatively low cost of a year of Grendon treatment compared to health service equivalents. A year in Grendon costs a fifth of the cost of a secure health service personality disorder treatment bed and about half the cost of a non-secure bed. Part of this saving is made up by the industrial scale of the operation, and there are savings in relation to the somewhat austere residential accommodation normal in prison settings. Most, however, seems to derive from the low ratio of professional/civilian staff to residents. This is possible because the residents do not suffer from psychiatric illness. If Grendon were to provide a treatment to dual diagnose people who had both a mental illness and a personality disorder, the professional input would need to increase, with psychiatric nurses, clinical psychologists and psychiatrists.

Offering treatment for those who have an active mental illness would become cost prohibitive.

The third reason is that the need for psychotropic prescription is a crude measure of the severity of mental illness. A guesstimate of the levels of psychiatric morbidity in Grendon might indicate that about a quarter of Grendon residents seen in a standard psychiatric setting might attract an Axis 1 psychiatric diagnosis and treatment. However, because all of the admitted men have been able to survive medication-free for several months prior to admission and in assessment, one can be reasonably confident that any psychiatric morbidity that does exist is on the milder end of the spectrum. Where this is not the case, and where there is a genuine need for the prescription of medication for psychiatric symptomatology, it is an indication that the individual might be too psychiatrically disturbed to continue in treatment, given Grendon's limited resource in this regard. Grendon provides treatment for those with personality disorder; those with complex dual diagnoses of personality disorder combined with psychiatric illness sufficiently severe to require active and ongoing psychiatric treatment require a more specialist psychiatric treatment resource.

The need for specialist treatment resources for particular groups extends to the issue of general intelligence. Experience suggests that residents need to have an IQ in the average range (i.e. above about 75) to be able to benefit. While there is no disagreement that therapeutic community treatment is an appropriate and helpful intervention for those with a personality disorder and learning difficulties, this would require specialist input that Grendon is unable to provide.

The other parameters are that people need not to be engaged in appeals against their index offence, that they need to be in remission from major physical illnesses they may be suffering from – in both of these cases because they would be too preoccupied with these issues to be able to engage – that they have to have had a few stable months prior to transfer, when they are not actively taking drugs or engaged in physically violent behaviour towards staff or other inmates and, finally, they need to be able to agree to abide by the three basic Grendon rules – no sex, no violence and no drugs.

The issue of active appeals has caused some controversy, because it seems unfair to refuse a person treatment for his personality disorder because he is seeking justice. The reason for this decision is more profound, however, and it relates to a fundamental difference between forensic psychiatry and psychotherapy, and the legal profession. The task of the forensic psychotherapy is to strive for the truth, and the task of the legal profession and process is to strive for justice (Kennedy 2001). Justice states that a man is innocent until proven guilty, so it is the barrister's task to hone, to prepare and to make as convincing as possible his or her client's account of innocence. In doing this, defendants are trained in the arts of rationalisation, minimisation and normalisation in relation to their antisocial behaviour. They learn a way of making the index offence sound everyday, making it understandable to members of the jury, as if any of them might have been in the same situation and made the same mistake. This is legitimate because it tests the process of justice: is the evidence of maleficence sufficiently proven to convict; is it 'beyond reasonable doubt'?

GEORGE

George is a 42-year-old man serving a 6-year sentence for a series of offences against young children in his capacity as a care worker in a children's home. Following the publicity about the abuse that took place in the 1970s and 1980s in homes in Wales, several complaints were made about George and his activities over a ten-year period while in the employ of a number of local councils. From his account, George would identify attractive young boys between the ages of nine and thirteen or so who seemed a bit lost and lonely, befriend and help them and, after several months, introduce sexual activity, depending on the response of the victim. One of the cases in the trial had been involved in a sexual relationship with George for seven years, and the two remain in contact.

George never met his father; he was an only child of a mother who worked as a prostitute. George's earliest memories are of asking Mother who the men visiting were, and whether one was his father. This was met with a telling-off, which is perhaps why the memory remains. Other memories include endless time having to 'play out' – i.e. play in the street because he couldn't be at home while Mother was with a client. At the same time, there was a series of 'new daddies', reflecting Mother's sequential love affairs which lasted no longer than six to twelve months. Aged eight, George made friends with the next-door neighbour, a single man who provided an informal type of child care that fitted in with Mother's activities. This man had a number of children visiting, and George remembers that he had a Chopper bicycle that he loaned out. It was much nicer being with the neighbour than Mother; sweets were liberally dished out, and presents bought.

In the neighbour's house George was first introduced to pornography that he found lying about, asked about it, and then was invited to try some of the activities depicted. Over several years, this extended to being introduced to some of the neighbour's friends from the estate with whom he and some of the other visiting children would also have sex, sometimes with the men and sometimes together. This carried on until he was in his teens, when he drifted off; perhaps the neighbour lost interest in him as he physically matured. George still has some fondness for this man, seeing the sexual activity as a deal in exchange for the friendship and support that the neighbour provided, much like the tricks Mother was turning. For him, the abusive villains were one or two of the clients of Mother's when he was much younger. Some of these men, while Mother slept, would come into his room and touch him intimately as he pretended to sleep, rigid with fear. This went back as far as he could remember.

At school he was a reasonable pupil, leaving aged sixteen with several O-levels and getting a job in a DIY shop, ending up working as a clerk in the office. At the same time, his interest in pornography and sex with children was developing, and he would save up to be able to pay for his habit. In his twenties, apparently believing in a wish to help those who had had difficult backgrounds like him, he got a job in a care home working with children. For the first few years, he maintained a boundary between his paedophilic interests and his work; but with one boy with whom he had formed a close attachment, a sexual contact took place. Over the next year, his interest became more predatory, and he settled into a sexual practice of having one active sexual partner in the home he worked and another that he was 'bringing on'.

By the late 1990s, he was heavily involved in the exchange of pornographic images of children on the Internet from his collection, and continuing his work, when the complaints were made about him. Faced with the detailed and corroborated accounts, he pleaded guilty, and it was only after he was charged that his other paedophilic activities came to light. Effectively, this current sentence is George's first offence.

He has not married, but has had some close female friends, with at least one of them being sexual. He is rather secretive about this, but all of these women have young children; although, when challenged, he vehemently denies any sexual contact with these children. His longest relationship seems to have been with the next-door neighbour/abuser, with whom he still keeps in contact. He has tried meeting men, and has a number of homosexual friends, but none of these relationships is sexual because he is repulsed by 'their hairiness'. He maintains contact with his mother whom he sees once or twice a year; she has now been married for five years and settled down a bit.

In prison, he was immediately placed on Rule 43, being segregated for his own safety. Because for many years he was able to keep his perversion separated from the rest of his life, he was horrified and traumatised by the process of trial, sentencing, and incarceration. The experience of being on the front page of the local paper, receiving death threats and being spat at because of being a 'bacon' (bacon bonse – nonce) in prison, George found horrifying. He responded by closing down, keeping his head down and becoming as unnoticeable as possible. He rejects fraternisation, networking and exchanging stories with others who share his proclivities, claiming to be a reformed character and to have renounced his former interests. He completed the Sex Offender Treatment Programme with flying colours, although it was noted that he struggled to be able to accept the trauma that he caused his victims, perhaps explicable by his own experience at the hands of the neighbour. Grendon was suggested to him by a former colleague from a care home, who had visited while George was remanded. This colleague had been shocked at the revelations and had persuaded George that he needed some therapy.

The legal profession do not want truth where this produces guilt, because it may hamper them in their task. Forensic psychotherapy, on the other hand, digs down through the rationalisations, minimisations and dismissals to get at deeper layers of truth. So it may not be in the interests of those engaged in the process of justice to be engaging in the process of psychotherapeutic truth-telling at the same time.

Grendon's admission process

The admission process consists of three stages: a pre-transfer paper triage, a two- to three-month stay in the assessment community, and the process of assessment in the first two or three months in the treatment community.

Most therapeutic communities, and indeed most residential treatment environments, are linked to some form of pre-admission clinical assessment process. Even emergency admission for a heart attack involves an out-patient assessment stage where the GP or ambulance man decides whether admission for treatment is appropriate. Unfortunately, with Grendon's rate of admissions (about three per week) and with its catchment area being national, pre-admission assessment, with a staff member visiting prospective Grendon residents in their sending prison, is cost prohibitive. As an alternative, a system of pre-transfer paper assessment has developed, where the applicant writes a letter describing his situation, is asked to fill in a questionnaire that includes some basic demographic and historical data, and a variety of other reports are sought. The rule of thumb is that there needs to be enough 'soft copy' to be able to get a feel for the individual. 'Soft copy' means descriptive data about the person, his family and social background, his offence and offending profile, and how this fits into other aspects of his life. Usually pre-trial or sentence reports from psychiatrists, psychologists and especially probation officers contain some softer descriptive material. The pages of rather opaque data that can accompany prisoners are less helpful but necessary to get some sense of previous convictions, previous institutional behaviour (numbers of prison rule infringements; does he attack staff or other prisoners?), performance on previous psychological programmes and actuarial data where available. Gradually an expertise has been built up among Grendon staff of making an assessment on an individual on the basis of this paper evidence, and a particularly important part of this is the individual's own written contribution.

Self-referral letters from prisoners are interesting phenomena that seem to mix heartrending supplication with acidic defiance. One for example starts with a rather stilted 'Please could you take me into Grendon because I need help with mi offending behaviour needs...' and '...I need help because don't want no more victims...', but peppered with murderous intent to '...officer X who lied to the governor, and mi solicitor is dealing with it...', along with gut-wrenching comments about the index offence. 'Katie was mi little princess, it was two weeks after her fifth birthday when I got her a bike, that I killed her...'

The main assessment point is to identify the extent to which the applicant can acknowledge some agency in his life. If everything is someone else's fault, then the applicant has little or no sense of being an agent in his own situation and there is little that can be done for him. For example, in the letter above, the incident over which the officer is alleged to have lied is that the prisoner disobeyed a direct order. The prisoner's account is that he debated it rather than disobeying it, and that the 'lie' is in the interpretation of his behaviour. The reality may be that this is a man who constantly sails close to the wind, who is always remonstrating about things that he is required to do, and that the officer lost patience. While the allegation of a lie might technically be true, this misses out the agency in the applicant's own precipitation of the confrontation. This level of awareness of agency is not to be expected in a pre-treatment group, or even for that matter in the less sanguine moments of the post-treatment group. More important is the acknowledgement of a degree of responsibility for the offence itself. The applicant's sense of agency cannot be expected to be particularly developed, but there needs to be a kernel that might grow.

The second stage of the assessment process is a stay of two or three months in the assessment unit. The assessment unit is run along therapeutic community lines, albeit modified because of the transient and constantly changing population. The aims of this part of the treatment programme are threefold. First, by spending three months in a community, attending groups, new residents can get a sense of the culture and feel of being in treatment. It is difficult to overestimate how profound the shock is for those who arrive in Grendon. Most have spent years hating prison officers, spent years being constantly afraid in the environment in which they live – of being attacked in the shower, being bullied and so on – years of keeping a guarded distance from the prison officers in their role as agents of an army of peacekeepers or occupation, years of being treated as a number as part of a necessary batch living structure. When they arrive in Grendon, staff members introduce themselves by their first name, with a shake of the hand. Remember that in most prison settings referring to or addressing a prison officer by his or her first name can be prosecuted under the prison rules as offending 'good order and discipline'. In Grendon, introductions take place in this format. In most prison settings, the culture dictates that the last thing you do with a problem is take it to a member of staff to talk about; in Grendon this is actively encouraged.

Prisoners describe 'feeling safe' in Grendon as a predominant change in culture. Because they have some confidence in their own safety, there is a global de-escalation of suspicion, mistrust and intimidation that becomes a virtuous circle. What it is that produces this is unclear, and is a broader theme of the book. The outcome, however, is that prisoners have to adapt to a very different culture from that to which they are accustomed and, for the protection of the treatment community environments, it is important that new-comers can be 'detoxified' to some degree from the hostile cultures that they are used to, and can learn to be in a more relaxed one. This enculturation process of the assessment unit may be its most important function – acting as a buffer between the usual default prisoner culture to be found in most prisons, and the different therapeutic environment found in Grendon.

Second, prisoners can begin to get used to the business of living in a therapeutic community, get used to living and engaging with other people rather than trying to ignore them and get used to the process of conflict negotiation and resolution with a peer group. The assessment unit staff discourage exploration of offending or background history at too deep a level. The agenda and discussion for the group meetings that take place is to discuss the business of the community – to air the frustrations of 'here-and-now' living together.

The reason for trying to maintain a superficial discourse, rather than allowing residents to delve too deeply, is to allow them time to become familiar with the treatment format prior to having to use the format to begin their treatment proper. For many, the way to deal with frustration borne out of close proximity living is to bury the resentment until it builds to a critical level, when it is unleashed in violence. The requirement to disclose anger that the person in the next cell is playing his music too loud may seem simple, but often represents a developmental task that has to be carefully facilitated. As well as this, there is no doubt that Grendon provides an environment where individuals are cared for actively, and concern for the residents is actively articulated and expressed. To those unfamiliar with this, there is a risk of gushing out too much that is later regretted. This risk is more profound than simply saying or revealing things that are later regretted. For some, operating within a hostile environment has been instrumental in creating and sustaining the structure of their personality. The psychological distinction between self and non-self is defined by self being good and non-self being bad and abusive. Coming into a caring environment, the perception of some good to be found in the environment leads to a profound sense of confusion between me and not-me – characteristic of a psychotic experience. What can be observed as 'spilling' or 'gushing' is in fact a result of the dissolution of the structure of the personality, so that the internal secrets emerge. To some extent, new residents need to be protected from this sort of breakdown, in order that they can more gradually disclose and explore themselves. By being clear that treatment proper does not start until the individual reaches the treatment community and his small group, the prisoner can learn to work with the caring environment instead of simply reacting to it.

As well as this, there is a debate about the harm that is done to people as they begin to attach to a community where their stay will be short. Without going into the whole meta-psychology of attachment, a simple model might be that, as infants and children, people learn a repertoire of attachment styles and strategies during their development. Children with parents who bring them up in a balanced and secure attachment environment and who are reasonably reliable carers and reasonably reliable figures of authority, will learn how to negotiate and rely on attachment figures and how to relate to authority. Conversely, those who grow up in an environment of capricious variable care-giving (heaps of presents at Christmas, with neglect and abuse the rest of the year), or with abusive or violent and unpredictable authority, will learn an entirely different set of strategies about how to manage their attachments – perhaps by not forming them, perhaps by forming hostile dependant patterns, and so on. While many Grendon men can be quite intimidating and frightening, at another level, this can be understood as a continuation of a playground bullying pattern of the kid from the unhappy family, carried on into adulthood. The paranoia, hostility and threat projected by the individual is appropriate for the world as he perceives it. If you believe yourself to be under threat of violence, you will practise your own violence as a defence, and try to maintain an outward façade of threat similarly as a defence. This pattern of relating can be perceived as a disordered attachment pattern for adulthood although, in many of the individual backgrounds of Grendon inmates, arguably it was both adaptive and self-protective. Many subsequently gravitate to environments where such an attachment style is normal, and even confers benefits, such as delinquent or criminal groups and gangs. If they end up in prison environments, such attachment styles might again be adaptive, allowing them to anticipate danger and, to some degree, ward it off.

This notion that the hostile, violent and threatening attitude displayed by Grendon men reflects an appropriate attachment style in the sort of environment in which they have grown up presents a model of therapeutic change for how the Grendon treatment works. Grendon simply provides a less toxic and violent environment and, by maintaining this, allows residents to explore the difference between it, and the environments that they are used to. Gradually, residents are able to recognise the difference between the attachment environment that they are used to and that which they find in Grendon.

From this perspective, the attachment concern about the assessment unit is clear. Many residents have a history of brief and intense attachments (for example, arrival at a new approved boarding school, misbehaviour and intense engagement with the school authorities for a short period, followed by expulsion and disruption of the attachment) and of being shifted around to different care-givers, for example foster parents or children's homes. The at times overwhelming experience of arriving in the Grendon assessment unit, of finding staff with the time and inclination to talk to them and hear their stories, and with a genuine interest in them and their well-being; this is a somewhat intense experience for residents that fosters an attachment which then is disrupted after a short period, when they are transferred to a different community, their assessment period over.

For this reason, an attempt is made to manage the depth and intensity of attachment that is formed during the assessment process in two ways. There is the aforementioned expectation that individuals will save discussion of their early and family histories and experiences until they have arrived on a treatment community. Second, the treatment regime is modified to reduce the contribution of the small group therapy and to increase the community experience. The task in the assessment community is not to delve deep and explore a person's innermost issues, but rather to begin to establish some community living sensitivity and skills and allow the resident to become aware of being in a different type of environment without breaking down: an environment that is to some degree caring, to some degree respectful of the individual and to some degree nonjudgemental.

During their stay on the assessment community, residents will be interviewed by their personal officer (part of the prison service key worker system), a variety of actuarial tests will be carried out and they will be the subject of two or three case conferences, 'progress reports', to establish within the team and then feed back to residents how they are getting on. Gradually, over the three months, the staff group will get to know each individual and will develop a strong position about whether he will be able to benefit from the treatment process. What the features of a 'good bet' are is difficult to determine, but include the extent to which the individual has been able to play an active part in the group structures; the extent to which he has been able to speak to and engage with staff; the extent to which he can 'psychologise' – have a psychological understanding of his situation or can develop one in response to problems that emerge – and the extent to which he recognises his own 'agency' – his active participation in the process – rather than having a hostile and passive attitude.

The other assessment process taking place in tandem is more specialised to prison environments and doing therapeutic work with psychopathic people. One expects a degree of duplicity between what the resident says and what is actually going on; the response to the question 'Have you got drugs?' will almost always be negative, irrespective of the situation. The expertise is in establishing the degree of malignancy and the extent of duplicity. Because this is expected to a degree, the task is not to be diagnostic about whether it is present or even, particularly, to establish what effect this level of duplicity will have on the treatment process. The task is to make an assessment of the extent to which this level of duplicity will undermine the treatment community to which the person goes. Is this person so duplicitous and malignant that he threatens the integrity of the therapeutic community or indeed the integrity of the whole prison? The potential power of the intelligent and very psycho-pathic individual in a democratised therapeutic setting and the risk that he presents cannot be overemphasised. The ability of pathology that is being treated to destroy its treatment process is highly respected by staff, and watched for.

When the staff group has a grasp on these indices, they are presented at a prison-wide meeting to staff representatives of the treatment communities, who carry out their own individual assessment. This usually involves an interview with more than one member of staff, a presentation at a staff meeting of the treatment community, followed by a conclusion, which is fed back to the assessment community team and to the individual.

One of the difficult dynamics in this process is distinguishing suitability from treatability. The assessment staff team struggles with a resident for three months, getting to know him, getting to grips with the way his offending is mirrored in his everyday relating, taking the risk of interpreting this and working with the response; then the team decides and agrees on a verdict, only to have one of the treatment communities decide that the person is not suitable. What the treatment community team means is that this particular person is not suitable for that particular community at that particular time, but it makes no comment about whether the person might be suitable for another community. The clinical management of a therapeutic community requires a sensitivity to its social and cultural mix and what effect different factors will have on this. For example, a local community issue might be that a community at this particular time is struggling with a large and overbearing bank-robber bully, thus an attempt to bring in another gangster-type large personality might not be a good idea. Likewise, if there is a concern about a covert nefarious drug racket going on, bringing into the community an international drug dealer might not be a good idea. Those who lead therapeutic communi-ties talk about 'fit' – whether a particular patient will fit into a particular community at that particular time. Those who do not may not be suitable for that particular community, but may indeed be treatable by a different community, and this is usually what happens.

FRED

Fred doesn't see himself as a criminal, rather he is a businessman. Going bankrupt is an occupational hazard of entrepreneurs in the city, going to prison is an occupational hazard in his line of work. Besides, prison is simply a different market, more challenging and more fun in some ways. At the age of 29, he got a 4-year sentence for possession with intent to supply. He usually got drones to do his drops, but he was going off for the weekend to a party and wanted to take some gear; he was caught and, because he was known to the police, he went down. They had been waiting for some time to get him. Fred has been in prison twice before, although he has a long list of convictions: fraud, burglary, and so on. The sentences were for burglaries. None of his convictions are for violence, he doesn't do violence, he has drones for that. When he was in before, he heard of Grendon; there was a bloke he worked with in the kitchens in the Scrubbs who had been to Grendon and had his head sorted out. He was back in prison, but he seemed to know a thing or two. So when Fred came in for this sentence, he thought he would give it a go.

Fred grew up in the East End of London. Father was in and out of prison on various sentences during his childhood. There was some involvement in the well-known East End criminal scene, but at the fringe. Fred particularly remembers going to see his father in prison on a sentence for robbing a bank in Vauxhall: a daring raid that had been successful. They would have got away with several hundred thousand pounds, had it not been for the fact that there was an informer. Even so, the kudos that derived in the neighbourhood from Dad being a bank robber made up for the absence of Father and the depressive withdrawal of Mother. Father had taken Fred's two older brothers out on burglaries. Fred was too young, but was well imbued with criminal values – that family and friends were to be protected, but everybody else was fair game.

Fred was uninterested in school and instead turned his intellect to devising plans for burglaries and robberies that he would carry out with his close group of friends in the evenings. He didn't particularly get in trouble with the school authorities, being too clever to be there when the discovery of some school misdemeanour was made or the teacher arrived. Latterly he truanted, so that school was increasingly irrelevant to him from the age of 14 onwards. His burglaries moved from local houses to houses in more affluent areas, and on to premises storing electrical goods. When he was 18 he was caught on video and, because this followed a history of lesser offences, Fred received a 10-month prison sentence.

Following this experience, he started to get others to do the actual robbing and burgling. Fred took care of the re-sale. All this time, he had been dabbling in drugs as part of the social scene he was engaged with. In prison, he used heroin on a more regular basis. Shortly after his release, his father died, beaten to death, apparently mugged, but there was considerable suspicion that there was more to it – that it was a contract. Fred took this badly, sought solace in heroin and for a while became addicted. Short of money he would need to burgle to get his next fix; in this state he was careless, and broke into one house that was occupied. He took some contents, so was convicted of robbery instead of burglary. On this occasion in prison (a three-year stretch) he withdrew and resolved to deal drugs rather than be addicted to them, having seen their power and how the money rolls in.

Fred had loads of 'babes'; he knew many women, had had many sexual partners and had a sideline in arranging for girls he knew to meet others who would pay for sexual favours. He denied that he had pimped, he was just popular and introduced people to each other. None of these relationships were particularly serious, Fred didn't like women 'tying him down' like that; but he often had a product that they wanted, – money, business or drugs – so he never lacked for female company and had no other needs. In fact, in his early teenage years, he had been very fond of a girl several years older than him, who was his first sexual partner, but she had humiliated him after an argument on one occasion, ending the relationship. According to Fred, this was so long ago that it wasn't significant.

Once in the new community – usually after a process of visiting, meeting the chairman and being allocated a mentor from the resident group – the resident begins the process of initial assessment in the new community. Effectively, this is another process of a staff group getting to know an individual and this usually leads up to a case conference after three months or so, where treatment targets and issues to focus on are decided and negotiated with the resident.

Who really comes to Grendon

After all this process of sifting, assessing and so on, what are the characteristics of the population that remains. The figures vary slightly, but broadly 50 per cent are serving a life sentence; 50 per cent score 25 or above on the Hare Psychopathy Checklist, making them psychopathic; 25 per cent score 30 or above, making them severely psychopathic. About 80 per cent of residents are imprisoned for the commission of a violent offence; for about 25 per cent this is a sex offence. Ten per cent or so have primarily drug offences, although 60 or 70 per cent have a significant history of regular Class A drug usage. Ten per cent or so are principally in prison for deception or theft-related offending. Of course, many have offending histories spanning across different types of offending.

For its first 30 years, Grendon did not admit life sentence prisoners, as they were seen as being too high risk. Anecdotally, in its first 20 years Grendon men were much more likely to have been imprisoned for more minor offences such as fraud. There are several reasons for the change, one of which is that those with more minor problems are now funnelled into the cognitive-didactic offending behaviour programmes and can obtain effective treatment from this resource. Grendon, as a more involved and exhaustive treatment, is perhaps appropriately being focused on the more severely disturbed and damaging prisoners. The fact that there is an increasing number of lifers in Grendon has a number of antecedents. First, the escalation of public and political anxiety about risk seems to have led to an increase in those detained for a life sentence; second, the statutory structures such as the Lifer Review Boards, which have the responsibility to make decisions about who to release on licence and when, may require more from the prisoners who pass through their committees. It is now expected that life sentence prisoners, prior to release, will have made considerable strides towards addressing their offending via a variety of psychological programmes. More may now be being invited to think about the possibility of a Grendon treatment.

Clinically, allowing about half the population to be long-term life-sentence prisoners seems to be a ceiling on what can be managed. Life sentenced prisoners may have been off the streets for five or ten years, and therefore have no experience of life as it is currently lived. Likewise, they cannot realistically expect to go back into society until three more years have elapsed following their move on from Grendon. So they represent a group that is very insulated from real life. Communities need to have a critical mass of people who know what life and the world is about in this decade, in order to retain some sense of contact with it, and so that the outside world retains some relevance in the communities' discourse.

There is a number of other variables that help to describe the nature of the population, summarised in Shine and Newton (2000). For example, more than 40 per cent have significant drug and alcohol problems contributing to their offending and have attempted suicide; more than 30 per cent self-injure and have a history of more than 10 guilty adjudications for breaking prison rules; more than 15 per cent have escaped in the past and assaulted staff and more than 10 per cent have been involved in fire-setting or rioting during their current sentence.

From a different perspective, the question can be re-framed, from 'What sort of people come to Grendon?' to 'Why do people come?' Going to Grendon is not seen as something to be proud of, with its reputation of being full of 'grasses, nonces and nuts'. The point is that deciding to transfer to Grendon as a prisoner is a highly significant step, not taken lightly.

One common story is that prisoners have spent years fighting the system. They end up in prison segregation units after being involved in violent confrontations, perhaps initially directed at a fellow prisoner but then directed at staff. Having fallen into a spiral of violence, they end up in a strip cell mainly to protect themselves from their own violence, or a stand-off develops so that they cannot be taken out of their cell without six prison officers in riot gear standing ready, so great is the threat of violence that they present. The spiral is that the violence from the individual is met with a potent resistance in the form of manualised control and restraint and other techniques to maintain order. In turn this is experienced by the individual as a taunt or a provocation to even more extreme violence, which is met by the need for more potent containment, and so the amplification of the disturbance goes on.

Grendon men are often those who have exhausted this avenue of expression of their resistance, and who recognise that they are making some contribution to the situation that they are in. For one prisoner, after the umpteenth battle, when (by his account) he had been 'folded up' and was lying on the floor of his cell, he wondered if this was how it was always going to be and why he always ended up like this. It then occurred to him that he might be able to change it by not always fighting back, which in turn raised the question of why it was that he had always fought back till now. Following this was a rather uncomfortable insight that, in some way, he might have contributed to the unpleasant situation in which he now found himself, and perhaps to other problems he had had in the past. He raised this idea with the doctor who visited the next day, and this began a quasi-counselling relationship which grew into a thought that a more sustained therapeutic intervention might be helpful in the form of transfer to Grendon

Not in this case, but commonly, this sort of insight collapses a defensive edifice that has been holding the personality together and there follows a period of breakdown, in the form of a psychosis and/or as a depressive picture with or without self-harm. When a breakdown has followed, in the process of recuperation, a staff member might suggest Grendon as a possibility which, in time, becomes a focus for the rehabilitative direction.

Another avenue is that by chance the individual starts some process of self-exploration, either in a counselling setting with a health care worker or chaplain or informally with another prisoner who has been to Grendon. Those who have arrived by this route describe a curious process of development, from initially being contemptuous but curious about the staff member or prisoner who has a different view, to recognising that he has something to offer. One prisoner describes a fat and slob-like male nurse whom the prisoner was rather ashamed to be seen talking to; who didn't wear any jewellery at all and wasn't interested in Nike trainers or any other hip stuff. To start with he talked to the nurse because he thought the nurse needed to feel as if he was doing something. After a while, a realisation dawned on the prisoner that the nurse was helping him, understanding him, and that maybe middle-aged people and those without cool training shoes might have some value.

So, after this process, the client group that Grendon ends up with has been described as the heavy end of the British prison population. Anecdotally, many of them are those who have been 'fighting mad' in the past, sometimes for years, but have got tired, have had a moment of clarity when their agency in their difficult situation is realised, have had a recommendation by a professional in one of the various court procedures they have been through, or who have been lucky enough to strike up a friendship with an ex-Grendon man or an interested staff member.

CHAPTER 3

Grendon's Process

In this chapter I will attempt to describe Grendon's work as a cross-section: in terms of the various structures and functions that make up the process in order to give a general overview. Following this, from a different perspective, I will try to give a more longitudinal sense of the temporal sequence of therapy from arrival through assessment to treatment and leaving.

The vision and brave thinking that went into Grendon the concept cannot be said to have extended to Grendon the built environment. Grendon's late 1950s design has a rather brutalist-flavour wall surrounding the two 80-bed house blocks that are further divided into two, making four of the therapeutic communities. The remaining two are testament to different, unfulfilled aspects of the brave Grendon vision. A smaller unit for 25 was for some years a unit for youth offenders and this is used as the assessment and preparation unit. A separately built wing was originally to house women separated from the male accommodation, but is now used for the specialist sex offender community. Currently the prison houses 230 men in 'Category B' security. Technically this is a medium to high security prison, but compared to current design for both health and prison accommodation, the physical security level is far lower than this.

Each treatment community has something like 40 beds in a block on four floors. On the ground floor, there is a large community room that can seat about 45 people, and a number of small group rooms used for the small groups and for staff meetings, as well as staff office accommodation. In addition, each community has a 'pod' – a small cookery area where meals are prepared and served, with a dining area adjacent. The three upper floors, the 'landings', consist mainly of single cell accommodation, some floors with a converted dormitory area at the end that has been converted to provide extra small group rooms. The 'lads' are allowed considerable latitude in the decoration of these small areas of home that they have, although there is enforcement of the 'volumetric control' – that prisoners' belongings have to be able to fit in a specific volume – two medium-sized cardboard boxes. In general, the corridors that make up the communal and corridor spaces seem somewhat oppressive and dark, with little or no natural light, and no room for communal areas or furniture.

Downstairs, the 'corridor' is the staff domain, there are dress code expectations and a sense of people being at their place of work, or at least engaged in something productive. The calm and uniformed efficiency of the staff and clients gives the impression of a 1950s psychiatric ward, with a sort of routinised caring; so practised that it need not be declared as such. This atmosphere sits uneasily with the smell of cooking or toast that reminds one that this is a place where people spend their lives rather than simply come to work. Upstairs are the 'landings', which are very much more clearly people's home; there is a sense of needing to knock, of intruding, of inadvertently coming across people swathed in towels on their way to or from a shower. The smell is of toiletries rather than toast, and snippets of music (often house) mingle with sights of loved ones' pictures and glamorous pin-ups to amplify one's sense of intrusion. Should this sense of intrusion by a 'suit' be resented by a prisoner, one is reminded of the fact that, were it not Grendon, such unaccompanied visits to the landings would be inadvisable. Grendon has the highest concentration in one place of hostage-takers; and civilians are favoured targets to be bundled into a cell and bound, then to become a bargaining chip for the prisoner or part of a possible collateral damage calculation of one or other strategy to resolve the 'incident'. In fact, Grendon clients are almost always helpful and facilitative of whatever one is on the landings for, calling, fetching or pointing in the right direction.

At times, a split can develop in the communities between a dynamics of the downstairs corridor and one of the landings. In the corridor and in its associated meetings (the community meeting, groups and so on) a particular culture may pertain; one with a degree of respect and engagement with the therapeutic process and a degree of renunciation of the old, more default criminal values of secrecy, intimidation, 'blag and graft'. On the landings, where staff go only to carry out specific tasks such as searches, a different culture can develop; one more like some standard prison cultures, with an evolved hierarchy enforced by bullying or intimidation. This dialectic between a democratised, respectful and open culture and a more default bullying and intimidatory one will be described in detail later. Suffice to say now that it can become concretised in the form of an upstairs/downstairs difference of culture.

The other structure that permeates the organisation is the structure of group and community meetings. There is surprisingly little variation in the basic pattern of therapy. In brief, each morning is devoted to therapy. Two days per week, the whole community meet (Tuesday and Thursday) and three days per week the community syndicates into its slow open small groups (Monday, Wednesday and Friday). The community meeting is chaired by the community chairman, and has a variable degree of structure. There will often be an agenda, with residents asking for permission to do various things – to do a particular job, get backing for home leave, start an education programme or whatever. There will often be reports from other groups such as art therapy or psychodrama, or if one of the small groups has had a 'special' (un-timetabled) meeting. The community meetings form the democratic backbone of the whole process so, in addition to these bits of everyday business, they will often have some ongoing contentious piece of business to tackle. For example, someone has been found positive for heroin on a urine test. Should he be discharged? Is he simply unlucky because everyone is doing it at the moment? Whom did he get it from? Even in this modified prison environment, would it be safe for him to say? Are the staff on a power trip by testing this person? Why did they choose him? And so on and so on.

In their work trying to identify the crucial aspects of a therapeutic community, Kennard and Lees' (2001) audit instrument contains a parameter that establishes whether there is a community meeting each day. In Grendon there is a community meeting proper only twice a week although the whole community meets briefly on the other three working days to 'feed back' after the small groups. The difference between these brief opportunities for the whole community to touch base about the current issues and concerns of its members and the more elaborate ritual and business of the twice-weekly community meeting proper point up different dimensions of the community's function. The first function – the function that the Kennard Lees audit parameter is going for – is the presence of a sense of community, a sense of a continuity of belonging and interconnectivity within a social unit. Group analysts have debated the nature of the group 'matrix' – a sense of identity that exists in the collective of the group that is a function of the collective rather than of any one member. The existence of a collective community matrix is clear and is potentiated and nurtured by the structure of frequent, daily, contact.

The second function of the community is its executive function – the need to have a political forum in which debate can take place and where policy and thinking can be forged about the whole community, about its subgroups and about its individual members. In the debate that will take place about, for example, whether someone should get a 'red band' – an armband worn by prisoners who have a position of special trust that enables then to move more freely within the prison – there will be discussion at various levels. At the first, and most superficial, there will be one about the applicant's current situation, in terms of being trustworthy, his 'previous form' (meaning how in the past he has reacted in positions of responsibility and how his pattern of offending relates to this) where he is in his therapeutic work and what obtaining the red band might mean at a meta level for him. How to understand and interpret his wish to have this position will be raised – for example, is this a reaction formation to last week's challenge that he is untrustworthy?

Operating in the debate at another level will be the internal politics of the community. Bloggs didn't support Jones for his application for home leave, so Bloggs votes down Jones' request for a red band. At a more sinister level, it might be that Jones owes Bloggs money for heroin supplied, as do half of the other community members, so everyone will vote in favour. At this level, the debate is about the interpersonal and inter-group dynamics within the community and the development of a sensitivity to the importance and relevance of these issues. Restrictions to honest negotiation and free will brought about by nefarious secret deals can be examined as part of this political process.

The third function of the community meetings is to test out the nature and legitimacy of authority. In the meetings, the staff are accountable for their actions. If there has been a request for Works to change a light bulb and the staff member has forgotten to pass on the request to the Works Department, then he or she will attract some criticism. Thus, the authority held by the staff group is identified as accountable. Likewise, the staff group will respect the authority of the client group, as articulated by their representatives, the chairman and office holders. In the same way, if the community seems to be colluding with something nefarious – for example, a client or staff member being bullied or bad-mouthed – then this will come in for some criticism. In this environment, of course, the bounds within which the criticism can flow are extended, so that the legitimacy and the authority of the communities' rules are tested, as are aspects of the more general prison rules. For example, brewing and drinking alcohol are forbidden in prison, but are not against the law. Discussion of this might then lead on to a questioning of how legitimate it is to have one's freedom curtailed by imprisonment, how legitimate the punishment is for the crime that has been committed, and the nature of the authority of law and the Hobbesian civil contract.

As a fourth function, the community meetings act as a large group, albeit a modified one. Practice varies. Either, when the business is done, an 'open wing' is declared and there is an opportunity to have an unstructured discussion, or alternate community meetings are unstructured, allowing a free-floating discussion. In large group settings more psychotic defences characteristically arise (e.g. Kreeger 1994), and these will become apparent in the meeting, with paranoid and annihilatory anxieties emerging and taking over that can be interpreted.

The small groups are more like psychoanalytic psychotherapy small groups, although with several important caveats. They are similar to small group psychotherapy in that they meet regularly for an hour and a half three times per week, that in such a setting a strong and coherent matrix is established and work takes place spontaneously at considerable depth; and as in group analytic psychotherapy there is the opportunity for the individual to explore his own history and issues in some depth as well as to benefit from the intimacy and sense of relatedness with others that evolve in such settings. They differ from psychotherapy small groups in several important respects. First, they are an ancillary mode of treatment, not the central one. They are an aspect of the therapeutic community treatment, and as such the boundary of the group needs to be permeable for information to pass in and out of the group and, of course, for relationships to develop outside the group, as one lives with one's group members. Porosity of information is a crucial factor; it is essential that the community is aware of what is going on in each small group and it is also essential that, if there is an issue that emerges elsewhere in the community, this is returned to and taken up in the group. The second issue is that most of the lead therapists in the small groups are not psychotherapists. They derive from the disciplines in the team and have a variety of training backgrounds and often considerable experience, but mostly they are not group analysts.

The foregoing presents a cross-sectional view of the community, but the work can be also conceived longitudinally. At its most simple, this conception comprises a period of assessment and 'getting to know' the resident, most of which has been described in Chapter 2, and includes both the period in the assessment unit and the first three months or so on the treatment community. This involves both the staff group getting to know the resident, and the resident getting to understand the mores and language of the treatment process in order for him to utilise it. Once this process is complete, he can enter a period of maximum usage of the treatment – the period where the bulk of the work will be done. It is interesting that it is during this period that many residents actively select themselves out. With Grendon's inclusive policy of offering everyone a go, we would expect residents who are for whatever reason unable to tolerate the treatment to select themselves out, and this they do, usually in the first six months of treatment. Some come forward and say that it is 'doing their heads in', but most commonly there is some form of acting out which necessitates the staff actively removing them. As a prisoner, one saves more face bringing in drugs or getting into a fight and protesting that one should be given a second (third or fourth) chance, then being 'shipped out' against one's will, than to declare that one can't handle the insights that are being provided. If this period can be survived, the therapy really begins to get to grips with the individual and he struggles with the work proper. After 18 months or 2 years, residents and staff will start to think about what might happen post-Grendon; about where the resident will go next in terms of transfer to another prison; about through-care and licence arrangements if he is to be released from the gate.

In their study of Grendon, Genders and Player used a semi-structured interview methodology to identify the treatment process, and proposed a five-stage model (Genders and Player 1995). This included first, the process of recognition of a problem; second, the development of a desire to do something about it and to change. Third, there was a recognition of the interconnection of different aspects of life and a dawning awareness of the complexity of the problem, with its links to cycles of current relating, behaviour and offending, to upbringing and developmental history, as well as to structural constitutional and personality factors. The fourth stage was the beginning of the development of solutions to these problems, and the fifth was the testing phase – putting into practice the new strategies for coping with issues that had formerly led to problems.

Anecdotally, there is a two-stage model which pertains and which was probably more prevalent prior to the professionalisation of the psychodynamic therapeutic input. It does seem both a bit crude, and also somewhat ritualised. In this model, there is a stage of telling the personal history where everybody sympathises, saying what a horrible time you've had, followed by a phase of telling the story of offending, when you are attacked and criticised.

Because these life stories are usually pretty awful accounts of neglect and abuse during childhood development, and sad and cautionary tales of the failure of services to prevent the slide into a cycle of violence and repetition, they do genuinely attract enormous sympathy. During this detailed account, the resident can deepen his understanding of his background story, with the ability, as an adult, to re-appraise responsibilities. For example, abusive experiences are often remembered as the fault or responsibility of the victim; with an adult perspective, the primacy of the adult's task to protect the child can be underlined, with the failure of care that the abusive experience will represent.

GEORGE

George felt he wanted to let the group know as much as he could about his background. He was anxious about being 'nutted off' and ostracised, and he thought that by talking about his own childhood problems, the group might be able to see that he was like the rest of them, and it might break down barriers. In his exploring of his personal story, the issue of his first contact with his abuser was raised. George found it difficult to talk about this, as the different emotions that the memories of these early days raised were very painful. First there was the sense of abandonment and being a nuisance in his mother's life, and the reality of being sent out to play all the time while the 'other daddies' and other men visited. The group wondered whether this extrusion from his own home might have made him more vulnerable to the local paedophile. Second, George found it difficult to say that he had actually *liked* being with the man – at this point his name emerged, Tony. Tony had fed him Spaghetti Bolognaise, which had been his favourite dish ever since. Some days it was cold when he had to play outside; he always knew that there would be a warm welcome waiting with Tony. The point at which the abuse started was even more difficult for George to talk about. He spent several weeks being unable to broach it, and accused the group of wanting to hear it so they could 'get off' on the story. Some were angered at this but others, including the facilitator, suggested that there might be some other reason why George was so anxious about talking about the events. Perhaps he felt guilty that he had enjoyed it, or felt responsible that he had started the sexual contact himself. After a period of angry silence, George disagreed. He had been frightened and ashamed when Tony first fondled him once when he had been looking at some sex magazines. He had been frightened because Tony discovered his secret, that he had an erection. Tony stopped when he ran away, but the next time, when George was reading the magazines, he didn't run. 'I wanted him to do it,' said George '...but I didn't want him to do it. It was my fault – I didn't run away, and I went back.'

Another paedophile member of the group said that in his own experience, 'that was the best way to do it – to get it so that the kid thought that they had started it. It was always a bit risky to threaten the kid with what would happen if they told; they might tell anyway. But if they thought that it was their own fault, so that they were telling on themselves first – that was always safer.' George was dumbfounded and disturbed by this casual revelation. He was overwhelmed by the idea that Tony might have had a plan to abuse him, rather than his belief that it was his fault for going back and reading the magazines.

Conversely, there will often be a deep hatred for a parental figure because of some aspect of abuse, such that contact has been dropped. Often, this type of relationship can be re-appraised and the problems identified, but the good parts of the relationship also recognised.

FRED

Fred has no contact with his mother. 'They had the film *The Jazz Singer* on the telly a couple of weeks ago, when the old Jewish geezer says his son is dead because he becomes a pop singer, it's like that. My mother is dead. Well, she's not, but I have nothing to do with her. Dead and gone, not important. Fred saw no point in discussing her in the group, either. No he didn't particularly feel anything about her either. 'She's just not relevant, you know,' he would say.

Sometime later, the issue of Fred's family came round again, and again there was a flat denial of his mother's importance or relevance. Someone in the group suggested that he was so angry with his mother that he'd killed her off in his mind. Physically she was alive and well somewhere, but he'd as good as killed her for himself. Someone else made a link between this and the way Fred treated his 'babes'; it was as if none of these were alive or had any meaning for him. This got under Fred's skin, and he angrily shouted that this wasn't so. 'Mind your own fucking business, my family are my business, keep your fucking nose out. Fucking bollocks. They wanted to fucking kill me. They fucking as good as did,' he shouted, 'they fucking should have done,' he went on, clearly upset, but then said no more.

With this outburst, Fred had given the lie to his notion that his relationship with his mother did not matter, or was somehow neutral for him. The group began to notice him become sullen when other members explored aspects of their own families. Eventually, following a dripping tap approach of remembering that Fred had an issue that he hadn't yet addressed about his family, the story emerged. Fred was the baby of the family, and there was a wall of hatred towards his mother about this. Underneath this slick gangster-dealer exterior, he had suffered because his mother had always called him her baby. She didn't allow him to go out burgling with his father before he died, as his other brothers had, because he was the baby. He had felt humiliated and demeaned by this. When his father died in during Fred's teens, Mother had been furious with him (Father) and the older brothers, convinced that he had been the victim of a professional hit, because of the scams he was running. A rift opened up in the family with him and his mother on one side, and his brothers and father's friends and associates on the other. As Fred's teenage years wore on, he found himself piggy in the middle, going out on jobs with his brothers, and keeping this secret from Mother. His short sentence when he was 18 blew this out of the water, and there was a huge row with his mother, then no more contact.

With this story in the open, other aspects of his mother emerged. She and Fred had been very close, especially during Father's periods of incarceration. Especially when Father was in prison, Fred and his mum would go out and spend some of the money amassed by Father from his latest heists. Together they shared a taste for the finer things in life, clothes and food, the delectation of which Fred had continued to enjoy.

The second phase is when the resident begins to give an account of the story of offending, and a detailed account of the index offence. Usually these stories present the resident in a less favourable light, and he will be subjected to a high level of challenge and criticism about his duplicity, violence and callousness in carrying out the offences.

EDDIE

Being in the group had been a revelatory experience for Eddie. Prior to coming to Grendon he had done an offending behaviour programme called 'Cognitive Skills'. In this, he remembered being told that he should think before he hit out. He could see that this made sense, but found it difficult to get a grasp on what this really meant. He still found himself in fights in prison. In the group, he had heard people talking about their offences, and about how they had made a choice to offend. Eddie didn't really think when he had his fight with Dan that he'd made a choice. Dan had died, and it was a mistake really.

Eddie had had a review meeting, where the staff group commented that he hadn't said much about his violence and his offence, so he was tasked to bring this to his small group. He felt quite angry about this, because there was nothing to it, really, it was just a mistake. He didn't want to kill his mate Dan, of course. Both him and Dan would go out tooled up with knives, just in case they needed them, but they didn't usually.

The group facilitator was a bit anxious about approaching the issue. Eddie was quite a loud and aggressive voice in the community and on the landings. All were aware of his language of violence and intimidation that he brought to almost every issue, and indeed it had become a problem that Eddie's offending pattern could be seen in his daily life on the community, but could not be addressed or spoken about. The facilitator wondered in the group whether the reason why Eddie had not explored his offence in much detail yet might be because people were worried what would happen if they broached it. Eddie complained that the therapist had it in for him, and that was why he had to bring it to the group. A fellow group member was becoming quite irritated. He and Eddie often sparred about things, and he took up the questioning. 'Eddie, that is bullshit, stop blowing smoke up my arse. You don't stick a knife in somebody's chest by accident. How many people have you cut, twenty or thirty that I know about. Maybe more than one of those died and you just don't know, mate. You're a bloody liability, you're fucking dangerous, you blow up at the slightest thing and it's straight to fists and treats. It's either violence or nothing with you, mate. Fucking accident, piss off. Was it a fucking accident that you're a fucking Nazi? What about being a fucking football boot boy – is that an accident? Piss off, it was bound to happen. I'm just glad you took away another of your fucking type, another stupid fucking murderous thug.'

Eddie had his head down, and another member of the group was talking. 'That's not fair, Ian, Dan was Eddie's friend.' Eddie's silence continued, and the group remained quiet. Another member spoke. 'Do you miss him?' Eddie nodded, still silent. There was a distinct sense of hidden tears.

The collective wisdom is that there are two phases to a Grendon treatment that are complementary. The first phase is that of articulating and expanding a personal history. Usually, these stories are full of abuse and neglect, and elicit genuine sympathy and empathy that enables the individual to build trust in the setting and in their group colleagues. The second phase is residents giving an account of their offending, violence, intimidation and so on. This account is given as a developmental account, and then more specifically in relation to the index offence. These criminal histories of Grendon men are often quite extreme, and difficult to hear. Attack and strong challenge of the individual by the rest of the group and the community will be inevitable, compounded by the probability of some form of acting out of the core delinquent dynamics in the community. However, following the first phase, these difficulties will be contextualised by the preceding account of the personal history, and within the context of knowing the individual well. These factors potentiate the group's ability to contain and work with the very difficult material of the individual's violence, cruelty, duplicity or whatever emerges during the course of the treatment. In addition, with the context of the individual's background developmental history, the meaning of the offending behaviour can be understood, and it can be put in the context of a cycling repetition compulsion that usually has its origins in childhood traumas.

CHAPTER 4

Grendon's Programme – Models of Change

The notion of a 'model of change' derives from the 'What Works' approach to offending behaviour programmes, and the associated literature and practice (e.g. McGuire and Priestley 1995). As mentioned in Chapter 1 the 'What Works' approach was a response to the collapse of the rehabilitative ideal in criminal justice from the 1970s. Its argument was that it was true that some treatment programmes for offenders were ineffective, but that these were not evidence-based, not theoretically sound and not rigorously and consistently applied. The fundamental elements of the 'What Works' approach are that the programmes are strongly evidence-based, have a coherent, legitimate and robust theoretical grounding and are applied in a consistent and audited way. The importance of the model of change is that it meets the second of these three requirements – it provides a logical and rational theoretical exposition of why the programme can be expected to work.

The problem with trying to articulate a model of change for a therapeutic community setting is that each person involved with a community has a different legitimate understanding of how it works, and this illustrates a reality that the treatment factors are indeed multi-factorial and complex. An example of a clear model of change is the way that anti-libidinal drugs reduce the risk of re-offending by sex offenders. Anti-libidinal drugs specifically prevent male sex hormones from being effective: sexual drive (libido) is dependant on male sex hormones so if these are reduced, sexual desire and libido are reduced, and hence the likelihood of any sexual activity that constitutes an offence. This is a simple and logical sequence that can comprise a model of change. Most therapeutic community workers will agree that the effectiveness of a therapeutic community experience includes social, psychodynamic and behavioural therapeutic elements along with attachment re-configuration, historical exploration and reconstruction, and the experience of membership of and a legitimate role in the social structure of a community.

A second problem in the creation of a model of change for a therapeutic community is that the philosophical tradition from which the 'What Works' paradigm derives is different from that from which the democratic therapeutic community does. As such, the task of trying to explain how a therapeutic community works in the 'What Works' language is like trying to translate jokes, poetry or puns from one language into another. It simply doesn't make sense in the new language – it can't be translated. The sense is lost in the translation because the new language does not have the idiom to be able to articulate the process. For example, all of the 'What Works' programmes rest on a recipe book of a progression and agenda for each session in the programme – rather like a teacher's lesson plan as part of a overall teaching curriculum. In a therapeutic community, most of the sessions are specifically unstructured. Furthermore, to structure the sessions would be to kill the therapeutic process. For example, the third essential feature in the 'What Works' triad of evidence base, coherent theoretical model and treatment integrity is the consistent application of the programme, of the centrally structured lesson plan, as an antidote to the problem of 'programme drift'. The concern is that allowing the content of the programme to drift according to the whims and trails of the facilitator, the clients or the subject being discussed will dilute and devalue the programme. Therapeutic community work is about drift; drift from subject to subject as the different lives of the residents unfold, as the history of the community unfolds, and as crises emerge and are managed. One way of understanding this difference of perspectives is in terms of the first of the 'What Works' triad – the evidence base or, more precisely, in defining the nature of evidence. 'What Works' evidence is positivist, empirical, whereas therapeutic community evidence, along with the more dynamic psychotherapies, is more qualitative, experiential.

In spite of these difficulties, and perhaps because of them, a number of different models of therapy have emerged during the iterative process backwards and forwards with the 'What Works'-orientated Home Office accreditation panel, and these will be summarised below in turn, starting with the medical model, which relies on the concept of the therapeutic community being an effective treatment for personality disorder. The second model is a more behavioural/cognitive formulation, where specific criminogenic factors can be seen to be tackled by aspects of the programme. The third has more of a social/milieu focus, where the therapeutic community as a whole is the effective agent of change. Because these models are meant to be complete and to stand alone as an explanation of how the community works, they do contain elements of repetition. However, they do capture different dimensions of how the process works and are relatively full for this reason.

Model 1 – therapeutic communities treat antisocial personality disorder

This model of change is probably the least satisfactory and coherent, but is historically important because it was accepted by the then UK Prison Accreditation Panel as a legitimate model of change for Grendon's work as a 'What Works' offending behaviour programme. As such it was the first successful explanation of how therapeutic communities work in the 'What Works' idiom. It starts at the point that the aspects of the individual that need to be changed are, in brief, the 'criminogenic factors' that have been identified by factor and cluster analytic statistical techniques as associated with higher risk of recidivism. These are widely accepted by the forensic psychological community (McGuire and Priestley 1995) and are divided into major and minor sets as follows.

Criminogenic factors (Andrews and Bonta 1994)

Major Set

1. Antisocial, pro-criminal attitudes, values, beliefs and cognitive-emotional states.

2. Pro-criminal associates and isolation from anti-criminal others.

3. Temperamental and personality factors conducive to criminal activity, including psychopathy, weak socialisation, impulsivity, restless aggressive energy, egocentricism, below average verbal intelligence, a taste for risk and weak problem-solving/self-regulation skills.

4. A history of antisocial behaviour evident from a young age, in a variety of settings and involving a number and variety of different acts.

5. Familial factors that include criminality and a variety of psychological problems in the family of origin and in particular low levels of affection, caring and cohesiveness, poor parental supervision and discipline practices, and outright neglect and abuse.

6. Low levels of personal educational, vocational or financial achievement and in particular, an unstable employment record.

Minor Set

7. Lower-class origins as assessed by adverse neighbourhood conditions and/or parental educational/vocational/economic achievement.

8. Personal distress, whether assessed by way of the sociological constructs of anomie, strain and alienation or by way of the clinical psychological constructs of low self-esteem, anxiety, depression, worry or officially labelled 'mental disorder'.

9. A host of biological/neuropsychological indicators.

(Shine and Morris 1999, p.11)

A parallel is drawn between the factors, noted above as criminogenic factors, and the descriptive content of the two major operationalised psychiatric classifications of antisocial personality disorder, DSM-IV and ICD-10.

The Antisocial Personality
(DSM-IV, American Psychiatric Association 1994)

The antisocial personality is characterised by 'a pervasive pattern of disregard for and violation of the rights of others', and the following features:

i.   Failure to conform to social norms and lawful behaviour, indicated by repeated grounds for arrest.

ii. Deceitfulness indicated by repeated lying, use of aliases or conning others for personal profit or pleasure.

iii. Impulsivity, failure to plan ahead.

iv. Aggressiveness, indicated by repeated fights or assaults.

v.   Reckless disregard for the safety of self or others.

vi. Consistent irresponsibility, indicated by repeated failure to sustain work or honour financial obligations.

vii. Lack of remorse, being indifferent to or rationalising having hurt, mistreated or stolen from others.

The ICD-10 version, the 'dyssocial personality', has the following characteristics:

The dyssocial personality
(ICD-10, World Health Organisation 1992)

i.   Callous unconcern for the feelings of others and lack of capacity for empathy.

ii. Gross and persistent attitudes of irresponsibility.

iii. Inability to maintain enduring relationships.

iv. Low tolerance of frustration and low threshold for discharge of aggression.

v.   Inability to experience guilt and profit from experience.

vi. Proneness to blame others.

vii. Persistent irritability.

(Shine and Morris 1999, p.13)

The second step is to propose that the behavioural clusters identified by Andrews and Bonta (1994) as 'criminogenic factors' are actually symptoms of the underlying personality disorder. The personality disorder is the disease, criminogenic factors are the symptoms of that disease.

Although there are enormous problems in defining personality and disorders of personality, the accepted rule of thumb is that the characteristics and idiosyncrasies that make up different personalities become disorders at the point when they cause suffering to the person or to society. A model of criminology based on personality disorders conceptualises offending behaviour as a symptom of the disordered personality. Offenders are those who come to the attention of services by virtue of their personalities causing suffering in society in the form of victims of crime.

The third step is to articulate why a therapeutic community is an effective treatment for personality disorder, namely that the complexity, disciplinary diversity and flexibility of the setting can match and stay on top of the variety of pathological manifestations of the disordered personality. Some of the complexities of personality disorder have been described above, but for the sake of this model of change the general descriptive frame for personality disorders from DSM-IV was articulated.

Personalities all display the following features (American Psychiatric Association 1994):

a.   An enduring pattern of behaviour that differs markedly from the expectations of the individual's culture manifested in:

   i.   Cognition – abnormal perceptions and interpretations of self, other people and events

   ii.   Mood – abnormal range intensity, lability and appropriateness.

   iii.   Abnormal interpersonal functioning

   iv.   Poor impulse control.

b.   The pattern is inflexible and pervasive across personal and social situations.

c.   The pattern is stable and long-lasting.

In this model of treatment the link between personality and crime was summarised thus:

> The personality disordered offender is disabled by distortions of perception, mood, interpersonal functioning and impulse control. These problems lead to social and intellectual failures which lead to social alienation and which compound the initial disability. The adoption of social deviance and crime is an alternative which is promoted by initial positive reinforcement. However, in the longer term the adoption of a deviant social framework continues the progressive social isolation except with pro-criminal equally socially disenfranchised contacts. The adoption of a criminal lifestyle, as described by the identified criminogenic needs/risk factors is the end stage of a long vicious circle that begins with disability of personality; extends to social failure and disenfranchisement and eventually to crime. (Shine and Morris 1999, p.11)

Personality disorder leads to multi-system failure: failure of emotional and relationship skills' development in childhood; failure of appropriate socialisation and pro-social attitude development and academic failure at school, with failure to achieve appropriate achievements for ability leading to low self-esteem, frustration and aggressive acting out in the form of deviant and law-breaking behaviour. Surrounded by antisocial peers, an individual may perceive a short-term advantage in the pursuit of criminal activity or substance abuse, which itself becomes an ingrained pattern. This often takes place in a setting where parents and relatives have similar antisocial characteristics, and the individual will have suffered to a degree from the neglect and/or frank abuse that will accompany this (Shine and Morris 1999).

Because of the degree of personality, attitude, value, social and behavioural distortion that comprises the clinical picture, the treatment process demands a similarly wide range of different treatment interventions taking place simultaneously. The therapeutic community environment provides this multi-factorial, multi-modal treatment environment in which the total personality can emerge and then be treated. In the therapeutic community, a multi-disciplinary and multi-dimensional approach specifically targets and challenges antisocial attitudes, values and beliefs; it specifically sets up an anti-criminal culture in which residents associate; it explores and challenges the antisocial history; it explores in detail the problems of the family of origin and it provides residents with experience of personal achievement as, through experience, they become leaders of the community.

Within the therapeutic community relationships between individual prisoners, prisoners and staff, and prisoners and the community as a whole, are under constant therapeutic scrutiny. Pathological behaviour is always a subject for discussion. Antisocial behaviour is repeatedly raised to awareness in groups and increasingly becomes available for informed understanding. Conscious management of behaviour is encouraged. Destructive behaviour is challenged by social sanctions. Creative and positive social and interpersonal behaviours are positively reinforced. The asocial and antisocial are anathematic in a therapeutic community. At the same time, at another level, the internalisation of these new appropriate social models and experiences leads to a structural change of the personality, diminishing the temperamental and personality factors that are conducive to criminal behaviour and reducing the sense of personal distress.

The explicit objective of this multidisciplinary team is to construct a social milieu that is conducive to the development of free social interaction and expression between inmates and between inmates and staff. In turn this sets up an authority structure similar to that of a pluralistic democracy, where different interest groups and perspectives jostle for position and decisions are made by consensus. All these contribute differing perspectives to the therapeutic milieu in general, and to the understanding and challenge of the members' personality, attitudes and values in particular. This multiplicity of models and the dialectic between them are all bounded by and contained within the therapeutic community social therapy structure; indeed, the pluralistic jostling of models forms the democratic social milieu. It also models for offenders vigorous disagreement, debate and resolution carried out in the community and staff team without recourse to criminal acting out.

The diverse disciplinary backgrounds of the therapeutic team enable them to maintain a social environment where residents feel safe and able to relinquish the aggressive and paranoid attitude that they will have acquired in the rest of the prison system (or which may have been present for much longer). Residents must feel sufficiently safe and trusting in the environment to be able to explore their own family and personal background histories, which for many will be traumatic and easier forgotten. Residents must feel they are in an environment safe enough for them to explore their criminal behaviour and be challenged and criticised about their rationalisations and avoidances of responsibility. There has to be a sufficient sense among residents of owning the process, and of belonging in the community; a sufficient identification with the aims of the community to help them tolerate the criticism and hostility that they may be faced with during their stay without their having recourse to assaultative behaviour or other destructive activity that would undermine the work. This sense of community cohesion is principally fostered in the numerous groups and structures that form the programme. The ongoing, 24-hour-a-day social environment, which is created by all the community members, is steered by staff towards health. This healthy social environment is in continuous interaction and dialogue with antisocial criminogenic need.

To summarise, within this model of change, criminogenic need and behaviour are symptoms of severe antisocial personality disorder. Personality disorders are ingrained complex multi-system problems, so their treatment needs to be sufficiently flexible to be tailored to individual need, sufficiently diverse to be able to respond to the variety of pathologies that will present and sufficiently robust to be able to withstand the organisational pressures that this group can bring to bear. The therapeutic community provides these elements in its environment via its combination of a clear pluralistic democratised structure with the disciplinary diversity within its multidisciplinary team.

Model 2 – therapeutic community treatment targets criminogenic need

This second model was developed to create a methodology for behaviourally-orientated forensic psychologists to be able to visit and audit Grendon. The task was to identify specific aspects of the therapeutic community programme that were observable and definitive of quality within the therapeutic community. The model eschews either an account of personality and personality disorder or one of developmental or upbringing environment to explain the treatment effect. Instead, it relies purely on the behavioural characteristics of offenders: those behavioural characteristics that have been associated with recidivism – criminogenic factors.

The frank behavioural component of therapeutic community work is clear; rule transgression leads to a fairly hefty negative stimulus, being 'dug out' on a community meeting – i.e. being confronted with the facts and challenged for the justification of one's actions. In their account of Grendon Genders and Player emphasise this more purely behavioural aspect of the work. 'The therapeutic community regime incorporates a strong behavioural component, whereby an individual's actions are examined with surgical precision and commented on by the whole community' (Genders and Player 1995, p.86).

The model is based on four assumptions that can, to a greater or lesser degree, be independently observed and evaluated. The first assumption is that the phenomenon of 'offence re-enactment' occurs, and that criminogenic factors contribute to offence re-enactments as they do to the actual offending behaviour. 'Offence re-enactment' has been described and defined by Lewis (1997) as the committing of minor infringements that in some way echo or mimic the index offence. The notion of offence re-enactment proposes that the resident's actual offences are not isolated events, but rather are a single manifestation of a longer cyclic repetitive process. The offence is one element of the cycles that has been more extreme or has come to the attention of the law. Because these cycles are part of the characteristic repertoire of the individual, they can be expected to exhibit themselves in the resident's everyday life. In a therapeutic community setting, with scrutiny of behaviour 24 hours a day, seven days a week, the pattern will be recognised as it exhibits itself in an attenuated form, will become linked to the core offending pattern and so will become available for exploration. This is best illustrated by the examples below. In order to allow these to take place, a setting has to be sufficiently tolerant not to clamp down on every minor enactment, and in order to allow the exploration of these enactments, the setting needs to have an active culture of enquiry.

The second assumption is that there is 'lateral linkage' between different treatment settings, so that offence re-enactments that occur in one frame are taken up in another. In case of Eddie described below, an offence re-enactment on the football field is tackled in the group and the community meeting. This is an essential part of an effective treatment because, in criminal activity, there is often a structuring of duplicity and feigning of good in one setting while nefarious activity takes place in another.

The third assumption is that, through exploration, the clients' under-standing of their offending and criminogenic factors is deepened and enriched, such that they recognise themselves much more as agents of the offence account, rather than victims or bystanders. In turn this promotes the acceptance of responsibility for the offending and the prevention of further offending. This deepening and enrichment of understanding does not take place via a structured programme of psycho-educative sessions as will be the case in standard offending behaviour cognitive programmes. Instead, the re-petitive cycles of offence re-enactment that take place will prompt an iterative process of exploration and re-exploration in the small group and community meetings.

The fourth assumption is that the criminogenic factors, or offending profile, of each individual are common knowledge across both the resident and the staff groups. Both staff and client members of the community will be aware of the criminogenic factors of individual residents in order that they are able to recognise offence re-enactments and characteristic antisocial strategies and risk constellations in order to challenge them and prompt exploration.

Together all of these processes are brought together in a regular case con-ference that reviews progress against treatment targets and identifies new targets to be focused on. These processes are best illustrated descriptively.

EDDIE

Eddie had always been good at football and was an active and regular player during the hour's exercise period in the prison's exercise yard. He played with gusto, exuberance and enthusiasm, and had a friendly contempt for the losing side, on which he rarely was. Staff had noticed this enthusiasm and had wondered about links with his football hooligan past, but had not been able to knit together a coherent strand. During the World Cup the prison had an internal knockout tourna-ment where teams took on the mantle of the international teams (and in the final England beat Brazil). Because of the tournament, there was more of an edge to the games than there had been previously with the kick-abouts during exercise. In one game Eddie was heavily tackled and exploded in rage, lunging for his opponent, and being held back by fellow members of his team.

The member of the opposing team who had tackled Eddie, Sid, was a member of the same community. He had been shaken by Eddie's rage and brought the issue to a community meeting, raising it as an agenda item. When his turn came, Sid rather falteringly described the incident, acknowledging that the tackle was on the edge of what was acceptable, but claiming that Eddie's actions amounted to an act of violence. Implicitly, this was a claim that Eddie should be discharged from Grendon because he had broken one of the three rules of no violence, no drugs and no sex.

Some of Eddie's friends remonstrated, arguing that the tackle was itself an act of violence. Prior to bringing the issue to the community, Sid had discussed the issue in his small group. In this discussion, Sid had been challenged that the tackle was heavy and had agreed that this was so. Sid said that in his group he had spoken about how he might have wanted a reason to get at Eddie, because Eddie always seemed to be threatening when he was playing football. Eddie's friends pooh-poohed this, and there was a *sotto voce* accusation of 'pussy'. Sid was more angry now. 'Eddie, you're always at it, and it's your offending behaviour. Before, you used to go out and get into fights – you would need a fight just to make yourself feel better, and there was some poor sod who you hammered that was in the wrong place at the wrong time. You can't do that here because you'd be on the bus, so you do it playing football.' Other members of the community were commenting now: 'It's true, Eddie, you give it large in football.' 'Look,' said another resident, 'Eddie, we all know what you're like, and you have done well by not getting into fights. You know that I'm one of the people that piss you off, so if you were looking for a fight then I might be on your list. But you haven't, and that's good. But what do you do instead? It's got to go somewhere. Maybe Sid is right – and you know that Sid pisses me off too, so that's not it – but maybe Sid's right, you're kicking it in on the pitch instead of in here when you get pissed off.' After some further discussion, the chairman proposed that the issue might go to a vote, but that Eddie needed to take the issue to his group to discuss first. The community moved on to its next item.

In the staff group discussion subsequently, the staff agreed that Eddie's boisterous football behaviour probably had an element of offence re-enactment incorporated within it, and more examples of a puppy-like over-enthusiasm that had an intimidatory quality were noted in different things Eddie did in the community. Staff members became aware of their own feelings of being intimidated; for example, Eddie had given out the coffee at the last family day, and had done this with an intimidatory bluster that had been difficult to pin down prior to this discussion. In his small group this was discussed, with more examples of a subtle edge to Eddie's interactions being noted. In the community, Eddie reluctantly owned that he did get angry playing football, and that he did feel better when he came back after a game – and that yes, it was a bit like the feeling he would have after a Saturday night fight or after a pitched battle as a football supporter/hooligan with opposing team supporters. In subsequent weeks in the group, the pattern of Eddie using different settings for a muted catharsis of his rage was clarified. Eddie struggled with this and often became enraged, which increasingly he would express on the group, feeling depressed and hopeless.

This example demonstrates two particular aspects of this model: one, the expression of the characteristics that have led to the index offence in a more mild and attenuated form – offence re-enactment – and two, the identification of such a re-enactment in one living setting being laterally linked to others, where is it examined and explored further.

GEORGE

By his third month of treatment, George was beginning to make himself indispensable, being a happy and willing worker, especially happy to do the sort of jobs that no one else wanted to do. He agreed to be the cleaner of the most dirty landing, after many had been approached and refused; and he agreed to be the film rep, whose job it was to arrange for the video hire and showings. This was a hated job because everyone was always critical of the film choice, and the work involved endless consultation and mollifying of dissatisfied residents.

There was a more sought-after job that George made it clear that he would like to have; that of catalogue rep: the holder of the Argos catalogue, through which items could be ordered. There was another person up for this job who was also keen. In the community meeting where a vote was to be taken, George made the case that he had 'shov-elled the shit' for the community and so should be allowed to get something back. He was asked why he wanted the job, and said that he didn't have much money, but would save it to buy something. When he was 'on the out', he would spend hours window-shopping. 'I don't get out much any more to do this,' he said, to laughter. 'The catalogues are a poor substitute...' Some of the community weren't happy in a non-specific way, but George got the majority vote. In the event several weeks later, the catalogue had to be replaced because it ended up in a shower where it got soaked. George was apologetic for his poor stewardship and nothing more was thought about the matter. George continued to work hard and reliably at his different tasks.

Three months later, during a routine cell search, a stuffed envelope was found in George's room, filled with pages from an Argos catalogue: pictures of the toy section and products with children in the photo-graphs. George was confronted with the find, and asked to take it to his small group. His group identified two parallels with his offending. First, that he had planned his access to the material, so that this was not an impulsive thing. They accused him of destroying the first copy to hide his tracks which, after confrontation, he agreed, and that this was also finely planned. Second, they found a parallel in his making himself useful. He had been a good worker in the children's homes, above suspicion, as he had tried to make himself in the community.

In the larger community meeting, when the issue was raised, there was anger at George 'taking the piss' out of the community, and those who had been suspicious of his volunteering for the post were able to explore their thoughts that George had been too good to be true. Some demanded a vote about George's commitment to therapy, thinking he should be 'chucked out'. They felt defiled by having been duped and inadvertently involved in George's perverse ritual.

George had been humiliated and shocked by the process of being found out and felt bewildered, having been stripped of his cloak of helpfulness, which was a lifelong defensive attitude beneath which much was hidden. In the following weeks, however, the issue that he struggled with most was the idea that he had been 'taking the piss', and the anger that this had generated in the community. His small group looked at how his sexual perversion and offending were themselves a cloak for his rage and murderousness and that, although he had not physically killed his victims, he had killed some aspect of them, their innocence or youth or trust in carers. George was painfully and powerfully put in touch with the violence of his offending and its lesser recapitulations.

In the examples above, it is clear that the total environment provided by the therapeutic community residential component contributed by allowing the offence re-enactment to be identified. It is much more difficult for someone to hide his characteristic ways of functioning in a residential environment than it is in a specific sessional treatment programme. So, Eddie's intimidatory attitude is noticed playing football rather than in the group settings, although once the dynamic was identified it could be traced through different settings. The community meeting functioned as the setting where George's offence paralleling could take place (he was 'grooming' the community in being elected) and also when the pattern could be confronted (George and Eddie's peers tackling them over their behaviour). The staff meetings serve as an opportunity for the staff group to process the information that has emerged, and to contextualise it, refining the formulation to then inform the facilitation of the small group. The small group functions as a place where the fact that has been identified in the community as worthy of exploration can be discussed further. This deepens the understanding of the particular behavioural 'fact' itself, maps out its links to wider issues and offending. At the same time the web of influence of the particular criminogenic dynamic can be rooted out (Eddie's boisterous intimidation being seen in his giving out of the coffee and in other settings).

In criminogenic language, the vignettes about Eddie and George above describe the identification and confrontation of antisocial attitudes and cognitive-emotional states and the rationalising of cognitive distortions. In the settings of the community and facilitated small group, the behaviour is modified, explored and understood through interaction with the staff group and the collective of the group and community who form a 'pro-social other'. Eddie and George are being offered alternative problem-solving and regulatory skills and are being engaged with by a pseudo-family rather than being isolated. This process of the emergence of criminogenic factors in real time, where they can be challenged, is augmented by a process of assessment and review.

Model 3 – the therapeutic community is a mutative environment

This third model is very much more simple and was evolved in response to concern about the legitimacy of arguments that treatments of personality disorder were poorly evidence-based: a concern that had sprung up around the issue of Dangerous and Severe Personality Disorder (DSPD). At its most basic, the model proposes that the offender is a function of an unhelpful developmental environment. The therapeutic community provides an alternative, more pro-social environment in which the offender may re-forge his characteristic repertoire. This model requires an account of how disturbed and disordered developmental environments give rise to criminal behaviour and of the characteristics of the therapeutic community that can maintain a more healthy environment in which people can recapitulate aspects of their development. The broad model can be expressed diagrammatically (see Figure 4.1).

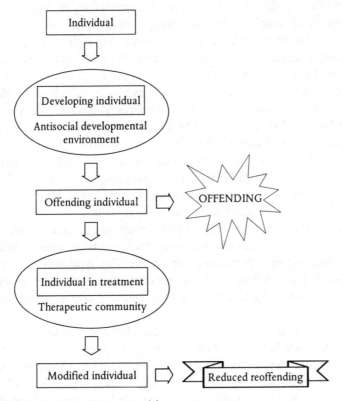

Figure 4.1 The mutative environment model

It was proposed that the environments in which Grendon residents had grown up were often abusive, neglectful and difficult. In a general way, survival in an abusive and neglectful environment might inculcate a negative set of values and attitudes as adaptive to the environment. Specific antisocial skills might need to be learned for one to be able to survive in this environment, and would become the norm. The use of this antisocial skill-set outside the specifically hostile home environment and in the more normal community settings such as school, shared community spaces and the homes of others would constitute offending behaviour.

An example might be the psychopathic symptom of callousness and lack of empathy, particularly noted in relation to the effect of the offence on the victim. One might imagine that if you had parents who were unconcerned about you as a child, who had not empathised with your childish traumas and so on, who had been abusive and unconcerned about the effect that the abuse was having on you, this would have an effect on your own development of the capacity to see things from another's point of view. If you were conceived by your mother in order to trap a wayward boyfriend or in order to obtain a house from the council; if you were simply a hassle as a child, only useful as a negotiating chip in relations between parents and grandparents or as a means of obtaining some more State hand-out; it might be difficult to grasp the sense of the inviolability of personhood as a moral starting point. If, as an adolescent, your worth was measured by the extent to which the older gang members could get you to steal and then, later, you were only relevant as a punter who could get money for the drug dealer, it might be rather difficult for you to develop a Kantian ethical principle that people should be treated as an end, not as a means. It seems to be a characteristic of such difficult environmental settings that the children are property: a part of the parent to be treated as the parent wishes. Later, in gangs and criminal peer groups, people are 'owned' by each other, continuing the same dynamic.

The developmental accounts of neglect, abuse and cruelty that are commonplace in Grendon and other criminal justice settings where offenders are given a voice suggest a common environment. The hypothesis is that this environment is the crucible in which cruel values and attitudes develop that become self-sustaining and that, in turn, become criminogenic needs and issues for individuals.

The next stage in the model is to describe the setting in which some recapitulative development can take place, namely the therapeutic community. This is described in four ways: that the environment has a 'culture of enquiry', the classical Rapoport dimensions (1960), the feel and culture of work in groups, of Yalom (1985), and/or using the more home-grown Grendon value set.

Broadly, the whole therapeutic community process can be understood as one that fosters and facilitates a culture of enquiry (Main 1983). Anyone with experience of small children will have played the 'Why?' game, where the child asks 'why?' to each question answered. Pretty quickly the adult becomes exasperated, but maybe this is in part because, pretty quickly, the questions become quite fundamental and philosophical, difficult to answer. This illustrates the power of the process of enquiry. In the therapeutic community, everything is up for question; it is legitimate to question and enquire about every process, every nuance, every activity, every decision, and so on. The maintenance of such a culture is not a passive process, but one that is very active and requires considerable effort because the pulls down to more regressive ways of thinking are so strong (Norton 1992). This culture is exemplified in one of the questions on the Therapeutic Community Audit Checklist, namely whether the residents feel able to ask a staff member why they feel grumpy that day (Kennard and Lees 2001). The point is that nothing is off-limits for enquiry.

This culture of enquiry is focused both on the process of treatment and on the behaviour and understandings of the residents as these emerge in the treatment process. For example, in the case material above, why did Eddy lose it when he was tackled? Someone might have asked why George was so keen to be the catalogue rep when he volunteered. Why did George go back to his abuser's house after the first inappropriate touching? Even though he went back, why does George think that it was OK for his abuser to abuse him? Why is it important to keep drugs off the community? Because it creates an alternative mafia like authority structure. Why does this happen, why can't people 'just say no'? Because this is a prison, everybody wants the 'walls to go away' and almost everybody has used drugs to make this happen for a while, so many people are vulnerable to the temptation. Why are people vulnerable to temptation? Everybody is, and so is the person asking the question – indeed why is the questioner pretending he or she doesn't understand this anyway, and asking stupid questions?

The second broad descriptive platform for the therapeutic community environment comprises the four themes of therapy abstracted by Robert Rapoport (1960) from his sociologically-based observation of the therapeutic community at the Henderson Hospital. These themes of therapy are:

- permissiveness – allowing sufficient space for pathological behaviour to become manifest and available for changing

- democratisation – modelling healthy society with group-based decision-making

- reality confrontation – enabling the consequences of behaviour to be returned to the person/people emitting this behaviour

- negative reinforcement of antisocial behaviour, and

- communalism – modelling a good community and encouraging appreciation of communal participation and experience.

Haigh (1999) has re-cast these characteristics as a developmental process, with an additional dimension of attachment being the starting point. When this is established to some degree, a sense of containment and safety (permissiveness) will evolve, that can create communication and openness (communalism). The process of finding a place will bring forward involvement and living/learning in the community (reality confrontation) and will be followed by a sense of agency and empowerment (democratisation).

A third descriptive aspect of the therapeutic community experience is that of being in groups, and this is best illustrated by reference to Yalom's work, where he described factors in group settings that he thought were therapeutic (1985). In a therapeutic community setting, residents will benefit from the following factors characteristic of groups:

- the installation of hope – by the sense of an ongoing treatment process and by observing community members who have made progress by virtue of being further on in treatment

- universality – it is striking how many hostile, macho, frightening prisoners think that they are the only person who is putting on a bit of a front, and who deep down can feel afraid, and contemptuous of that fear

- imparting information – the cognitive therapeutic process – learning about how people's minds work, the notion of choice, the methods of denial, rationalisation and minimisation, and so on

- altruism – that genuine affection and attachment grown between members of the community and group such that altruistic feelings emerge

- the corrective recapitulation of the family group – this is in essence the whole model as depicted in Figure 4.1

- development of socialising techniques – learning social skills and having the opportunity to rehearse newer and more appropriate ones in the group and community setting

- imitative behaviour – modelling more appropriate behaviours, such as expressing anger without recourse to violence

- interpersonal learning – for example, learning how others cope with overwhelming emotional impulses, or learning from others' reconstruction of their histories

- group cohesiveness – a sense of belonging somewhere

- catharsis – a place to emote. At a basic level, in Grendon there are fewer fights in the showers because people fight verbally in the groups. When the groups are cancelled, for example in holiday breaks, one can feel the pressure building up

- existential factors – being alone in the universe and recognising that others have the same dilemma.

In this model the function of the small group is to facilitate the community process. The small groups are not psychoanalytic groups in the classical sense. Their character and content are entirely changed by their location in a 24-hour community therapy regime. Their contents are not confidential, but a précis of each small group is fed back to the larger community at the end of each group. The group therapist is not a 'blank screen' figure seen only once or twice a week on whom intense transference rests. Usually, the group therapist is not a qualified analyst, shrouded in unchallengeable mystique. He or she is most often a prison officer who, at the end of a group, may have to carry out a mandatory drug test or cell search. The group therapists are more like community group facilitators than analysts. The aim of the groups is to facilitate the wider work of the therapeutic community. This is not to deny that the facilitation and maintenance of the therapeutic community relies heavily on psychodynamic ideas and approaches; it does. However, it is not true to say that the aim of the groups is group analysis. The psychodynamic therapists work to empower and support staff who are engaged in the broader social therapy work which underlies the functioning of the therapeutic community.

Finally, the Grendon set of values and understandings of its function need to be touched upon. These represent the local perception of how the therapeutic community culture is different from others, promoting positive mutative change in the personality.

Respect is a starting point. Individuals are deserving of respect irrespective of their history (and offending) and irrespective of their occupation (e.g. prison officer). It is easy to say that, but the maintenance of respect is quite a difficult task for both residents and staff. For residents, years of hating 'screws' and 'filth' (the police) have inculcated a judgementalism about the uniform and tasks of staff, as have poor experiences at the hands of staff in the past. Abuse and neglect by civilians in authority often fosters a similar suspicion of civilian staff by the residents. For the staff group, the task is about trying to respect the perpetrator of what may be horrific crimes, and the holder of a frighteningly callous attitude. Thus the maintenance of bilateral respect is quite a difficult task on both sides. Also, within the prisoner group there is a rigid hierarchy of crimes, with the armed robbers as the royalty on the top, the burglars in the middle, sex offenders and offenders against women and children below that, and paedophiles at the bottom, universally disrespected. Residents struggle to respect their fellows whose crimes are perceived to be beneath their own. Also, within the staff group, it is easy to become contemptuous about the skills and expertise of those from different disciplines as well as those at different managerial levels.

Honesty and accountability are the next important underpinning values, and there are several levels to this. First, honesty is a central value in the therapeutic process. It is assumed as a starting point that individuals are not honest with themselves about their own minds. To paraphrase Nietzsche: my memory says I did that; my will says I did not. My will prevails. Anna Freud (1936) [1966] extended Freud's description of the defences of the ego – psychological mechanisms that the ego uses to minimise and water down unpleasant facts about the self. Basically, all these are about being dishonest. The process of exploratory psychodynamic therapy is one of unearthing and facing unpleasant aspects of and facts about the self. This requires honesty from the outset. Eddie was being dishonest with himself in believing that his killing his friend was an accident – as pointed out by the group, this level of violence was a lifestyle choice and something like it was bound to happen sometime. His 'accident' hypothesis was dishonest. A more honest and truthful account would own his violence and recognise the risk that he poses.

Second, the accountability element is where the staff group become involved. Because the staff group are in charge, they hold the position of authority in the community. The staff group need to be able to be honest and accountable in their decisions and actions. In the services, there is a phrase, 'sloping the shoulder'. The policeman who catches the burglar red-handed can have a laugh with him on the way back to the station or complement him on his technique, by 'sloping the shoulder' of disapprobation. It is the judge, the court or society who disapprove of theft, not the policeman. This process is actually quite important, because it allows those who have to be in actual contact to maintain reasonable relationships with the perpetrators, while confronting or preventing the behaviour.

In a therapeutic community setting, an authority needs to own its own authority, because a significant part of the task is to help residents get to grips with their relationship with authority. If the officers and the inmates are chums and all the unpleasant stuff is the fault of the governor whom they both hate, the officer and prisoner can get along but not make any therapeutic progress. The prisoner's hatred of authority rests with the governor whom he rarely sees and with whom he will be unable to work the issues through. The officer needs to own the governor's decision or to protest to the governor that the rule is inappropriate. If the officer owns the rule, then it is the officer's fault that the rule is being enforced, and the prisoner can work through his frustration face to face.

The issue of safety is a particular issue for treatment environments where the resident group might be damaging to oneself and others. It recognises that there are boundaries that need to be drawn for the safety of all. In Grendon, these boundaries are drawn at the 'no violence, no sex no drugs' level. There has to be a general ownership of the legitimacy of these boundaries. This is not to say that they cannot be challenged and, indeed, will be when a transgressor is defending himself; but the reasons for them are so strong that they cannot be shifted. Broadly, the reason is that in their different ways sex, violence and drugs can corrode and undermine the community process itself, creating allegiances that are hidden so cannot be explored and enquired about, and creating obligations that can compromise an individual's freedom to speak.

The treatment hypothesis is that the therapeutic community provides a setting where the prevailing culture present in the residents' antisocial, developmental environments can be reversed. In the therapeutic community, each person has the right to deserve respect and a say; each person is accountable for his or her actions, both staff and residents, and there is a clear structure of rules which is respected and adhered to. Violence – the currency which enforces much of the anti-social environment – is not tolerated. Drugs – the currency that continues and refines the antisocial culture into adulthood and primes the bullying and intimidatory cultures found in some prison – settings are not tolerated. Within such a setting, individuals can re-address their own histories, and grow.

CHAPTER 5

Diverse Perspectives –
The Multidisciplinary Team

Working with personality disordered people, there is one truism that recurs. The biggest risk of all is certainty. If, as a practitioner, you start to feel certain or confident about anything, then it is pretty clear that you are being taken for a ride. People – we – are complex, contradictory and unpredictable things. From this perspective, the process of getting to know people and deepening relationships is a process of getting to understand the rhythms and patterns within the chaos and unpredictability that is the human condition, while accepting that you can never really know. When one is treating this group, this presents quite a number of problems, most notably in the area of risk assessment and prediction. Closely related to this is the problem of the process of clinical decision-making. Decision-making is not a science but, rather, always an educated guess.

This account may seem a little exaggerated – we all know people whom we can set our watches by so regular is their carrying out of their rituals and daily routines. Paradoxically, it may be these obsessional people who are the most disorganised, needing to construct for themselves an outer order to counter the inner chaos. Expressed technically, the illusion of certainty that one has about obsessional people is a projection; they are managing to make you believe that which they wish to believe about themselves, that they are ordered. Meanwhile, internally they struggle with all sorts of madness and chaos. This perspective can be criticised as over-psychoanalytic – namely seeing extreme pathology in the normal and everyday. The assertion might be re-stated as a medicalisation so that those whose personality is very unpredictable and chaotic have a disease – personality disorder.

Either way, the truism remains that in work with personality disordered people the certainty of the practitioner is a significant risk. Team decision-making is a technical device to get around this problem. Stated simply, the personality disordered patient can fool some of the team some of the time but, one hopes, not all of the team all of the time. The illusory certainty of one practitioner in the team can be challenged by a colleague, and a debate can ensue. The result of this debate will be closer to an accurate formulation of the current situation, from which more accurate predictions can be made, and so better clinical decisions.

This chapter explores the nature of these teams as they are constituted and function in the Grendon communities, arguing for their multidisciplinary constitution, and provides some illustrations of their work. After an impressionistic account of the complexity of personality pathology that is being dealt with, and the reason why this complexity is best treated and followed by a team combining diverse disciplines, the contribution of the different disciplines to the teams in Grendon is explored in more detail, with clinical illustrations.

The need for multidisciplinary teams

Arguably, the problems stated above about personalities can be reduced to looking at the complexity of mind. One of the problems of the study of mind is the vast and bewildering number of apparently legitimate theoretical models to account for human nature. On the one hand, there are accounts that understand a person's personality and nature as explicable in terms of family and upbringing, there are those that emphasise the importance of observed behaviour and those that lay stress on a more biological understanding of the functioning of the brain. On the other, are the even larger number of more purely psychological accounts of human nature to be found in the psychotherapies: from attachment-based understandings to drive theory psychoanalytic ones; object relations, trauma and so on.

The reason for this bewildering array of apparently coherent models of human nature is not so much that 'no man is an island' but more that each man is a continent. It makes more sense to refer to a sociology of mind than a science: a sociology of mind populated by a chaotic and disparate number of different sub-personalities, cultural affiliations, attitudes and mores. One can also compare the sociology of mind with a sociology of a continent with competing interests, political allegiances, agendas and relationships that are constantly moving, constantly changing and evolving. Different models and disciplines describe different aspects of this sociology of mind. Neurology describes the physical geography of the land mass of the continent; neurophysiology describes the communication links; neuropharmacology, the influences that determine the dynamics of this infrastructure; dopamine, leaves on the line; or an anti-depressant, a new bypass to resolve a bottleneck.

At another level, the study of familial and traumatic influences on character are an account of the political history of the society that is the mind, and the ways in which this affects and influences current functioning. The behaviourists are the media observers of the actual activities of the society of the mind. The cognitive psychologists explore the political and civil structures beneath the actual activities that make more sense of the observed gross movements or behaviour. In this model, wherein the mind is best conceived of as a society rather than as a singular entity, the more psychodynamic models are the humanities and arts faculties of this continent of man. The impressionistic accounts of what is going on may be to a greater or lesser extent systematised into coherent academic theories but ultimately can be no more than impressionistic statements.

This model of personality and character as a vast and largely chaotic system derives from a psychoanalytic perspective. Other perspectives can be more clear and simple. For example, a Skinnerian view of behaviour emanating from a 'black box' reduces character to that which can be seen and observed. The account of human nature is simply an account of those things that can modify behaviour – for example, prevention of a phobic response to a stimulus or reinforcement of a behaviour by associating it with a positive stimulus. The next level down – a cognitive approach – assumes that the mind is rational and that adverse aspects and behaviours can be changed by persuading the individual of the logical and rational reasons for doing so.

From a psychodynamic perspective, one can learn as much about human nature from the study of cognitive psychology as one can learn about a Big Mac by studying the pattern of sesame seeds on the bun. From a psychoanalytic perspective, man's much vaunted rationality is merely the icing on the cake: an illusory cloak beneath which a much more animalistic, monstrous and chaotic organism lurks. Rationality is a veil of order and coherence concealing a mass of disorder and confusion. The fact that so many people believe that they are rational beings is testament to the effectiveness of this evolutionary development. Sustaining this illusion makes life much easier to live and, for the most part, it is a healthy and beneficial illusion. However, at times, for some people, the mask slips and some of the chaos leaks out. When this becomes a pattern and a problem – this is when it is important that the chaos and confusion are tackled for what they are, rather than a pretence being maintained that the illusion of rationality is either effective or relevant.

The reason for this rather suffocating account of personality is to introduce the need for multidisciplinary teams. Multidisciplinary teams are difficult, confusing and chaotic animals wherein schism and dissent reign. Being a member of a particular professional discipline means that your world view has been configured according to a particular perspective. Indeed, an experienced member of a particular discipline becomes an expert in the interpretation of the world according to that particular view. Having to work with a colleague from a different discipline on a particular issue involves the threat of your own world view/perspective about a particular issue being undermined by a different one. As a professional, you don't just 'do' medicine or psychology or law or whatever; as a professional you 'are' a medic, psychologist, lawyer. Therefore, the experience of having your professional perspective undermined by a colleague professional threatens your own identity. In an interdisciplinary debate about an issue, the stakes can be high, and the debate that begins from different perspectives can be fuelled by personal and identity issues. Multidisciplinary teams lead to decisions that are contested, controversial and ambiguous: decisions that nobody is happy with, but which are the best that can be brokered in the circumstances.

Simple, clear decisions about people with personality disorder are usually wrong. Because personalities are themselves complex, ambiguous and unclear, their management will similarly be complex, ambiguous and unclear. The beauty of the multidisciplinary team is that the different disciplinary perspectives and personalities that constitute it allow dimensions or degrees of freedom to articulate the complexities of the personality that is being worked with. Decisions made by a multidisciplinary team enshrine a balance of perspectives and interests that will be the best possible compromise in the circumstances. To outsiders not involved in the decision, a clearer and simpler path may be evident; but this is an illusion born of their monodisciplinary perspective.

FRED

Fred had six months to go prior to his release, and among the staff team there was some debate about whether he should have a home leave as he had requested. Fred had made good progress in looking at how his whole life and lifestyle were linked to his offending, and his probation officer was working hard with him to try to find some accommodation for him so that he would have a home and a place to live, rather than living his previous nomadic life from hotel to hotel, leaving no trace. Fred had decided he wanted to get a flat in the East End of London, but his group had deconstructed this thinly veiled attempt to get back on to his old stamping ground, taking up his drug-dealing business where he had left off. Fred had protested, and this had been rather a difficult issue for some time, with Fred having to face his wish to return to his old ways and his ambivalence about change.

The probation officer had found a hostel in Birmingham that was interested in offering him a place. Fred had been interested as he knew it a little from childhood, having had an uncle whom he had visited in the suburbs there as a child. He had relatively good and pro-social memories. The hostel wanted him to visit, and this had led to the discussion about the appropriateness and advisability.

Two different disciplines were fairly certain about what should happen. The probation officer was quite clear that this was an important opportunity for Fred; he had made very considerable progress in agreeing to consider Birmingham and the officer felt certain that Fred's motivation to go out and visit was genuine. He felt that Fred should be allowed to go on his own, ideally; after all he was getting out in six months. Two of the officers had a different view. Fred was more offish with these two and in the past they had had their suspicions about some of his activities. At their extreme, these concerns were that he had established something on the wing and more widely in the prison and was now one of the central drug dealers. They believed he had ways of bringing stuff in and was distributing it, making money, as he had always done, and staying one step ahead of suspicion, as he had always done. The two officers were convinced that Fred's demand for a day out was a ruse to be able to pick up drugs and bring them back in. Fred's own view was that he would feel humiliated going out cuffed or with staff, and would rather not go if he was going to be accompanied.

When the issue had been discussed in the community, Fred had turned round the discussion to the question of why he was not trusted or, more particularly, who it was in the community that didn't trust him. The staff had attempted to interpret this as Fred preventing a debate by intimidating those who would question his integrity and being unable to accept that it was legitimate to ask questions about his trustworthiness. In the staff meeting this performance was taken as further evidence of his nefarious motivations, but his group facilitator didn't agree. Fred always operated in the background, he was very intimidated by being in the community and his bullish and intimidatory presentation was a function of this. In his subsequent small group, he had agreed that he had raised suspicion by his performance, and felt a bit foolish when this was pointed out.

Fred was an item on the staff meeting agenda and, quite quickly, the issue became rather heated, with different members of staff strongly holding diverse views. The probation officer, with some support from the therapist, tacitly accused the officers of making a macho response to a man (Fred) who might outwit them in his circumvention of the security structures. 'The fact that he could get stuff in if he wanted doesn't mean that he's doing it.' The suspicion that Fred would use the visit to bring drugs in was ridiculed: 'He never does it himself, he gets others to do it. There is no way that he'll be bringing stuff in, he just wouldn't do it himself, he's far too clever.' The officers were angry about this, quoting chapter and verse of the release risk assessment procedure which emphasised the importance of intelligence, and there was intelligence pointing at Fred. 'He may not do it himself,' they returned, 'but he might go and meet a man who can.'

The psychologist contributed that although they didn't have a psychopathy test score, they were quite certain that Fred would score highly, and that the controversy in the staff group confirmed this as he seemed to have split the staff group. With this, the meeting became a bit more reflective. Someone commented that it was interesting that Fred's contribution was that he wouldn't want to go if he was accompanied. 'If he had someone with him, he could do all the stuff about visiting, and so on, but he couldn't pick up gear. He may not be planning to, but he might be anxious about having his options closed.' Another officer suggested the plan of agreeing to the visit, but that the staff group view was that he needed to be accompanied. Fred could propose two members of staff who could go with him, to acknowledge his sensitivity, and then the package proposal would be put to the release of temporary licence board, who would have the final say.

The disciplines that are combined in Grendon's work consist of psychotherapy, forensic psychology, probation and custody – prison officers. In addition there is input from art psychotherapy and psychodrama, and primary care medical and nursing. In exploring the way the team works, a distinction will be made between task and dimension. Each of the different disciplines in the team has different tasks, but in addition to these concrete things that they do, they bring to discussion and debate about the clinical work different perspectives and points of view that constitute the disciplinary dimension. Particularly important in Grendon's work is the flavour of this teamworking, which will be explored below.

In brief, the tasks of the different disciplinary groups are as follows. The therapist's task is to provide clinical and community leadership. The forensic psychologist provides a behaviourally-focused contribution, keeping in mind the individual's criminogenic profile and the actualities of the offending behaviour. The probation officer maintains and establishes links with external agencies and families; in particular preparing release plans for those who are discharged from the gate. Most Grendon men move from Grendon on to other prisons prior to release, but determinate sentence prisoners may lead up to and then be released from Grendon itself. The discipline informing the majority of the staff group is provided by the discipline officers. Their contribution is to be prison officers and to 'maintain good order and discipline', to quote the manuals; they bring a sceptical perspective, drawn from years of working with difficult people.

Tasks and culture – the therapist

The task of the psychotherapist in the team is to provide clinical leadership. At its most technical, the therapist's task is to facilitate the multidisciplinary team conceived as a group in its own right. Many accounts of the work of the therapist in a group focus on the task of conducting the group: of oiling the wheels of group functioning. It is not the therapist's role to have all the answers; it is assumed that most of the therapeutic input will be found within the group and that the group itself will do the work that its members need. However, from time to time, the group will become hooked on a dynamic that hijacks its ability to work. Bion (1961) identified 'basic assumptions' that can preoccupy a group, including a dependency dynamic on the leader; a fantasy that a messiah will come to save the group; a 'pairing' fantasy – that a couple will get together and solve the problems – and a 'fight/flight' group, that is self-explanatory. In a psychotherapy group – or in a staff team – it may happen that all the discussion and interest of the members moves away from the issue at hand, the risk assessment of whether prisoner Bloggs can go and visit his ill mother, and turns instead to the far more exciting issue of whether officers Teddy and Edwina are having an affair. Or whether prisoners Ted and Edward are. From a group analytic perspective, this would be known as a 'pairing dynamic', and the risk is that this debate rather than the task issue saps all of the energy of the staff group. In this situation, it would be the task of the therapist to deal with the dynamic, by interpreting it or in some other way, in order to refocus on the task.

A much more common group dynamic that emerges is the fight/flight or the scapegoating one. In a fight/flight dynamic, it may be that a particular resident has become a bit 'mouthy' – inappropriately verbally critical of staff, the work or a decision that has been made. As the staff group process this, somebody reviews his history to find that in a previous jail when he has been confronted over an issue he has taken a hostage whom he has injured. Suddenly, there is a will within the staff group to have him removed as a security risk and a paralysis of the clinical work because of a fear that he may once again become dangerous. Clearly feeding into this anxiety are the twin factors that the resident is undoubtedly a dangerous man, as evidenced by his previous behaviour, but also that groups tend to fall back on fight/flight type dynamic when under strain. In the debate about what to do in this situation, the therapist will comment on the possibility that the fear about the resident is a chimera created by a group dynamic.

FRED

One night, after lockup, Fred had raised the alarm, thinking that the person in the next cell had cut himself. This was indeed the case, and the resident was 'blue lighted' to the local casualty department. Over the next few days, while the resident was still in hospital, the story filtered out into the community that the resident had nearly died, having lost so much blood from the wrist wound. Over the past few weeks there had been a number of community residents feeling depressed, a number of '2052' forms opened (the suicide watch log), and the community and staff team had been rather jumpy about a number of those with a history of severe self-harm.

Surprisingly, and quite disturbingly, the resident who had cut up wasn't one of those who was on the worry list, further undermining the staff group's confidence, and that of the community. The cutter instead was an addict. The sense of anxiety did not diminish several days later when the resident returned, apologetic about the scene and the mess he had created, and attributing the crisis to a letter he had received from home, saying his little brother had been convicted of burglary, for which he felt responsible.

This account was greeted with some scepticism by the staff group because, with this resident, letters from a chaotic home life were something of a regular diversion. For the staff group, the question of why the self-harm had taken place was still open. Discussions in the staff group became more focused on the resident's drug history; about the fact that there was some memory of difficulties in the days leading up. He had seemed a bit distracted, a bit distant. Also, the vaunted letter could not be produced, having been allegedly destroyed in the angst leading up to the self-cutting.

Fred had raised the alarm, and Fred was thought to be involved in drugs. Fred might have been squeezing him for money owed, or whatever, or been aware that he was 'clucking' (strung out and needing a heroin dose). Concern ignited about Fred's complicity. There was a view in the staff group that Fred was a real cancer eating away at the heart of the community, poisoning it with his drug dealing, and now leading people almost to suicide.

The therapist resisted, interpreting the staff team's wish to be rid of Fred as displaced anxiety about the current wave of feelings of self-harm. He reminded the team that in Grendon there was the highest rate of self-harmers in the prison service, but that the suicide rate was low. Yes, the resident's suicide attempt had been frightening, yes, the whole issue needed to be taken up at a community meeting as an issue of why the only language to express distress currently seemed to be to articulate suicidal thoughts. These things were true; but discharging Fred wasn't going to impact on the current wave of depression in the community, even though it might make the staff feel better in the short term.

Another dimension of a fight/flight scapegoating dynamic can be illustrated by the next example where the annihilatory fear within the staff group is not directed at the resident, but instead at other members of staff.

FRED

After the discussion, concern about Fred did not abate. There seemed to be a widening split between the officers as a group and the civilian staff about his commitment to treatment, and whether he was genuine or using his therapy as a shield behind which to carry out his trade. The senior prison officer (the officers unit manager) was neutral about the issue, having discussed it with the civilian staff, but in response to his own team's concerns agreed to make some enquiries. He found out that Fred had spent some time in previous sentences in Brixton and, as the senior prison officer had quite a good friend in the segregation unit there, he telephoned to get an inside track on Fred. Fred had been in and out of the segregation unit on several occasions, and one occasion was when he had almost taken a woman teacher hostage but had been prevented by staff. The woman had been working closely with him, persuading him to do some work on his drug habit. Suspicion had arisen that Fred was bringing drugs into the establishment, and that possibly she was involved. Fred must have got wind of this, and the next time he was in education there was a scuffle that had been interpreted as an attempted hostage incident.

The senior officer reported this back to the Grendon security department, who were also reasonably sanguine about it, being aware that a high proportion of Grendon men have such histories in their background. However, when he fed back to the staff group, there was considerable anger and some of the officers insisted that Fred must be discharged, for their safety. An anxiety arose that Fred could easily bundle a member of staff into his room. After all, Fred was a professional who might not have been convicted of violent crimes, but must have been involved in many over the years. Fred would have the staff member in his room and possibly dead within minutes. One staff member went off sick and others talked the situation over with more senior managers and union representatives.

From the therapists' perspective, the peculiarity of the situation was that there were genuinely people in the community who had killed within minutes of apprehending their victim and who were still capable of doing so, but that Fred was not one of them. He was more interested in the money and clothes of gangsterism than the violence.

Within the therapists' group, the issue was discussed, and then between the governors and the therapists. The first question was, did Fred present the sort of level of risk that meant continued work in Grendon was untenable? The governor team recognised that there were strong feelings about the issue, but was curious about why these strong feelings and anxieties might have alighted on Fred rather than any number of other more acutely dangerous men. In summary, when Fred's level of risk was objectively evaluated, it was found to be unnecessary to remove him from Grendon at that time.

The second question was that, if the dynamic about Fred was not related to his actual risk level, what was really going on? This was the question posed in the therapists' meeting. One of the therapists noted that in the account of the anxious fantasy of Fred pulling someone into his cell and killing him or her instantly, the victim would have to be entirely passive; and, indeed, to be killed in the time frame that was being envisaged (seconds rather than minutes), the victim would probably have to give Fred a helping hand in his or her own demise. Perhaps the anxiety was not about the resident killing the staff member, which would create a struggle, but really about the resident killing himself, which would not create a struggle – and against which the staff member would be entirely passive. While you can fight for survival in a physical struggle, and bring to bear your 'control and restraint' and 'breakaway techniques' training, you can't do anything if one of your patients decides to kill himself. As a staff member you are indeed entirely passive. Perhaps the unbearable anxiety about a quick, silent killing was about suicide rather than murder.

Fred's community therapist described to the therapists' group the discussion of several weeks previously when Fred was in the frame for setting up another resident to cut his wrists. He remembered his own ridiculing of the position of the two officers who had proposed that Fred was behind the incident, by saying that it might make the officers feel better in the short term. Other therapists commented about how some officers find it difficult to examine their own dynamics and, while as therapists we might welcome that sort of insight, they (the officers) might be threatened, intimidated and humiliated by it. A hypothesis emerged that, psychically, the therapist had taken the officers hostage and 'killed' their sense of professional identity in seconds with the interpretation. This had led to a staff group dynamic that itself had to be exorcised by the discharge of Fred.

Fred's community therapist decided (rather sheepishly) to raise the issue in the subsequent staff team sensitivity meeting, setting it out in just these terms – that Fred might be a scapegoat for a staff team dynamic where he, the therapist, had been dismissive of the concerns of prison officer colleagues, and that this had fuelled a sense of anxiety and impotence in the face of the problem of residents' self-harming rather than helping to abate it. In the discussion, the therapist's proposal was discussed, with a gradually swelling tide of criticism from the other staff over his imperious and condescending attitude and his failure to listen to the concerns of staff. He was asked to consider whether he was being duped by Fred and so could not see where Fred was swinging the lead. After this rather uncomfortable meeting, anxiety abated somewhat.

In this particular case, the dynamic was contained by reference to senior managers in the prison, and then the sense of professional ablation that may have been felt by the officers could be articulated and worked with in the staff sensitivity meeting. Sometimes the situation goes the other way: the anxiety levels caused by a particular resident get to such a level that they cannot be contained and are discharged, even when the therapist and therapist group believe the anxiety is a dynamic rather than an appropriate appraisal of the situation. When this happens, the sense of professional ablation goes the other way – the therapist feels that his or her contribution has been destroyed.

The importance of the whole team being able as a majority to overrule any one held opinion, however firmly held and however senior the person holding it, is paramount. The reason for this is related to the issue of certainty in working with personality disorders mentioned above, that anyone in the team can be bewitched by a certainty and the majority of the team needs to be able to override this. The downside is that whole staff teams can at times become duped, or can follow a group dynamic; the majority are not always right either, but they are more so than any one individual.

Managing this sense of professional ablation amongst staff when a team decision goes against their strongly held view is one of the most difficult aspects of working with multidisciplinary teams. Staff members in this situation seem to get driven into a crescendo of activity to ensure that their own view holds sway (for example, the tracking down of the account of Fred's behaviour in Brixton). Threats of resignation are not uncommon, nor are consultations of the terms and conditions of employment and staff complaints procedures, and scrutiny of trade journals to find alternative employment. From a psychodynamic perspective, possible formulations of this behaviour might include a simple understanding in terms of narcissism. The individual's professional identity may contain within it omnipotent and un-challengeable elements that are a bit unstable, so that a challenge to him or her is potentially catastrophic. In situations like this, there does seem to be an element that by being overruled, the whole sense of identity of some staff members is somehow undermined.

The hypothesis at the beginning of this chapter was that certainty in working with personality is always suspicious and probably reflects the adoption of a patient's dynamic. If you feel certain about something, this cannot be a reality but, instead, you must have accepted a patient's projection. It may be that these certainties of staff members that are overruled are so painful for staff because they do genuinely represent a lapse from professionalism. Being overruled by a majority staff decision confirms that the individual has been thrown a baited line by the patient and has swallowed it, hook, line and sinker. The task then is to accept being able to learn from mistakes – they happen to everybody. Part of the therapist's contribution in his or her role as the clinical lead is to be sensitive to these issues as they affect the staff team, and aware that he or she can get caught up in them like everyone else.

As well as the task of being the supervisor/facilitator to the staff group, a second task of the community therapist is to supervise the work of the small group lead facilitators. After the community syndicates into its five small groups three mornings per week, the staff group has a supervision meeting where the content and process of the small groups that have taken place is discussed. Taking place three times a week, the small groups are quite intensive and spontaneously take on a significantly analytic flavour. However, they are not all facilitated by group analysts but also by the staff team probation officer, psychologist and specialist prison officers who have received an introductory group therapy training. It is the therapist's task to provide clinical supervision for these groups.

Much has been written about the task of clinical psychodynamic supervision (e.g. Martindale 1997). The task seems to be a combination of maintaining an awareness of the patient – where he or she is in relation to the process of therapy – and, at the same time, maintaining an awareness of the therapist or facilitator – where he or she is in relation to the unfolding process of the therapy. This bilateral awareness enables the supervisor to monitor the most crucial aspect of the process, the ebb and flow of the relatedness between the two. The supervisory process involves getting a sense of the flux and feel of the session as well as the material from both sides of the therapeutic encounter to understand what is going on, and then to formulate this for the group facilitator-supervisee to inform his or her ongoing work.

There are five small groups in a community, and a meeting that lasts about an hour; this allows ten minutes or so per group, which is not much time. So the effective chairing of this group is an important aspect, flexibly focusing on the issues of concern and being able to move on from those that are not 'hot' at that particular time. It is one of the paradoxes of psychodynamic work that there is always too much material generated and one can only skim the top of what can be understood. The therapeutic supervisory skill is in choosing the most fruitful things to focus on and discuss. Also, at another dimensional level, there is the task of gleaning information from the process and dynamics of the supervision group itself. Only so much of the clinical material can be articulated verbally; often the more difficult material is brought into the supervisory room as an attitude by the facilitator.

GEORGE

George's community therapist noticed how the group facilitator of George's group was increasingly rarely bringing sexual clinical material. The account of the group would be summarised by a reference to 'fantasies' or 'offending' without giving an account of what these were. The therapist was intrigued by this, and wondered if it was his own perverse voyeuristic impulses that made him want to hear the sexual details of the accounts. It was noticeable, however, that when thinking about the different groups in his community, he was less in touch with the dynamics of George's group than the others, so that there might be a dynamic involved. He also remembered how his justification for wanting to know the sexual specifics of fantasy and offence was that they often contained the concretisation of the core-object relational conflict, so that actually they were quite important to hear.

Privately, he raised the issue with George's group facilitator, wondering about whether he was right in thinking that the group facilitator was reticent about giving an account of the content at that level of sexual detail, or whether it was a phenomenon in the group itself and that level of detail was simply not being discussed. The facilitator at first denied that this was an issue, but agreed to think about it.

Several weeks later, in a sensitivity meeting, with quite an anxious introduction, the group facilitator outlined an issue that she had with the community therapist. She felt that the community therapist was almost harassing her to divulge the explicit content of the group, even though she felt uncomfortable doing it. The rest of the team were interested in her concern and, with some help, she went on to articulate her concern about being observed closely as she gave an account of the sexual content to the therapist. Another member of the staff team clarified the issue: 'So you think that (the therapist) is getting off on your reaction to the more sexual material.'

The therapist was a bit shocked and silenced by this suggestion, which he felt as an accusation, but he held onto an acceptance that the discussion of sexual material was always in some way an intimate and sexual process, but in this case it was one that had to be borne and contained in order to do the work. The issue couldn't be taken further at the time, but the therapist was left feeling as if he had been accused of a perversion that was not his.

The following week, George had been disclosing some of his offending pattern. He was describing how he would befriend slightly lost children and how the most exciting part of the process of engaging them in a sexual act was studying their reaction to the moment it became clear to them that this was what he wanted. Someone else in the group pointed out that what he was getting off on was the moment of trauma of the child; this was what he found sexually exciting. George was upset by this, and it triggered memories of both his own moments of trauma when caressed by the clients–men who would visit his mother, and the way in which his next-door neighbour who had abused him had watched intently when George found the pornography that was left.

Hearing this account, the dynamic that had evolved between the group facilitator and the community therapist made sense. The facilitator realised that when explicit disclosures were being made in the group, George's eyes were fixed on her with an intensity that she found both disturbing and intrusive. George was getting off on her reactions to explicit sexual material, as he used to with his victims. This dynamic had been too disturbing for her to realise and describe it and, instead, it had been brought into the supervision setting as a dynamic between her and the therapist.

In the subsequent sensitivity meeting, the group facilitator was able to describe the similarity between the feeling of being intruded upon by George's perverse watching and her feeling about the therapist wanting her to say more about the material in the group.

In this example, several different confusing dynamics have been elucidated. The group facilitator has been subjected to a perverse enactment by George. Because this was rather overwhelming for the facilitator she was unable to discuss it in supervision but instead projected the sense of a perverse process onto the therapist. In this case, it has simply been contained by the therapist, who is left wondering if the perversion is indeed his, or whether it derives in some way from the clinical material. Instead of acting, he awaits the emergence of an explanation, which in the event George supplies. The therapist's function has been to contain and continue thinking about what the material in the supervision and other staff group settings might mean.

Having looked at aspects of the therapist's function in the staff team as the facilitator of the multidisciplinary staff team, a task to which he or she brings his or her group analytic skills, and then as a supervisor of the work in the small groups, we can explore his or her cultural contribution. This cultural contribution is best described as client centred. Following the medical and clinical approach, the therapist's main interest is in the well-being of his or her patients. For the therapist, the process of therapy is to free the patients from some of their overbearing personality difficulties so that their lives in future are a little less wretched. The assumption is that creating victims and offending is a symptom of the wretched lives that people have led and that, if they can be helped a bit, if their personality disorder can be treated a bit, then the alleviation of the symptom of wretchedness will mean they have to make fewer other people's lives wretched. From this perspective, reducing re-offending is not the aim, but rather is a beneficial side-effect of the aim, which is to treat people who are suffering.

At its best, this approach to the work puts the well-being of the patient in the centre of the process. While it is easy to criticise Rogers' (1967) approach to counselling with its articulation of the need for unconditional positive regard for the patient as simplistic, the therapeutic or medical approach to the patient is imbued with this sort of ethos: that the task is to help the patient or client, to treat the patients' illnesses so that they can improve in their own situations.

It is useful to articulate a critique of this position to define it more fully. The criticism would be that in the context of Grendon, it can be manipulated by the offender to throw the focus away from his destructiveness, deserving of censure and challenge, and onto his own status as victim. This situation is complicated by the fact that there is almost always a pretty awful history of abusive experience of one sort or another. The danger is that the therapist with a naïve focus on the history of abuse – either as a central trauma that

---

EDDIE

In a staff meeting following a community meeting in which Eddie had participated, the therapist was trying to articulate a view of Eddie as actually rather a pathetic figure and that his hostility and violence had a rather childish quality to it. He said that it seemed as if somebody just needed to say 'boo' to Eddie, for him to run away in tears. Eddie's group facilitator partly concurred with this view, in that she had noticed that he just seemed to collapse when confronted or when an accurate formulation was made about him, but she only partly agreed. There was a silence in the room, broken by the therapist, who queried it. The group facilitator went on to say that, although she could see this, he still was pretty frightening and intimidating in the room. Another member of staff who had had a run-in with him described how he had gone from reasonable to extremely frightening and intimidating in an instant.

The therapist persevered, pointing out that his bluster was like that of the kid who had been terrified by the drunken father. 'He had to sit and watch his mother being beaten. His father wanted him to see it. Wanted him to be aware of how utterly powerless and impotent he was. I think that his bluster is a rather sad reaction to an inner feeling of total impotence.' The group facilitator and other staff member were now a little upset. 'How can you say that this is bluster – he is a murderer – you don't bluster with a knife. He meant it. He regularly fought; there are countless people who have injuries that have never been brought to court; he's a dangerous man – I think it is irresponsible to dismiss the way he behaves as bluster.'

needs to be worked through or as in some way an explanation of the subsequent offending – can miss the other element of the client as perpetrator of the same type of abuse on others.

In this discussion both points of view may be correct. Eddie's violence can be formulated in terms of a little boy's impotent rage and violence that needs to be understood as such; however, it is also true that the expression of this infantile rage and violence by a big man with a knife is very dangerous and represents a considerable risk to the public. The therapist's perspective is most closely with the patient in experience and outlook and there is a risk that this perspective can become too narrow. The dilemma is that there is both risk to this perspective – that of seduction into an attitude of minimisation – and a need for this perspective – to preserve the attitude of enquiry into the meaning of the behaviour. To some extent the balance is retained by the dialectic between the therapist and the forensic psychologist whose focus is more on the victim – the task of reducing re-offending.

Tasks and culture – the forensic psychologist

The next disciplinary perspective to explore is that of the forensic psychologist. In reading this account, and that of the culture and tasks of the other disciplines, it must be borne in mind that these accounts are necessarily and unavoidably partisan, at least to a degree. As a psychiatrist and a therapist, with a professional identity rooted in a particular value set, over the years, in multidisciplinary team settings, I have clashed and argued with colleagues from other disciplines. Traditionally, psychiatrists and psychologists vie. In Grendon, it seems more to be therapists and forensic psychologists.

Within the psychology profession, there is a large raft of people whose first degree majors are in psychology-relevant subjects. The British Psychological Society oversees those who can join on the basis of the extent to which the degree subjects are psychology-relevant. However, most professional psychologists, as distinct from psychology graduates, have postgraduate training experience in the different disciplines of, for example, educational psychology, social psychology and so on. Within the forensic world, psychologists from two different disciplines contribute. The first of these are forensic psychologists, whose substantial experience is in the Prison Service, who work in prison settings and who, for promotion, are expected to complete a master's degree in criminology. The formal training component is an academic programme, with a strong emphasis on empirical research, and usually a research thesis. The other group is clinical psychologists, broadly those whose substantial training is in the Health Service and who complete a three-year postgraduate degree which involves a rotation of supervised practice in different areas of psychological therapy practice, including a substantial experience of psychiatric settings and patients. Clinical psychologists who practise in forensic settings (usually secure psychiatry) sometimes entitle themselves clinical forensic psychologists but, clearly, confusion is possible.

This difference in training leads to a cultural set of the forensic psychology discipline that is very much more rooted in an academic positivist research approach than that of a clinical psychologist who will have the supervised casework experience from which an awareness of clinical pragmatics grow. Arguably, this focus on an evidence-based approach from the clinical psychology background is further fostered within a criminal justice setting, where the court's verdict represents an arbiter of truth that is inherited by its servants, including those in the Prison Service. Whereas those with a clinical psychological therapy background come to the work with a sense of flexibility and personal and professional fallibility, those from a more forensic psychology background have a firm confidence in the positivist empirical method and the hypotheses that emerge from it.

The effect of this is that for the forensic psychology discipline there is a risk that derivatives from the empirical method, such as actuarial indices of risk, are not taken as a contributor to a whole picture of an individual, but are taken as the whole picture and the final word. This concretisation is best illustrated in the way that the Hare Psychopathy Checklist (Hare 1991) is used, not as a contributory indicator of risk, but as a means of exclusion from cognitive programmes because of a notion (and some equivocal evidence, e.g. Rice, Harris and Cormier 1992) that high scorers are not helped by them.

In the same way as empirical evidence can be concretised and used as the final definition of reality, the evidence present in the depositions of the crime for the Grendon resident are utilised as the final statement of the reality of the individual. This perspective provides an important and valuable counterpoint to the therapist's empathetic position in relation to the offender. The therapist's natural inclination will be to see the offender as a victim of his upbringing and a victim of abusive developmental experiences. The forensic psychologist will criticise this account as conjectural and based on possibly fabricated childhood accounts for which there is no independently corroborated evidence. The clearest indication of the nature of the offender is to be found in the deposition and witness statements about the offending history. These accounts comprise the evidence that was presented to the court, and that were accepted as true accounts of what took place by virtue of the conviction for the crime, the forensic psychologist would reasonably argue; the account of the offender as perpetrator is the safest foundation on which to build a therapeutic intervention. In short, therefore, the therapist might see the offender as victim, where the forensic psychologist sees him as perpetrator.

EDDIE

The community was in the process of preparing for a family day. As usual, in the months leading up to it, there was much excitement and anticipation; the practice of allowing prisoners to bring in their relatives so that they could meet fellow prisoners and see the environment in which their loved ones were imprisoned was very unusual, and very special for prisoners. Each person who had family members whom he wanted to come to the day discussed them with his small group and, if it was approved, would bring the proposal to the community before completing the paperwork that would be scrutinised by the security department.

Eddie had asked for Dawn, the mother of two of his children, to be allowed to be his guest, along with his mother. Since his imprisonment, contact with Dawn had been sporadic; she had not married, but there was an impression that the chaos of her and Eddie's relationship had continued as a pattern with others. The sequence of contacts with Eddie during the years of his imprisonment was that she would get in touch with him following the end of a relationship, maintaining contact until she had found someone else. Contact would diminish, Eddie would confront her about her infidelity and there would be a severance of contact. Meanwhile, Eddie would become violent and irritable, often ending up in the segregation unit of the prison that he was in. This account of the relationship had emerged in the discussion of his request in his small group, with the other group members asking him why they were in contact again now, with the implicit taunt that she was simply in between men again.

Time was running short – the staff team had to make a decision whether to recommend her visiting or not. The therapist and probation officer argued that this was an important step Eddie was taking towards re-integrating himself with family elements in the outside world. Eddie's request should be supported. The psychologist had a different view. Eddie had killed his best friend after an argument with Dawn. After almost every contact that he had had since then there had been some violence. Allowing Dawn into the family day presented a considerable risk, both in terms of what might happen on the day, and in terms of what might happen afterwards, with Eddie spoiling for a fight. Furthermore, the psychologist argued, the staff team were mini-mising risk, as Eddie did all the time himself. This was a serious risk. Eddie didn't agree that there was a risk of violence if Dawn visited, and this made it more of a risk. If the staff team couldn't see this either, the risk was even greater.

It was agreed that the staff group's concerns would be fed back to Eddie to see what his position was. Eddie took the issue back to the group and discussed it further. Over the past year, his and Dawn's children, who had been taken into care prior to Eddie's imprisonment, had been adopted. Eddie claimed that this contact between the couple was different in that Dawn was still in a relationship, it was not the case that one had finished. The two were back in touch because the children had been adopted, and it was more like being friends. The therapist seized on this, saying that this was the beginning of a more mature contact between the couple as they grieved the statutory loss of the children, but the psychologist still had concerns because of the instability that Dawn seemed to generate.

A compromise was agreed. The risk of an incident on the day was agreed, and it was thought that the strain of having two guests might be too much. Eddie could have either his mother or Dawn, but not both. Also, a member of Eddie's group who did not have visitors agreed to 'mind' him and be aware of Eddie's potential. Predictably, Eddie chose for Dawn to come, but there was some confidence in the staff group that the situation would be manageable.

In the event, the day seemed to be enjoyable. Eddie and Dawn talked calmly, and Eddie introduced her appropriately to some of the community staff and residents. The family day was (as usual) on a Friday. Over the weekend that followed, Eddie was morose, sullen and irritable. The group member who had agreed to 'mind' him during the day suggested to him that this might be his 'post-Dawn syndrome' and was shouted at in a scene on the landing, where Eddie was talked down by other residents before the staff arrived. The community chairman suggested a 'special group' (an un-programmed small group meeting in response to an emergency) where Eddie was tearful about his situation with children who had been adopted and who had no contact with him, and no contact with Dawn who was effectively lost to him. With the help of the group, Eddie recognised that since the family day he had been looking for a fight exactly as he had done the night he had killed Dan. He recognised that again he had chosen a friend to attack – albeit verbally this time – exactly as on the night he had killed Dan and that exactly as on the night he had killed Dan, his wanting to fight was a way of escaping from a feeling of total isolation and desolation following his desertion by Dawn.

The content of the special group was fed back in the following community meeting. The community collectively still seemed to be a little unsympathetic, as it was not long since the football tackle incident when Eddie had 'thrown his dolly out of the pram'. Hearing the content of the group, some discussion was stimulated. Eddie was quizzed about why, if he was going to shout at anyone, he had shouted at his minder, whom he was close to. Why didn't he shout at someone else? Sid, for example; those two were always fighting. Eddie was at a bit of a loss, shaking his head slowly.

The minder spoke. 'I think it was me because we get on,' he said. 'Eddie, mate, I think it was me 'cos you like me. It was like, because Dawn was gone, and you couldn't do anything about it, you had to get rid of someone else that you could do something about. So that you could feel you had some control. You killed Dan because you liked him, and because you needed him with Dawn gone; because you needed him he had to go so you could pretend you didn't need Dawn, or him, or no one.' There was silence in the community, as the truth and profundity of the statement dawned on people. 'Bloody hell,' the minder went on, 'I guess that makes me quite lucky, doesn't it!' There was a ripple of laughter, and the chairman moved onto the next piece of business.

In the staff meeting that followed, the therapist acknowledged that Eddie's offence re-enactment had been a little too close for comfort, and reflected that it might be rather easy to be taken in by the puppy-dog depressed part of Eddie, losing sight of his dangerousness.

In this example, the advantage and importance of a rigorous, more evidence-based approach can be seen as it impacts on both the process of clinical decision-making based on assessing risk and on the ability of the therapeutic process to contain the individual and enable him to get to a deeper understanding of his offending. If Eddie had been uncritically allowed to bring in Dawn, without the arrangements being made and the thinking that went on beforehand; had Eddie ended up in a physical fight in the weekend following the family meeting, he might have been expelled from the community, arresting his therapeutic progress or, worse, he might have caused serious injury. With the treatment of those with personality disorder who have ended up creating victims and offending, each side of the debate that conceived the individual as a perpetrator or as a victim needs a reality check from the other side. This almost adversarial process of debate keeps the treatment process on track and safe.

The specific task of the forensic psychologist is to maintain the offending behaviour focus of the treatment. In the structure of the treatment programme, there is a process whereby initial treatment aims are set in the assessment unit and are reviewed and re-set once the resident begins treatment proper on the treatment unit. These treatment aims have been termed 'Criminogenic Personality Factors', as an effort to combine the process of identifying the specific criminogenic factors that an individual displays with the more prosaic, 'simple psychology' formulation of people's problems that are characteristic of therapeutic community discourse.

EDDIE

Eddie's Criminogenic Personality Factors were summarised as follows:

1. Poor impulse control of aggression.

2. Inappropriate attitude to aggression – enjoyment and use of it to solve other personal and emotional conflicts.

3. Developmental contributors to aggressive pattern.

4. Criminal/aggressive social circle and lifestyle.

5. Disinhibitory use of alcohol.

6. Distrust in intimate relationships and relationships with authority.

In the process of treatment, the aggressive problems were increasingly seen as a cloak to hide a potential depressive breakdown, linked with abusive experiences from an alcoholic and violent father, and perpetuated by experience of relationship and other failures in adulthood. In his sequential reviews, Eddie was asked to focus on his impulsive aggression, as highlighted by the tackling incident. As this was explored, it became clear that the violence was not sporadic and random, as it had seemed, but rather that is was more focused on specific people and related to particular constellations of circumstances, in particular when he felt abandoned or impotent and humiliated as he had been with his father. Sequentially, Eddie's treatment focus moved towards exploring his relationship with his father and how this was linked to his feelings about those in authority and his relationships generally.

The task of the forensic psychologist in the team is to retain a more objective criminogenic focus. There is no evidence base to the hypothesis that reconviction rates of murderers are related to feelings of abandonment, but there is one to the hypothesis that those rates are related to antisocial values, for example. This tension between exploring the depth of the offender's personality and the need to keep the presenting symptom in mind is a constant dialectic of the work. The need to focus on the presenting symptom – the offence and the risk of further offending – this focus is held by the forensic psychologist.

Tasks and culture – the probation officer

In a psychiatric multidisciplinary team, there is a need to have a social focus and input – a professional brief that starts at the point of the social environment and setting from which the patient derives and that can put the clinical picture into its context. In a prison setting, where there is a physical wall between the individual and his environment, as well as an even higher cultural and procedural wall, the need for a brief to maintain the social contextual perspective is that much greater. It would seem as though this contextualisation takes place in three different dimensions: first in terms of the resident's past and historical context; second, in terms of managing and an awareness of the co-existence of his former (pre-prison) context outside his presence in prison, through maintaining links with the home probation service; third, in terms of planning and preparing for release and resettlement – i.e. the future.

Proceedings in the judicial process are often adjourned in order to establish the social background and context of the offence that has been committed, which involves a probation officer meeting with the family and preparing a report. This contextual account informs the judge in the decisions about the appropriate sentence and establishes a link between the Probation Service and the familial and social context in which the offending has taken place. In the process of therapy, there will be an expectation as well as a natural inclination for the resident to explore his background history. Gradually, an account of childhood will be developed and refined by the resident which, as with Fred's and George's explorations of their relationships with their mothers, will illuminate different dimensions of the resident's experience. It needs to be remembered, however, that these recollections and reminiscences are reconstructions of the past rather than being accurate accounts of the past. At times a gulf will open up between the resident's memory of what took place and what actually did take place. In a therapeutic setting, where experiences in the past are seen as important and relevant, an interest grows during the exploration in what happened back then, and so, often, does a hunger for independent accounts. It is common for Grendon inmates to re-establish contact with family members and raise the issue of past experiences to compare memories, and this is encouraged. For example, what was it actually like when the abusive father used to come home drunk? What are the different memories of different members of the family?

EDDIE

In one group, another group member was talking about his violent and drunken father and about how he had spent hours talking to his brother about what happened, who had been too young to remember. Eddie realised that he had never spoken to his older sister about his own experiences. He had never thought of doing this because they were in the past, and he'd always seen them as not important, and because he'd lost touch with his sister. One member of the group wondered if he had lost touch with her to try to forget what had happened – to keep it out of his mind. Eddie didn't accept this, but became more intrigued about what her memories would be. To him now, talking about his father beating his mother, about how he used to get beaten about, they all seemed like a bit of a dream; and while he knew it had happened, somehow he wasn't sure. The social services had been involved, he remembered, and the group suggested he might speak to the probation officer about it, because there might be some records he could get hold of.

In this way, the probation officer is the link with the past outside context for the resident. The next dimension is being the link with the present outside. Many of the families of prisoners are in low income groups and the task of travelling around the country to visit prisons is a disincentive, so that there is a continual process of isolation of the prisoner from his former social networks. This is a problem for all sorts of reasons, not least of which is that the risk of re-offending will be increased by the development of stronger antisocial social networks – for example, with fellow prisoners – whereas non-prisoner friends and family links and integration into the community reduce the risk. In Grendon, the second task of the probation officer is the awareness and facilitation of the maintenance of these external social networks in real time – maintaining a connection with the current outside context for the resident.

EDDIE

The probation officer made some enquiries within the local probation team, and there were records of Eddie's sister's address that were still current. Eddie discussed at some length both in his group, and with the probation office the pros and cons of contacting his sister, the best way of doing it, the need to recognise that she might find it difficult to hear from him and if so he had to accept this and that, even if she was keen on re-establishing contact, she may not wish to explore the past with him.

The other lines of current outside context that need to be maintained are an awareness of the victim, and of the impact that any events in prison might have on him or her. For example, it is not uncommon for there to be film crews in Grendon: what effect would a TV interview with the perpetrator have on the victim? This would be something that might need to be discussed with the local services and the impact of it assessed. Also, there is a need to be aware of the network of other professionals involved, such as the home probation team and previous psychiatric and other involved professionals.

FRED

Fred had decided that he wanted to go back out to live where he had been before his sentence. In the community and in his small group there was criticism of this idea, because he would have all his old contacts knocking on the door wanting him to get involved in his old patterns. Fred argued that this would be more likely in a new patch, the temptation to take over – to get to learn who the men were and what they were doing – would be too great. 'I'd need to get in there man. In my own place, I know how to stay low.' The probation officer facilitated this debate with the hostel where it was proposed he would stay and found an alternative possibility in a different locality. A case conference was convened attended by the local probation officer, who knew Fred well, and others of his group, and the issue was discussed further. The possibility of his attendance at some form of community drug programme at the same time was raised, and the possibilities were explored.

The third area of context in which the probation officer takes a lead is that of the future context – preparation for release and resettlement. In the UK there are current policy developments that promote the importance of public protection in the resettlement of offenders. From this policy direction, along with the outcome of many different enquiries which identify problems in communication between agencies as a cause of things going wrong, a model of resettlement is emerging where risk assessments of offenders being released into the community will be carried out by multidisciplinary teams with input from police, probation, social work, psychiatry and other interested groups. This model structures the current probation resettlement practice in Grendon where, in an individual, cogwheel manner, the different relevant agencies would be liaised with in the process of devising a resettlement plan for an individual.

Taken together, the functions of the probation officer in a Grendon community are those of a traditional social care role. Social services and probation together seem more broadly to have moved towards a care management and commissioning function rather than care provision, so some have seen the role of the Grendon probation officer as anachronistic. Nevertheless, this function is an essential and central component of the multidisciplinary team that needs to assemble around the Grendon resident as part of his treatment package.

Culturally, the probation officer maintains a balance between the individual care focus of the therapist and the offence focus of the forensic psychologist. The therapist's preoccupation is with the experiences, progress and psychological development and growth of the individual Grendon resident, seeing this as the most important factor to be pursued. The forensic psychologist's focus is more on the victim, the crime committed and the risk of re-offending posed by the individual. Culturally, the natural inclination of the probation officer is to be socially therapeutic, to see the relationship developed between him or her and his or her clients as an important factor, 'befriending and guiding'; however, this approach is very clearly applied in a criminal justice context with a very clear focus on the primary importance of reducing re-offending and assessing risk. Set between the two poles of approach, the probation officer acts as a mediator between the two divergent briefs in the multidisciplinary team: the therapist's focus on the resident as victim of a negative developmental experience and the forensic psychologist's brief of the resident as dangerous perpetrator. The combination of casework, integration with wider systems and offence focus that the probation officer brings maintains a balance and discourse that can lead to compromise.

Tasks and culture – the officers

In the more general description of the Grendon regime above, I have drawn a parallel between the officer's role in Grendon, and the psychiatric nurse's role in a hospital setting. The officers must be present 24 hours per day and are the first line of containment and care for the residents, being the most numerous and the most junior group and responsible for the management of the setting and the fabric of the setting. In medicine, it is common to hear doctors in the coffee room complaining about the practice of one nurse or another, or complaining about their culture as a group. At the same time, it is also very common to hear them being given credit and tribute and being praised highly in public settings which, given a knowledge of the difficulties in the relationship, can sound a little hollow: an idealisation of them as 'angels' rather than a recognition of their genuine contribution and the work they do. The tasks of the prison officer are clear and listed in a manual, but in Grendon there is an added dimension of work required which might seem at odds with the default task. The same can be said of the cultural position of the prison officer.

The prison officers own the setting. They do this in two ways. First, within the team of two senior officers and ten or twelve basic grade officers on each community team, the senior officers are the overall managers. Technically, the civilian staff are only allowed onto a prison wing with the permission of the senior officer. Technically, he makes a risk assessment of the state of his wing, and decides whether or not the situation is sufficiently safe to allow group meetings and therapy to take place today. The therapeutic activity in Grendon takes place within the gift of the operational line managers so that, extending this dimension up the organisation, Grendon is a therapeutic environment only, and for as long as, the operational line manager – the governor – is happy and content for this to be the case. In practice, situations in the wings only become sufficiently risky for civilian staff to need to withdraw once every two or three years for each community – most commonly around the time of the discharge of someone who has reverted to a violent and threatening means of communication – as part of the plan for safe and effective removal.

Second, the officers own the setting in that staff team decisions are democratic, and the officers are in the majority by a considerable margin. The officers hold the balance of power in the clinical debates about the residents and if there is a failure of the staff team to agree, the matter is put to a vote, where the officers' opinions hold sway.

The difficulty with this apparent clarity is that such a clear managerial accountability and authority combined with overwhelming majority of numbers might mean that the officers would be culturally and managerially dominant. This is not the case, because of the cultural influence of a therapeutic perspective, both at the level of clinical decision-making in the community and at a managerial level within the prison. The interface between these two cultures and broadly between the two disciplines of therapy and governorship is a constant dialectic, discussed further in Chapter 7.

EDDIE

Several months later, a new member had joined Eddie's group, and was talking about his experiences. The new boy said that he had spent time on the 'merry-go-round', explaining that he had been so difficult in whatever prison he was in that they could only cope with him for a short time, needing to move him on to a new staff team after only a few months. He described his time on 'dirty protest', as a theme emerged in his account of hatred of the prison officers. 'They hated the smell of my shit. I hated the smell of my shit, but I got used to it, and they hated it more – so it seemed worthwhile,' he said. 'When they opened me up for something, it just felt good to have landed one of them, just one.'

In the group, a more general discussion ensued about people's feelings about officers. A slightly competitive atmosphere was emerging in the group, about who had been the toughest to control or who had formerly hated officers the most. Eddie spoke about the segregation experiences he had had, that on one occasion there were eight 'of 'em' trying to control him and transfer him to the segregation unit. The new boy said he had been completely amazed by the staff on the admissions unit, when he had arrived, shaking him by the hand and introducing themselves by their first names. This was followed by an awkward silence. The group facilitator was an officer, who looked and felt a bit uncomfortable, but said nothing.

In the staff group's discussion following the group, the incident was summarised as a brewing rivalry about who hated officers the most that had stopped in midstream. One of the officers suggested that Eddie, for example, had, at times, defined himself in terms of his hatred of and violence towards authority figures like his father, police and prison officers. 'When you don't give them back the violence that they give to you in the first place, sometimes they don't know what to say.' He proposed that a version of this had taken place in the group. There was general agreement in the staff group about this interpretation. Eddie, for example, got on well with one of the senior officers, whom he seemed both attached to and able to trust, to the extent of Eddie sharing his concern about goings-on in the wing that formed part of an intelligence jigsaw. This attachment was in stark contrast to how he felt about officers when he arrived.

The community therapist reflected on the reason why the group had been rendered speechless, proposing that the gulf between the hated image of the authority and the reality of getting to know officers as people – people who have families, hopes, dreams and frustrations just like everyone else – was indeed difficult to articulate.

The 'black and whites' (the officers) in prison settings are traditionally the enemy – the opposition – the filth – the screws. They attract all this contempt because of the authority that they represent for a group for whom authority is a problem. In Grendon, they still have to have the absolute authority that their position as prison custodians demands – authority to search, to instruct and so on. But they have to discharge this authority within a relationship setting.

FRED

Early in his stay in Grendon, Fred had been aware of how there is a throughput for the complementary therapies, and that at some point there might be a push for him to go to one. Years ago, on a youth-offending project, Fred was in a drama group that he'd enjoyed, so he thought he would keep people off his back by doing psychodrama, as it had been quite fun. The psychodramatist was a bit concerned about accepting him given this motivation, and the staff group were curious about his wish to start relatively soon in his Grendon stay. Nevertheless, he did start, and his psychodrama group became a place where he seemed to engage in a way that he struggled to in other settings. In his small group, he recounted an experience that had given him pause.

In a psychodrama session another resident was sculpting a scenario. This other resident's friend had died of an overdose. The other resident and his friend had shot up together, in the friend's house. The other resident had been woken by his friend's mother who was hysterical because she couldn't rouse her dead son. For the other resident, the experience had been devastating, waking up groggy, realising he had lost his friend and that he was in big trouble. In the investigations that followed he had been prosecuted for supply.

In the psycho-dramatisation of the scene, Fred had played the friend, lying on the floor, while players in the drama came and went around him. In talking about it afterwards, Fred had been struck by being in the centre of things, and yet somehow isolated from them. Fred was more used to being in the centre of things in all senses, in demand from all quarters. Somehow the experience put him in touch with mortality, and with the fact that his attitude to drug 'punters' was blasé. There had been occasions when there had been deaths from overdosing on heroin he'd supplied, and in the past he'd laughed these off, merely cursing himself for not diluting the base heroin more fully. Somehow, the idea of trying to wake someone up, then realising gradually that he was not sleeping but was in fact dead was horrifying.

Complementary therapies

There is a variety of complementary therapies in Grendon, including art psychotherapy, psychodrama, drug counselling, and formerly a sex offender treatment programme and a cognitive skills programme functioned. Art psychotherapy and psychodrama are community-based, with a small group continuously running on each community, for which community members volunteer or are recommended as part of the assessment/review process. Drug counselling is set up differently with a consultative model, and the cognitively-orientated offending behaviour programmes were centrally delivered – i.e. with a single group running, attended by men from different communities. The contribution made by these activities is at two levels. First, they make a contribution consistent with the modality and function of the treatment process that they provide and second, they provide vantage points from which the therapeutic community process as a whole can be critiqued.

One of the strengths of the therapeutic community approach is that it incorporates in its treatment modality a spectrum of different psychological modalities, ranging from the very behavioural through to the psychoanalytic. Likewise, to some degree, there is opportunity for artistic expression in other formats – Christmas reviews, crafts to sell to the public and interior decoration – and these can be commented upon and explored in the group settings that exist. In the same way, via the flexibility of the therapeutic discourse, there will be a full discussion of the various aspects of drug addiction and options for treatment that might overlap with the work of the drug counsellor; and the hope would be that insights and formulations of behaviour from the various offending behaviour programmes would contribute to the community discourse. In spite of this, this informal ability to be modally flexible is inferior to a structured professional input of the complementary therapeutic modality. The contribution of the psychodramatist and the fact of having a psychodrama group running in the community are more potent than having a theatre group, even though the therapeutic community will make use of issues that are raised in the latter.

The caveat in the integration of these complementary therapies is that they do need to be complementary in two senses of the word: there needs to be a recognition and acceptance that confidentiality is held by the community team – and that progress and problems in the complementary treatment are fed back to the treatment team – and second, there needs to be a recognition of managerial complementarity, in that the case management remains the responsibility of the therapeutic community team. The reason for this need for integration of the clinical activities derives from the potential for splitting that

GEORGE

Gerry, another member of the community, was undertaking the Sex Offender Treatment Programme. Convicted for sexual offences against children, he had been challenged in the programme about a cognitive distortion that had emerged, namely that he believed that the children whom he had abused had not been that badly damaged. He had argued that he had been kind and gentle and they had enjoyed it. He felt that he had helped them by teaching them about sexuality.

This account was being fed back in the community meeting, and provoked a long discussion. The gist of this was that Gerry's belief was crazy, and the community couldn't understand how he had retained this view, now being six months into treatment. 'How did you feel when it was done to you?' shouted one resident who knew Gerry's own story. Gerry struggled to respond, but said that he'd just never been asked before, not directly and outright.

George watched the debate intently, but contributing nothing, simply shaking his head occasionally.

would be exploited, and indeed will be exploited anyway. The following vignette about Fred illustrates a breakdown of communication between the team and a complementary therapist.

FRED

Several weeks after Fred had nearly been discharged, one of the staff team had a few words with the prison's drug counsellor, having been surprised to see him in the community. It emerged that Fred was having drug counselling, and that plans were now advanced for him to move to a drug therapeutic community. The staff group were astonished when this was reported back. Fred was cagey about his discussions, as was the drug counsellor, but what emerged was that Fred had asked for help because he felt that the treatment available for drugs in Grendon was inadequate and that his addiction needs would be better met in a specialised unit. The drug counsellor was invited to a staff meeting to discuss the situation, where he in turn was astonished to hear the wider story about Fred. Fred had painted a picture of himself to the drug counsellor as a victim of a community culture in which drugs were being tolerated and that he was in on a possession charge because he'd had some for his mates when he slipped off the wagon. The counsellor was shocked to hear the well-founded suspicions that Fred was thought to be the drug problem on the wing himself.

It was clear that Fred had opened and then was about to utilise a staff split between the counsellor and the staff group. This was taken up with Fred by the community therapist who explained her awareness of his plans to move onto a different unit, and her view that, while it was his choice, it seemed a bit odd for him to be wanting to move because of the drug culture when it was odds on that he was the main force behind creating this. She suggested the formation that things were getting a bit hot in Grendon and Fred was starting to be a bit restricted in his operations, so he was punting to be moved to a new pasture. In the meeting Fred denied all this, but in his small group, as the story emerged, the others laughed at the idea. Eventually, Fred did as well, claiming that it was worth a go; he had a mate who was in that same drug unit at the moment who had said he was having a good time.

The dynamic complementary therapies, art therapy and psychodrama, provide an alternative dimension in which the disclosure and working through of personal traumatic events and aspects of offending can take place.

GEORGE

For some time, George had been dubbed 'the auxiliary therapist' both in his small group and in the community. The assumption was that this was to be expected – George was familiar with care settings and how to function in them but, as time went on and there was still a sense of stagnation, concern grew.

In a review meeting, a tentative conclusion was that George struggled to make his mark – that he was too content to be in the shadows, watching things go by. There had been recently a breakthrough with a withdrawn man in his art therapy sessions, and this was suggested for George. This was proposed to him and he accepted, as was his acquiescent way, but with murmurings of having no ability.

In art therapy, George would try to draw still life; in the discussion at the end he would comment on his technical difficulties. Gradually, a sense emerged of George controlling himself and the setting to a large degree. George didn't want to articulate messy emotions in his work and didn't want the rest of the group to either; he would subtly undermine the accounts and comments of others who would broaden out discussion of work, and restricted his own comments to the work itself rather than implications to be drawn from it.

In a discussion with the staff group, the art therapist commented that this now seemed to be presenting a problem for the whole group; that it is of course easier, neater, safer and much less painful to do art criticism than art therapy and, with George's influence, the rest of the group seemed to be learning this, stifling the whole process. George's small group therapist was intrigued by this account, recognising a pervasive dynamic in the group, and the rest of the staff group could relate as well on the basis of George's functioning in other settings. The community therapist proposed that George must be struggling to keep inside something very messy indeed, to be exerting all this effort at controlling things.

The art therapy medium, where there is the possibility of mess and smearing with the materials available, seemed to be the place where the dynamic was clearest. As George drew his small, controlled still life pictures, the therapist began to comment on how controlled they were, suggesting that he might risk working with something a bit more expansive. In the art therapy group, this led to a discussion of control vs mess, and George began, gingerly, and with some scepticism, to draw people and events. He began to be a bit more moody and isolated in his sessions. One week he did a simple, highly controlled and detailed pen outline of a man – probably himself. Within the outline was a mess of fiery colours, reds, oranges, yellows and blacks. In the discussion, and carrying over into his small group was a discussion of how people didn't want to see what was inside, it was so messy.

The following week, George spent his art therapy session smearing finger paints on large A5 sheets, consuming six or seven sheets in his 90-minute session. With each he would start with a relatively ordered form of a person, then on this he would superimpose different colours until there was a brown mess with some suggestions of forms within.

In the community, George became depressed, and began losing weight, causing some concern. Even though he had no active suicidal plans, he was put on a 2052 suicide watch, if nothing else to manage the anxiety of the staff and to register the staff group's concern. In his small group, George was talking about how in his life it seemed as if everything turned to shit. In particular, the perfect little lives of the kids he had abused he had turned to shit.

George's depression was going on and he had been on a 2052 for two weeks. The health care centre, which is required from a primary care perspective to monitor as part of the 2052 process, was expressing concern about George's psychiatric state and wondering if he was becoming psychotically depressed. In the staff group discussion, views from his small group and the community were pretty negative. George was struggling to communicate in these settings, and was either silent or monosyllabic, except when directly challenged, when he would quite reasonably say that he was struggling through some difficult stuff at the moment, so being depressed was to be expected.

The staff group were considerably reassured to hear that in his art therapy sessions there was some evidence of movement. The messy chaotic material that had heralded the emergence of George's more chaotic side had evolved from being an all-or-nothing total mess or ordered pen outline to being more integrated. His work was more impressionistic. Recently, after a family day, he drew a picture of a family in a car going to Grendon that was clearly discernible and emerging from a chaotic background. George had understood this as him beginning to review his own family experiences – his real family rather than one of the myths he had created for himself.

This experience of being in a situation and reviewing how it feels to be in the different roles is extremely powerful and disturbing. In particular, offenders will usually enact incidents from their own offending, at some point playing the part of the victim, when they become aware of the fear and terror that they have inflicted.

The importance of more structured cognitive/behavioural complementary therapies is that they add a dimension of rigour and structure to the multidisciplinary debate between the treatment modalities described above. For example, the Sex Offenders Treatment Programme is quite explicit about the ways in which sex offenders evade responsibility and reduce the importance of their offences.

In a more dynamic treatment process such as that of the therapeutic community, attention and focus on the centrality of the offence can be lost, often with the active playing down or avoidance by the resident of the issues. After a while staff can become conditioned to this. In such a situation, a complementary therapeutic process that focuses on these issues that is being fed back into the community meetings keeps the awareness of the different dimensions acute.

Primary health care

There is a number of curiosities about the provision of primary health care in prisons, the most notable of which is the activity of health care services. These are largely catering for fit young men who in the community would extremely rarely attend a GP's surgery. In prison, as has been mentioned above, the doctor has an important statutory role, 'fitting' prisoners for adjudications, for confinement, prior to being moved and so on, that can be understood in human rights terms. Alongside this, and possibly more important than the health care role, primary care is care. Care in a setting where people struggle with the deprivations of imprisonment; where people's liberty is removed;

FRED

Several more weeks after the incident with the drug counsellor, Fred had to miss a community meeting because of a hospital appointment. The senior prison officer noted that this was the second or third time that this had happened, and that he would ask Fred about it. He learned from Fred that he was having heart investigations, and that there were plans for him to be transferred to another prison nearer a specialist hospital for more extensive investigations of these. This was immediately seen as a further parachute or way out that he was setting up. He met with his small group therapist and the community therapist, who made this formulation, pointing out that if he wanted to leave

Grendon, he simply had to ask. Fred protested that his pathology was genuine, telling a story of palpitations that had been particularly bad when there was the security debate about removing him, and that would be worse in a group or community where he was supposed to speak.

The therapists used the timing of his palpitations as evidence of their being related to anxiety rather than any more sinister pathology and Fred became angry, refusing to say any more, and rightly claiming that his medical history was confidential. In the following week, Fred opted out of his small groups and one of the community meetings because of feeling unwell and also refused to meet staff for the same reason.

The health care staff were unhappy about discussing him because of the confidentiality issue, Fred being clear that he didn't want his medical history passed to the community team. The community staff group felt over a barrel, unable to work with the issue because they didn't have the facts and, at the same time, worried that he might genuinely be unwell, and that their confronting him with the dilemma might itself exaggerate the condition.

In a staff meeting, a position for the staff group was agreed. First, it was accepted that they couldn't demand that Fred disclose his medical history, as this was confidential. Second, it was accepted that the staff group had to make a decision about the safety of Fred continuing in therapy and the ability of Fred to engage in treatment given his condition. Third, it was clear that they couldn't be sure Fred was safe without more information about his medical decision. The staff group could make a decision to discharge Fred on the basis of the little medical information it had. If Fred wished to argue that it indeed was safe for him to continue in treatment, he would have to disclose some more medical details to support this.

Meanwhile, Fred had decided to start attending his small groups again, although not the community meeting. There was interest from his peers in the small group, and the issue was discussed there a little. One member of the group talked about his own experiences with panic attacks; about how he had been convinced of having a heart attack, and that it took a long time before he could accept that he was not. 'I was always absolutely certain I was going to die,' he said, 'and it was terrible to think I was going to die out in the open where I was. That thought just made it worse.' 'You just had a brush with your mortality recently, didn't you, Fred' said another member. 'All that stuff in psychodrama. If you snuffed it in here, your mother wouldn't find you, would she. Maybe that's it.'

Following this group, the issue abated. Fred decided that after all he could attend community meetings. His palpitations continued to be investigated but, somehow, the issue lost some of its urgency and moved into the background.

EDDIE

Eddie had an old back injury, sustained while playing football in his early teens. Most of the time it wasn't a problem but, according to him, sometimes he fell badly and that would set it off again. Unfortunately, this happened shortly after arriving in Grendon, and it had been grumbling away in the background. Apparently unrelated, there had been a concern in the community about the availability of opiate painkillers, DF118 and Codydramol, that could be abused, and were being used as currency. It was with some surprise to the staff team that Eddie said he was being prescribed them at the maximum dosage, as part of him was saying that they didn't work at all, his back was still sore. Eddie was predictably pugnacious in his response to scepticism about the appropriateness of the prescription, and angry when it was pointed out that, for an invalid requiring so much medication, it was odd that he was still able to play such a full part on the football field.

There was surprise in the health care department when staff learnt that this invalid, who carried himself carefully in the department because of back spasms, was the community's star in the recent World Cup Competition, and his medication was gradually phased out.

where people are removed from families, friends and the usual caring networks; where not many people have time to care on account of the numbers imprisoned. In response to this need for care, there has grown up a whole industry of demand for and provision of special diets: extra milk, protein supplements, vitamin supplements, onion-free diets, egg-free diets, and so on and so on. The theme running through is of being looked after in some way, of some part of the prison's structure recognising the inmates as individuals and responding accordingly.

So, if primary care in prison settings fulfils these three functions, primary health care, a statutory human rights function and that of being a generic care agency, in what way is this modified in Grendon as a specialist setting? First, alongside the primary health care function, there is a preponderance of psychiatric morbidity although, paradoxically, the Grendon primary carers probably do less psychiatric work than in normal prison settings because the therapy absorbs most of it. What remains are those who choose to create a split by telling a different story to the GP from the one they tell the community staff team, and those who become genuinely and uncontainably psychiatrically ill or who require statutory monitoring for a 2052 suicide watch. In Grendon the statutory functions of health care are the same, but the hope is that the GP will resist requests for different complex dietary supplements, in that the therapeutic process needs to discuss and explore these issues of care and deprivation face to face, rather than have them treated by a prescription of banana-flavoured 'Build Up'.

The difficulties occur with those individuals for whom somatisation is a significant element of their psychic functioning.

Clinical pluralism

The task of the Grendon team in its residential work with personality disordered clients is to make the least bad decisions. In coming to such a compromise, one has to bear the disappointment of the different individual disciplines which individually have a much clearer and more succinct plan. One has to trust that, in the same way as democracy is imperfect, but the best form of government overall, pluralistic clinical debate and decision-making is imperfect, but the best overall. The histories and activities of Grendon's men evoke sound-bite responses: 'Lock him up... Get rid of him... Give him a chance'. The task of facilitating a therapeutic process for such a person needs to be more complex than simply enacting one of these reactions. The multidisciplinary process structures this complexity by providing a forum for debate in the different meetings that take place and differing starting points for the views that will contribute to the debate, different views that will be synthesised into the decisions that are made. In the same way as in a pluralistic societal structure, no one pressure group holds a hegemony of influence; in the therapeutic community, different therapeutic models combine in a rich and dynamic forum of debate and creativity; from cognitive behavioural through psychodynamic and expressive artistic therapeutic approaches, and on to spiritual and educational dimensions.

Management of these teams and of this diversity is not easy because one perspective often undermines another; so that the interdisciplinary debate can easily veer into an interdisciplinary battle, and all of this is prior to the inclusion of the added dimension of personalities. But at the same time, management of these teams promotes an intellectual and clinical rigour that is exhilarating and adds a sense of legitimacy and stability to the work. This takes the form of a confidence that, although they may be undermined by hindsight, at the time and with the information available, the decisions reached can probably not be bettered.

CHAPTER 6

Grendon as a Psychodynamic Treatment

One of the difficulties of putting together a psychodynamic model of therapy to describe how Grendon works is that it would be misleading to provide one consistent account. Unlike the 'What Works' framework where a rational and linear understanding of how a programme works is a pre-requisite to legitimacy, psychoanalytic understandings derive from a different epistemological root. In some children's play parks there is a game where an object is hidden in a box which has hand holes. The children cannot see the object in the box but can feel it, and the game is to describe what they feel. Several children (and often their parents) have a go at feeling the object: its texture, its shape and so on. Together, people's different accounts lead to a description of the object and a solution to the puzzle of what it is. If the object is a person's personality, then the different psychoanalytic approaches are like different attempts to describe the thing that can't be directly observed. The best one can do is collect these different accounts and get an overall sense of the shape.

The more positivistic type of knowledge that underlies an empirical, science-based 'What Works' approach would measure the object's dimensions, length, weight, and so on. A psychoanalytic perspective would see this information as a valuable contribution, but not the whole truth. In the children's parks, in one of these games, a dried sheep's skull was the hidden object. The descriptions came about it being pointy and light and thin, and like a container with holes in it – with two or three shiny hard things at the front – the qualitative descriptions. The skull's measurable dimensions would have added to this, mass, length, breadth and so on, but it was a qualitative account that gave the experiences meaning – the hard things are a bit like…like teeth! Squeals of delight from the children as the adults look a bit queasy with the recognition. In the same way, each of the psychodynamic accounts of how Grendon works are qualitative hypotheses that in themselves are unbalanced and exaggerated, but which together begin to provide a sense of the shape of the problems being tackled.

A psychodynamic model of criminality proposes that the unconscious becomes a vast storehouse of all the unacceptable thoughts and fantasies that a person has. What distinguishes the criminal is not the existence of an unconscious full of repressed violent and sexual material, because this is relatively normal. In the course of normal development people go through stages of incestuous wishes as well as wishes to kill parents, siblings and others. From a psychoanalytic perspective, what is interesting is that so few people *are* homicidal or sexual offenders. According to Freud, the struggle in life for an individual, and the struggle more generally for a civilisation, is how to manage and channel the rapacious and murderous elements of personality. The perpetrator of a crime simply does that which we all have the capability (and unconscious wish) to do. The criminal enacts in reality that which the rest of us manage either to maintain in fantasy or retain deeply buried in the unconscious. The objective of therapy, therefore, is not to remove or eradicate the criminal wish or thought (because this is an endemic part of the human condition). The objective of therapy is to enable the perpetrator to avoid acting on the impulse in future. The way to do this is a long exploration of the perpetrator's mind and internal world in a psychodynamic process.

If therapy helps people who have committed crimes by enabling them to choose not to re-offend it does this in four main ways: first, by re-integrating aspects of mind that have become fragmented and separated. Second, therapy can clarify what was actually going on in the person's mind at the time of the crime – clarifying the 'internal crime scene' and distinguishing this from the real external situation. Third, as mentioned above, a psychodynamic process clarifies a sense of self, agency and choice for the individual. Finally, in a more general sense, a psychodynamic treatment moves the process of development forward, increasing the emotional repertoire of clients.

Often, an offender will simply not recognise his responsibility for his crime; it feels 'as if' it were done by someone else. Clarifying for the perpetrator his own responsibility for what happened and challenging the various obfuscations that will get in the way of this recognition enable the offender to exercise a choice not to re-offend. In the structural model of the mind, the ego is assailed by unacceptable, lewd and violent impulses from the id, at the same time as being bombarded by harsh criticism from the superego. To maintain equilibrium and sanity, it develops a series of defensive strategies to counter these assaults. These include repression (mentioned above), denial, projection, reaction formation, and so on. Someone who has committed a crime that not only society but the person himself finds unacceptable, will use a variety of these strategies to avoid the emotional reaction.

Psychoanalytic theory distinguishes between these defensive strategies and more primitive ones including splitting and projective identification. When splitting occurs, it is not that the ego does something with the memory; the ego (and therefore the personality) itself splits, leaving a fragment of the personality that committed the crime and another fragment that is entirely innocent. A perpetrator who splits off the part of himself that committed the crime genuinely can say that he didn't do it. It was someone else; another part of himself. Re-integration of the personality is fostered by challenging the defences that prevent the person from recognising his own complicity and re-sponsibility in his crimes. The work is an attempt to re-integrate fragmented personalities by following them through the psychotherapeutic process, where the fragmentation will recur, and enabling the person to become aware of the split-off fragments.

EDDIE

Some way into his treatment, Eddie was talking in his group prior to a review. He was being directly challenged about killing Dan, and about the fact that he couldn't remember anything of the events. 'This sounds like bullshit,' said another group member. 'You were too drunk to remember anything – that's a cop-out. I think that you thank God that you were too drunk, because it means you don't have to think about who did it. It wasn't you, it was a drunken man. It was you, Eddie – get used to the idea.' Eddie was silent, but angry. 'It's true,' another group member said, 'all of us have to look at the fact that we've done what we've done. None of us like it, but you don't have to because of this drunk thing.' Eddie remained silent, which was itself challenged. 'It's right,' he said at last, 'it doesn't feel like it was me. People told me that it had happened, and because I really was out of it, it sort of wasn't me, and that felt OK.'

If the primary therapeutic task is re-integration, the second task is to establish the 'why' of the event: to begin to unravel the meaning of the crime. When a crime is committed, the police gather evidence at the crime scene. In fact, there are actually two crime scenes; the first is where the concrete act took place, the second is the 'internal crime scene' – what was happening in the mind of the perpetrator at the time of the incident. What actually happened in the index event is the crime. Its meaning, its personal relevance to the perpetrator, its internal resonances – these are the dimensions of the internal crime scene. If one man kills another in an argument over a £5 bet, it seems absurd. But it didn't seem absurd at the time during the struggle, it was a matter of life and death. Suppose the man who died had lost the bet but refused to pay, confident that the winner wouldn't have the courage to insist. Suppose the winner had all his life been humiliated by people who took liberties with him, confident that he didn't have the courage to challenge them. Suppose there was one occasion as a child when he had challenged his abusive and bullying father about a bet he had won. Suppose his father utterly humiliated him in front of the whole family, and beat him for his impudence. Whom did the perpetrator wish to kill? Whom was it important to kill? Was it the drunken friend who owed him a fiver? Or was it the father who utterly destroyed his identity with years of cruel and abusive taunting?

The incident with the father in this example is the internal crime scene; something about the argument with the friend in the real crime scene triggered off the utter rage prompted by the internal one. At the moment in which the crime is committed the person is in a psychotic state; he believes that the victim in front of him is the person in his mind's eye. After the crime, the killer realises that he has not killed the most evil thing that his mind has conjured up, but rather that he has killed his friend. More important, the horrific memory that sparked the killing is still very much alive. It wasn't killed with the offence, and it may spark further offending. The external crime-scene victim is dead, but the memory of the incident with the father is alive and well, and waiting to trigger another catastrophe. The aim of a psychodynamic treatment is to enable patients to become aware of the characters in their internal world who are seen as evil and frightening and to learn to distinguish these internal world figures from people in the real world even in times of great stress.

Gradually, in treatment, the various emotional elements that comprised the internal crime scene will be rekindled. The individual may become attached to the therapist or senior officer as if they were father figures, for example – developing a need for these two figures to respect him. A competitive dimension may creep into the relationship, with bets being laid where a difference of opinions arises, and where once again the spectre of being belittled stalks with its potentially disastrous consequences. As the elements of the internal crime scene are replayed in real time in the transference – with feelings and attitudes about the core players of the internal crime scene transferred to those in the immediate environment – the two crime scenes can be explored and their significance understood. The trauma can be excavated, its main elements reviewed, and the individual can start to work through the implications. In the brief example of the humiliation over a bet triggering a memory of a humiliating and belittling father, the individual may be fiercely protective and idealising about this father, in which case the reality of a more difficult relationship will have to be accepted.

In the process of therapy, the person is likely to feel the same way about the therapist as he did about the person against whom the crime was committed, as part of the transference process. At this point, what triggers off the momentary psychotic state can be explored. Did the perpetrator feel belittled? Was some provocation unbearable and, if so, what was the provocation, why was it unbearable and why did it conjure up the image or memory of the person from the internal world who had to be killed? What happened back then that was so awful that it has to be repeated in adult life mentally and then at times physically, with disastrous results?

FRED

In one group, Fred was being challenged about his offence – what the exact details had been. The group had noticed that Fred was a bit slow in talking about his actual criminal activities, and this slowness itself had become the group issue. This particular group followed developments in the implementation of the Prison Service personal identification number (PIN) for telephones – an initiative whereby, rather than operating prisoners' phone calls via the sale and use of phone cards, a PIN system would be introduced. This, of course, had implications for the tracking and monitoring of the telephone activity of prisoners and prisoners' ability to conduct their affairs both business and personal – both legitimate and nefarious. There had been mirth in the community about some 'big capitalists' going to the wall, and the general theme of continuing connections with nefarious activity on the outside.

A link was made between Fred's reticence about the *actualité* of his activities and the possibility that he didn't want to compromise an ongoing concern. Fred protested that he was not active at the moment – that he was detained at Her Majesty's Pleasure, so business opportunities were few. But his light treatment of the challenge amplified the challenges, with specific questions about what happened when he got caught, and why.

Reluctantly Fred told the story. It was simple, he and some babes were going to a mate's caravan; they were going to meet some people there, and party all weekend. He had a few drinks on the way, had the babes in the car, was showing off, and got caught speeding. After a chase, he crashed the car, no one was hurt, they found the gear, and that was it. The group was intrigued, thinking that for a slick gangster he'd been a bit stupid, both ostentatiously speeding while carrying drugs when he might attract attention, and taking them in the first place.

Fred managed to stem his irritation, so that the conversation could continue, but disagreed that this was an issue, it was just chance – fluke. In the face of Fred's refusal to explore more deeply, others joined in, raising possible motives for this display of, at best carelessness, at worst stupidity. One suggested that it was the 'baby dynamic' that Fred was always having to prove that he was not the baby – he always had to be larger than life. He had to take the gear to the party, so he could be the big man. He had to speed in the car with the babes, so he could be the big man.

Another took up the theme, linking Fred's efforts to be one of the big men in the community with this need, linking his account of running the rackets at school as part of the same theme – needing to get away from being the mummy's boy, needing to get away from being the baby of the family.

So the main objectives of treatment conceived from a psychodynamic perspective are first, the establishment of agency and responsibility via the process of re-integration of the disavowed parts of the personality and second, the establishment of the meaning of the crime as a repetition of an earlier trauma – the internal crime scene. The first of these objectives is more complicated than it sounds, and cannot be brought about by a mere bullying into accepting personal culpability – as can sometimes seem the case in the Grendon groups. The process of re-integration of the personality is best conceived of as a developmental process.

A developmental slant on offending brings forward the different stances on the development of the self taken by the different psychoanalytic schools. As mentioned above, these are not so much theories in conflict as different efforts to describe something felt, not seen, and are best considered as complementary. The different psychoanalytic theories can be grouped into three broad areas: more classical Freudian, largely based on Freud's earlier ideas that were subsequently developed by his daughter Anna; the more British object relations perspective developed initially by Melanie Klein; and a third group of theoretical perspectives that are derivative to some degree from these two – either psychoanalytic, such as the independent group in the UK or allied, such as the Jungians, or based on different techniques of therapy, such a therapy in groups.

The different psychoanalytic perspectives that form the polarity between a classical Freudian and a Kleinian approach are best understood with reference to other sociological debates – for example, the doctrine of original sin, or the nature/nurture debate – or the question of whether criminal behaviour derives from an innate evil or from good people learning antisocial survival skills in deprived social circumstances – for example, in sink housing estates. A more classical Freudian perspective would be that individuals are basically born good; that they are frustrated in some way by the environment in which they grow up; perhaps they are abused or traumatised and, as a result of this sub-optimal developmental experience, they become embittered and destructive. While there is certainly some truth in this account, it is also true that many survive difficult developmental experiences without becoming criminally destructive, and many who are criminally destructive have had a good enough upbringing. The parallels between this and a more straightforward debate about whether criminal activity is about nature or nurture, genes or the environment, is clear. A Kleinian psychoanalytic perspective would propose that the child is born with some innate destructiveness, and might criticise a classical account as an over-romantic view of the innocence of youth.

Every so often, in popular culture there is a debate about the violence present in children's stories and activities – from the big bad wolf blowing down the little piggies' houses and then eating the cuddly occupants, or the eating of Red Riding Hood's grandmother, to today's wall-to-wall video game and cartoon carnage. Is violence inculcated in children by these images and accounts, or is it an avenue for the expression of innate violence? If the former, then the sanitised version of the piggies' story, where the wolf puts the piggies in a bag which is cut open at the end of the story, rather than his stomach, would have the same appeal to children. It doesn't, so the traditional violent one lives on, and the sanitised version is forgotten. At the turn of the century, Freud caused a stir by proposing that childhood might be a time with some innate sexuality (Freud 1905). The notion that children might be innately violent seems similarly difficult.

Classical psychoanalytic models

At its most concrete the classical psychoanalytic account of development sees childhood as the negotiation of different phases of development. When a child is born, her whole world is experienced through her mouth. She has the task of learning to survive without an umbilical chord mainlining nutrients, to take in food through her mouth and to take in air to breathe. This is the oral stage of development.

GEORGE

For a while in the community there was an issue about how second helpings of food were distributed at the servery. The pod workers were being criticised on the community for having favourites. George was one of those who spoke accusingly. The pod workers protested that any food left over was distributed as second helpings on a first-come, first-served basis. If George was late asking he wouldn't get any, it was as simple as that. In the community meeting where this issue was aired, a suspicion lingered that there was some favouritism amongst friends about second helpings, but as in Scottish law, the case was 'not proven'.

George was angry about this and brought it to his group, complaining about the community not working if this obvious problem couldn't be sorted out. The group listened for some time as George vented his anger, then one member pointed out that George had argued with that particular pod worker, Harry, before, so it was possible that the two of them were just arguing again over a different issue. George complained that this issue was being turned against him, when they were all being short-changed at the hot plate where the food is served.

After a silence in the group, one member asked George why he wanted seconds. 'You usually have quite a lot on your plate when you sit down, and, well, you're not exactly skinny.' George is a big man, not tall, but stout verging on the fat. He carries it well, but he clearly chronically overeats. The issue of his weight or eating habits had been raised before, and the group seemed a bit nervous about raising it again. George said nothing more, and the group moved on. Several weeks later, he raised it again, spilling out how hurt he felt about what had been said. The group were surprised at the ferocity of his reaction and

---

said that he wasn't that fat, but that it was clearly an issue for him and perhaps he should use a group to discuss it.

Another week or so later, George took some time. He described how as a child, from as early as he could remember, his mother would be away from the house when he got home and he would have to get his own tea. This wouldn't have been so bad, he said, but there was never anything in the fridge or the cupboards for him to have. He would scrape around, making a meal of dry cream crackers, or the stale bread that was left on the side. As he grew older, he would start to go out with his mates, hanging round the local fish-and-chip shop. But while his mates were there for the social contact, he was there to cadge food. One of the main draws into the lair of his abuser was the fact that he would be given a meal. Since leaving home, George had always been keen to feed himself well; often junk, but with sufficient quantity – hence the debate over the second helpings being precipitated by there being no chips left for him. He remembered that a family friend remembered on one occasion that as an infant he was 'always screaming'. The friend had commented that she concluded at the time that George's mother wasn't 'feeding him enough', and that whenever they looked after George as a baby, he never cried, but just wanted bottle after bottle.

As the story unfolded, the issue of food was largely forgotten as George described the loneliness and desolation as a child of not knowing when mother was going to be there, and when not. 'I just couldn't rely on her,' he said, through tears, 'so I had to find other things to do. Tony [the abuser] was there.'

One of the group commented on a phrase that he had used, that he wanted 'more and more' food. When he talked about being driven to offend, when he had identified a victim and was in the process of grooming, George had described wanting 'more and more' from the boy. At the time George didn't recognise any link, and the issue was dropped. But increasingly it became clear that George wanted 'more and more' in quite a number of areas, and that a drive into deeper perversion and more risky situations was influenced by a needing 'more and more' dynamic.

In this example, a hypothesis might be that George's infantile feeding regime and a failure of dependable mothering prevented his successful negotiation of the oral stage of development. George was unable to rely on being regularly fed and so has spent the rest of his life making up for this via a direct symptom of overeating and via a perverse symptom, sexualising some of his unmet need.

GEORGE

Six weeks or so later, in response to a fellow group member giving an account of a difficult relationship with his own parents, George returned to the issue of his mother. The other member tried to formulate for his peer a way that being in Grendon and being in the group might somehow heal the damage that had been done. 'Don't you think,' he said, 'don't you think that somehow this place is, well is like looking after you? My mum was never there, you know that, and, well, it's funny, because you lot are. I can't really explain it, but it's like, no one has ever really been there for me before you lot. Yes, I piss you off, and some of you particularly piss me off, but like, you are still there even so, session after session, week after week. I think that with my mother, she was never there, and I kind of believed that no one ever is, but people are. It's like, I can now see that my mother was unreliable, not that everyone is unreliable and that I can never rely on anyone. You've had a shit time with your parents too. Being in Grendon doesn't make them any different, or doesn't make what happened to you any better, but it meant you can see that it was just them, and that there is the possibility at least that other people will be different. I think that's why I never had a partner, that it never occurred to me that someone I met and liked might not let me down like my mum did.'

In the weeks that followed, George described a different side to his relationship with his mother: about how they would together tease and taunt some of her punters, laughing at their mode of dress or at things that had happened. In particular, one of Mother's clients was an army sergeant-major, complete with handlebar moustache, who wanted mother to spank him but who was sexually impotent. He remembered shopping trips where his mother would take him to cafes and buy elaborate ice creams.

George seemed to have been able to identify and encapsulate a problem with his childhood experience, so that his experience of his mother moved from a simple one-dimensional traumatised hatred, to a more complex memory of good and bad times. In the group, his mother became a three-dimensional person, with qualities and failings, rather than simply an object of traumatised hatred.

The hope was that in future George would be able to sustain more of his relationships, reducing his sense of anomie in society and developing relationships, rather than having perverse fantasy or enactment as his only outlet.

The next classical stage of development, synchronous with the popular conception of the 'terrible twos', sees the infant as having mastered the process of ingestion and becoming aware of a degree of control that she has over the environment. In particular she has power over that which is expelled from the body – faeces. The links between anality and control-freakery are difficult to persuade critics about, but the links are positively physical. The child decides that she can and will deposit her faeces wherever she wants; that this is one of the few things over which she actually has control, when almost everything else is under the control of parents. This control over an aspect of the child's own environment feels like intoxicating power.

FRED

There had been another wave of concern in the staff team about the level of drug ingress and use. There was a certain characteristic feeling in the community meetings, where the residents seemed intransigently critical of the staff group. The staff group was criticised on the one hand for raising the issue of drugs as a current concern and on the other hand, for not solving the problem. The therapist pointed out that this is quite a characteristic pattern: because many residents will be implicated, they will feel paranoid about the subject being raised but, genuinely at the same time, they cannot cope with drugs being available; the temptation is too much. It is the staff group's responsibility to sort out the problem because it is one the residents can't do for themselves.

Staff noticed that, in the community meeting discussions about the issue, Fred was silent, and this was odd because he must be centrally involved. His group facilitator also commented that he hadn't been saying much recently, and that the small group somehow felt constrained. 'Constipated!' said someone, to laughter in the staff group, as this feel of things dammed up and held back captured the feel of the community meetings as well.

In discussion with therapy colleagues, the spontaneous laughter at the 'constipated' comment was reported and the situation discussed. Following this, the therapist decided that a strategy to tackle the problem might be to pursue the usual regime of drug testing, but at the same time to go with the hypothesis that Fred was somehow controlling things behind the scenes, and to interpret this in terms of his need to control everything – the drug market in the community, the discussion in his small group and the discussion on the community. This formulation was taken back to the staff group and, as issues emerged, the 'Fred-control' interpretation was made. In the community, the therapist wondered about why it was that Fred was in prison for dealing, and yet said nothing in the communities, suggesting that those who spoke loudest might be his puppets doing his bidding.

In the small group, this theme was taken up in terms of the suggestion that Fred might be arranging and controlling the agenda in advance. It was quite a struggle to get the issue into open debate, but eventually there was an angry outburst in a community meeting about 'bloody parrots being told what to squawk, and doing their master's bidding all the time'. The 'parrots' responded, denying the accusation and, for a while, most community meeting debates and subjects degraded into an accusation of block voting by Fred's parrots.

The staff group agreed that the therapist and the small group therapist would jointly meet Fred to outline the concerns. Fred was told that although he was of course too expert at his work for there to be any evidence to pin on him, the staff group was fairly sure that he had a quite tight control on the whole community. While it was possible that the security implications might mean he would need to be removed if things didn't change, the more important issue for the therapy was to understand why he felt the need to be in such tight control of everything and what was he worried might break free if he loosened up.

Following this, in his small group, Fred continued to deny that he was behind the control and compromise on the community but, at the same time, spoke about how he would control his business when he was 'on the out'. Everything had to be just so, 'every i dotted, and every t crossed'. Gradually, members of the group could talk about how they all felt controlled by Fred in the group about what they could talk about and so on. As the dynamic loosened, Fred's controlling behaviour could be identified when it occurred as an issue was raised that he didn't want talked about; he would then change the subject or close down the discussion in some other way. On one occasion when this occurred, one member teased Fred about his 'anal sphincter playing up again', to the same sort of laughter in the group that had accompanied the 'constipation' comment in the staff group.

The third classical psychoanalytic phase of development is the genital where, having become aware of and familiar with the process of ingestion and expulsion, the child notices the difference between the sexes, leading to the Oedipus complex. The child recognises that she or he does not simply own Mother; there is a third person to be considered, Father, and this is a considerable trauma and blow. An intense area of interest becomes the nature of the difference between the parents and so the awareness develops of genitalia and sexual difference. The Oedipus complex is a solution to this dilemma in the child's fantasy, which involves being rid of the parent of the same sex, in order to be left with the parent of the opposite sex.

EDDIE

As part of the programme of films on video that are shown to residents, The Matrix had been shown. This is a science fiction story proposing that reality is a persuasive programmed illusion. There had been some discussion about this in the community, prompted by a resident saying that thinking about what happened on the night of his offence was like that – as if he woke up afterwards and it didn't feel real. The community in the meeting seemed split between one group in a rather intellectually elitist way discussing the nature of reality considered philosophically as raised by the film, and the reliability of memory. Another group, with Eddie as part of it, were making lewd *sotto voce* comments about the tight leather clothing worn by the film's attractive female star. The discussion had been in the closing minutes of the meeting, and neither the split nor the lewd giggles could be addressed but continued as people drifted out. In the staff group's meeting afterwards, some of the female members of staff said that they had felt a bit uncomfortable, and one or two accounts of Eddie in particular being at the centre of such ribaldry and lewdness towards female staff were recounted. There was a sense that once or twice the usual banter had been exceeded, making female staff uncomfortable. One remembered that before she was going on holiday, a nudge-nudge comment made about 'her lucky fellah' had felt uncomfortable, but not challengeable.

At the following meeting, one of the community philosophers from the previous meeting wanted a 'minute'. He said that he felt that Eddie should take his attitude to women to his group following comments he had made after the last community. Gradually, by challenging the philosopher to say more and adding the fragments witnessed by others an account was pieced together. Eddie had made another *sotto voce* comment about 'those fucking wankers up their own arses about the film, when the real point was how shaggable [the female star] was'. The philosopher to whom the remark was directed had felt humiliated about this, as well as intimidated, as Eddie's comment had been met with raucous laughter by those around.

Gradually the names of those who had giggled during the community meeting and afterwards emerged. They defended themselves by saying it was entirely normal to be sexually stirred up by the film and, indeed, they would be abnormal had they not been; and, furthermore, the staff had to realise that they were young men imprisoned, without access to wives and girlfriends, so sexually frustrated. Such attitudes were to be expected; indeed the elicitation of such attitudes was the aim of film-makers. The female star would be quite aware that she would be the object of male sexual interest and fantasy. The therapist commented that the main protagonist had seemed to be Eddie, and that maybe this was something that he could take to his group to explore further. Eddie was cross, protesting that it was all being 'put on [his] toes. What about all that bollocks about philosophy, that's rationalisation, that is.'

Nevertheless, Eddie's small group questioned him about it next time. An account emerged of a macho cultural attitude to women bred on the football terraces. Yes, it had got him into trouble, and had been one of the problems in his relationship with Dawn, she being upset about his language about women when he was with his friends. 'She couldn't see that it wasn't about her, what I would say. I wouldn't disrespect her,' he protested. One of the group asked how he would have felt if someone else in the community had found Dawn 'shaggable' when she had visited for the family day. Eddie went very quiet, clearly overwhelmed; he agreed to think about it and come back to another group.

Several groups passed, with Eddie not feeling he wanted to address this matter. Instead he was talking to a group member he was close to, on an individual basis, who protected Eddie, saying that it was a difficult issue for him. Several days later, the friend said that Eddie had something he wanted to talk about. 'Go on then mate. Get it out. You'll feel better.' With a lowered head, Eddie spoke about how he had become jealous about Dawn, thinking that she was indeed very attractive; that he couldn't possibly hold onto her, 'being a bit of a shit and all'. His account included times when he would sit her down and question her about whether she was having an affair. He was particularly enraged about the possibility that she was having an affair with Dan – his victim. 'The fight that we had, I think that that had something to do with it, like I thought he was having it away with her.' The group pestered for details about whether he was. Eddie said that she'd always denied it, but they were close. After a long pause, he spoke about how he would hit her to get her to confess, sometimes overseen by the children, just as in his own family.

In the post-group supervision, the therapist drew attention to the Oedipal dynamic: that in his up-bringing Eddie had fought with Father over Mother, and that there was a dimension to his offence of two men fighting over a woman. Another possibility was a sense of being 'a shit' – small and insignificant – as he would have felt in the face of a competition with Father as a child – and being convinced that he was unable to be a potent father himself. Instead of being able to be a mature genital father, he is a boorish braggart making lewd comments. In the staff group, as not uncommonly happens, veering too far into a psychoanalytic understanding of what is taking place is met with blankness. 'Suffice to say,' the therapist continued, '[the philosopher] is probably right that Eddie needs to explore his attitude to women.'

The psychoanalytic hypothesis might be that Eddie's father's violence and drunkeness interfered with Eddie's ability to work through his Oedipus complex and find some sort of resolution, so that this remains a fixation point for him. Traditionally, two things happen to resolve this. The child recognises that getting rid of the same-sex parent would be wrong, and this sense of something being wrong is internalised and becomes a proto-superego. In Eddie's case, his father's chronic violence and murderousness to his children made this super-ego so savage that Eddie is left feeling like a 'bit of a shit'. The second aspect is that the child recognises qualities in the same-sex parent that he or she wants to have for him- or herself, which is difficult if you hate an abusive same-sex parent. Nevertheless, tragically, in some way, Eddie did internalise his father's distorted solution to Oedipus – jealousy and violence.

Another significant contribution of the classical school is the conceptualisation of the self in terms of an ego (as distinct from a largely unconscious animalistic id, and a conscience-containing super-ego), an ego constantly engaged in a process of psychic management and employing a set of defensive strategies to protect the self from being overwhelmed by some aspect of the mental contents. Eddie clearly failed to protect himself from a wave of jealous rage towards Dan with disastrous consequences. Alternative (more normal) strategies might have been to use denial (to ignore the possibility of Dawn and Dan's affair) to use rationalisation (to reason that even if she were having an affair she would return to Eddie, as the father of her children) to use reaction formation to adopt the opposite emotion to the one he felt and wish them well, with a small gift to celebrate their relationship) and so on.

Freud described the ego as a person trying to ride the horse of the instincts, barely able to control this powerful strong animal. This is a particularly apt metaphor to use when working in a psychodynamic way with offenders, because there is a strong sense that many offences are committed when the impulsive urge overwhelms the mental regulatory processes. The psychodynamic tasks then become to identify and sort out what are the instinctual drives that cannot be managed, why developmental strategies have not been evolved to manage them, and to make the individual aware of the risks so that he can manage them better. The sense is that civilisation for humans is a struggle, that humanity and goodness are not a default position, but need to be strived for, that a more natural position is more animalistic.

Object relations models

A significant theoretical difference between more classical and more Kleinian or object-related psychoanalytic theories is that, according to the former, the infant enjoys a period of blissful union with the mother before she or he realises that they are separate at all. This is a blissful period of narcissism when Mother is simply part of the baby (which in one sense *in utero* she is), and the world and Mother revolve around the baby (which again, *in utero* and very early life, Mother and the world do), so that the baby is simply the centre of the universe. Following this, and stimulated by the fact that bits of the universe do not revolve perfectly (Mother is late with a feed, for example, leaving the baby hungry), the baby has to recognise and then work through the idea that Mother and baby are in fact separate, that the baby needs to ingest orally, control anally and then come to terms with the realisation that there is not just Mother and baby, but that there is Father too – the genital or Oedipal phase.

From a Kleinian perspective, the baby is object related: he or she can perceive a difference between self and mother from the beginning. Be it placental insufficiency or an uncomfortable maternal internal organ sticking into them, the infant has a sense of 'me' and 'not me'. From the beginning the infant has a sense of anxiety about whether the 'not me' that is Mother can be trusted, and from the beginning the baby has a sense of whether 'me' has an internal space 'vagina, so female', or something to prod with 'penis, so male'. Consequently, from birth, the Oedipus dynamic operates, with the infant engaged not only in a struggle about the trustability of Mother and survival, but also about the third object – Father – and what that means.

Faced with these anxieties, the infant adopts two characteristic 'positions' or psychic constellations. In the first, the 'paranoid schizoid position', the infant attributes all the anxiety and fear that is generated by his or her situation onto an outside person – it is someone's fault that the infant feels so terrified, and that person is trying to destroy him or her. The only way to survive is to destroy that bad person first. The mythology goes that the infant perceives two breasts of the mother and decides that one of them is good and supportive and that the other one is the attacking one. They try to destroy the attacking one and destroy it by biting it (e.g. Segal 1973).

EDDIE

As a lifer, Eddie was used to receiving special treatment. He knew that prisons (following the Woolf Report into the Strangeways riots, Woolf and Tumin 1991) all had to have a governor whose task was specifically to manage the progress of lifers in their prisons. After a year or so in treatment, Eddie decided that he was cured and that he was ready to move on a 'progressive move' – to another prison at a lower security category – i.e. to take his next step towards release. He took this idea to his small group and there was a brief discussion in the staff meeting. The staff group's view was that he was nowhere near ready, that he was someone who, after two or three years, might be ready to move on, but that he still had a long way to go.

Eddie was angry and contacted the lifer governor, who said that it was an issue for him to negotiate with his community staff team. Eddie was even more angry and put in a formal complaint about the governor, which was investigated by the most senior governor, who found that the junior lifer governor had acted properly.

Eddie still wasn't satisfied. He had brought the issue to his small group several times, who on each occasion said that he still had a long way to go, so Eddie shut himself off from this avenue of discussion by withdrawing from therapy. He stopped attending his small group, but carried on attending his communities in protest. The community got fed up with him, leaving him to stew on his own.

He contacted his lawyer, who was aware that life sentence prisoners usually do two or three years in Grendon, and tried to persuade him to 'chill out', but he agreed to write to the therapeutic team. Eddie wasn't satisfied and wanted to find some legal redress. Eddie began to threaten the staff team with legal action, saying he would ask for a judicial review of the decision not to recommend him for a progressive move.

The therapist was by this time feeling quite persecuted by the increasingly intimidatory letters from Eddie's solicitor, asking for more and more detail about why he was not thought suitable for a progressive move, and with the spectre of being taken to court. Discussion took place among in the senior team about how to handle this should it occur, and about what the potential damage to Grendon as a whole and its reputation might be.

The therapists' group took the view that there must be some issue that Eddie couldn't face; that by arresting his therapy by wanting to leave, or opting out of his small groups, he was in flight from something. The most likely cause was developing and exploring further the revelations that had emerged about his morbid jealousy in his relationship with Dawn. The point was also made that the lot of lifers is pretty dire – they are completely helpless and dependant on the opinions and good reports of the professional staff and jailers in their prisons. This must be pretty difficult to bear.

The second position follows on from the biting of the bad breast. At some point, the infant realises that both breasts are attached to the same mother and that, while Mother is imperfect, she is good enough. By attacking a part of her the infant has damaged the mother. The infant becomes depressed.

EDDIE

As time passed, Eddie seemed to get wind of his lawyer's ambivalence about pursuing a judicial review. Eddie was further incensed, deciding to pursue a complaint about him as well. As he had to find another lawyer to do so, he decided to return to his small group to discuss this. In the small group, he was shocked to find that the culture was much the same as when he had last been in it three weeks before. He was welcomed back, but the group didn't take particularly seriously his complaints. One member of the group was angry with him, accusing him of harassing the staff and being unfair, saying he was stupid because the only person he was hurting by not being in the group was himself.

In spite of himself, Eddie carried on attending the small group, where he became aware of the effect that his threats of legal action was having. The same member who had been angry accused him of damaging the therapy for everyone. 'The staff have had their heads in a shed over this – I don't care if you want to fuck up your own therapy – that's fine by me. What pisses me off is that you're fucking up everyone else's as well. Dan was good to you – you killed him. The staff here have been good to you and look what you're doing to them. Bloody dangerous to know, mate, that's you – even more dangerous to be good to.'

Eddie continued to attend the small group, and the talk of legal action, as well as his anger over the progressive move abated. For some time he was quite subdued, so that the staff team worried about how depressed he was and whether he was a suicide risk.

Running through a Kleinian or object relations perspective is a central problem of the issue of the dual instincts. How, as a developing child, do individuals integrate their hateful and destructive feelings with their loving and nurturing ones? How do they square the circle that they hate Mother for not doing whatever but, on the other hand, love and are attached to and dependent upon that same mother? Older Freudian theory identifies these two instincts as thanatos – the death drive – on the one hand, with its destructive impulses attitudes and actions, its hatred of and envious attack on the good and its destruction of union; and eros – a life instinct – on the other, loving, creative, pulling together and so on. Life and its struggles are about how to manage these two opposing drives, and about how to sustain relationships when these two are constantly operating in conflict.

The overlap with the doctrine on original sin is that more classical Freudians would argue that the destructive thanatotic drive is born out of frustration – that it is not innate – that humans are born pure, untainted with destructive sin. The holder of more Kleinian opinion might argue that, prior to birth, the baby may have been tearing at its own placenta in the uterus in a rage that it was not sufficiently nourishing, that therefore destructiveness is innate. An idle game in addressing this question is to speculate whether human kind spends more time, energy and money on constructive activities (building cities, health services) or on destructive activities (arms, prisons to contain the destructiveness in society) – it might be surprisingly evenly balanced.

Different psychoanalytic models have striven to understand the way that these two forces are integrated. Earlier Freudian models posited a structure of the mind in which these different elements resided – the topography of mind where the destructiveness was in the unconscious and the constructive (equated with the) more rational part of the mind was in the conscious. The evidence was to be found in the violent and chaotic content of dreams where unconscious material evaded the psychic censor (Freud 1900). A second model was that of the id – the animalistic part of the mind where destructive and perverse sexual impulses lay, and from which the ego had the task of controlling such impulses as they attempted to emerge, with the help and support of a super-ego which was the repository of a moral conscience.

If these models proposed a structure of mind within which the different life and death instincts could be housed, a structure of horizontal splits into different functions, Kleinian theorists proposed a different splitting mechanism – a vertical split of the ego itself. The effect of this vertical splitting is to create sub-personalities: let's say one who is good-natured and considerate and another who is violent and unpleasant. The effect of these vertical splits in the personality include the sort of non-recognition of the agency of the self, described above, when the individual can legitimately say that it feels as if he didn't commit the crime. To some degree, it is true that the penitent individual sitting in front of the professional did not commit the crime. The crime was committed by an entirely different part of the personality that took over in a moment of madness, or truth or, more likely, both.

Another significant aspect of this style of defence is that of projective identification. In this, the sub-personality, or aspects of it, are projected out into the other, who is then attacked because he or she are supposed to have it.

EDDIE

Several weeks after the issue over Eddie's reaction to *The Matrix* film, an issue arose about a resident who had been disrespectful to a female officer. The officer had asked the prisoner to do something, and was brushed off with an inaudible comment, but the concern was that it had been sexually demeaning. Eddie was angry – in particular, he had got on well with this officer and he was enraged that someone could treat her disrespectfully. The issue had been broached in the community meeting, and the resident involved wasn't in Eddie's group, but Eddie brought it up in his own group quite energetically.

Some of the group joined in with Eddie's anger, but others were critical, accusing Eddie of hypocrisy; only weeks before, he had been the one in the frame for being disrespectful to women in quite a serious way. Eddie denied this and an argument raged about the issue, with force of numbers impressing on Eddie the fact that he had displayed these same attitudes himself. Eddie's response was to be confused. He couldn't deny it, but on the other hand couldn't deny the fervour of his criticism of his fellow resident.

Eddie's confusion when confronted by the fact that he was attacking his own attitude reflects a psychotic confusion. Eddie was deluded into believing that he does not harbour these attitudes himself but that they are to be found in his fellow resident. These are delusions in the psychoanalytic sense – they are held to be true until they can be effectively interpreted, so that insight can be achieved. The delusional sense and fixity of some of these defences have led to them being termed 'psychotic defences'. The hypothesis is that there is a hierarchy of defences, with some being more primitive and some more developed and more neurotic. The more primitive include the vertical splitting of the ego described and the projection of aspects of the self into others, who are subsequently attacked.

This process was illustrated in a fictitious account of a murder in the film *American Beauty* – a father of a young man becomes convinced that the male next-door neighbour is having an affair with his son. As the film progresses, it becomes clear that there is a split-off homosexual part of the father that is projected into the male neighbour, who is subsequently killed. From a psychoanalytic perspective, this is a reasonably familiar situation: that the perpetrator projects some unacceptable aspect of him- or herself onto the victim who subsequently has to be killed in order to keep the unacceptable aspect at bay.

EDDIE

In a supervision discussion between the therapist and the lead facilitator of Eddie's group, the issue of how Eddie re-enacts his offence was being discussed. Over the issue of the football, his anger had been directed at the person in the group with whom he got on well, not his usual sparring partner. The discussion centred around the idea that there was some way in which people Eddie was close to represented more of a risk to him. The therapist wondered if it might be that, *in extremis*, Eddie needs to destroy the person who represents his vulnerability. At the time of the index offence, the relationship with Dawn was again collapsing, exposing him to his vulnerability; and his friend Dan was someone who, because of the dependence, may have reminded him of his vulnerability. The facilitator remembered that on one occasion Eddie had talked with contempt about people in a fight who are just about to go down – just about to be beaten. Eddie had said that there comes a point when they are 'pussies' – meaning vulnerable.

A hypothesis emerged that the opponent in a fight becoming a 'pussy' represented vulnerability, and that in the fight with Dan, Dan had shown this vulnerability stage, but, because of Eddie's extreme vulnerability – with the kids taken into care and Dawn threatening to leave – Eddie had to extinguish that vulnerability as manifest in the person of Dan nearly beaten in a fight. Dan had become vulnerable, Eddie projected his own extreme vulnerability onto Dan, and then had to kill it off.

From this perspective, the external crime scene represents an enactment of an internal conflict projected into the outside world. In committing the act, the perpetrator is confusing his own internal reality with the reality of the outside world, and so the act is a psychotic breakthrough.

One aspect of a psychodynamic approach to criminality that is particularly distinctive is the deconstruction of a 'them and us' dynamic. Psychoanalytic theory hypothesises that fantasies of murder, perversion, cruelty and violence are part of everyday life for everyone, as part of a developmental heritage. The difference between the life-sentenced bank robber behind the prison wall and the bank teller recovering from post-traumatic stress disorder is that the victim has managed to keep her murder and mayhem in the realm of fantasy, perhaps by enjoying action films, whereas the robber has enacted some of this in reality.

To some extent this dismantles the moral aspect of the differentiation between those within the walls and those outside, but it identifies a more important aspect of the work. This is that, just because we have not done it (the robbery, the rape) doesn't mean we can't understand it, because we will have done it in fantasy. This means, for example, that within a psychodynamic approach, the therapist draws upon his or her own understanding or murderousness to understand the perspective of the murderer. The mentation of those who have dome terrible things is *not* beyond understanding, because we have all done these things in fantasy, for our own reasons.

CHAPTER 7

Dilemmas in Management

The managerial dilemmas and challenges thrown up in the process of the management of an organisation like Grendon boil down to four main issues. The first is that in its role of containing a residential environment full of high-risk people it is a prison, imbued and structured by that disciplined culture. The second is that in an open and communicative therapeutic culture, management will be synonymous with authority and the nature of authority, so management will be controversial and debated. The third is that the management function mirrors the dilemmas present in health care management in general, with the divide between executive operational management counterbalanced by influential clinical leadership. Finally, the organisational culture itself is a variable in the clinical process of treating the personality disordered client group. The organisational culture can and will at times become a stage on which the personality disordered person's pathology will be played out, and this needs to be monitored.

Using Grendon as a case example to explore these issues, the structural managerial frame in which the work is contained is as follows. The chief executive equivalent is the prison governor. A second tier of senior managers comprises the senior management group, including the lead therapist, lead forensic psychologist, deputy governor and a selection of other functional managers, including generic organisational functional directors such as personnel and finance, and prison-specific ones such as regimes, security and so on. The line management governance of this senior management team group is via the standard civil service performance and appraisal process. Technically the whole team work to the governor, the deputy governor takes a lead in day-to-day operational management and the director of therapy takes a lead in therapeutic issues. The prison's management structure reflects current prison practice, with a senior management team as the organisational board, comprising the disciplinary leads and functional managers. There are two subcommittees: the Grendon executive chaired by the deputy governor, overseeing the operational management of the prison, and a therapy executive, overseeing the therapeutic function. Introduced in the mid-1990s, this configuration has been relatively stable for some time, but is constantly under review. Feeding into both of these is a series of statutory and *ad hoc* committees.

Democratisation and authority

For most managers, there are jobs to be done, things to be arranged, and there is little time for a philosophical consideration of the nature of authority. In Grendon, however, this issue cannot be avoided or ignored, as every policy and decision has in parenthesis a comment on the nature of authority. For example, is it appropriate for the authority to make this decision – is it within its aegis? Has this authority (the prison's management) contradicted any other authorities, or any current policy or practice? Has this authority contradicted itself, and if this is so, what does this mean about whether this authority can be trusted?

All managerial process is subject to this sort of scrutiny, but in Grendon, this is amplified for two reasons. First, the organisation is a therapeutic community and is therefore a learning organisation. The fervour of managers striving to achieve the latest management fad at times tarnishes managerial innovations that may not be a panacea but do make a contribution. To some extent, the learning organisation concept is suffering from this ubiquity and lionisation in management literature and ideology at this time. However, from a therapeutic community perspective, the usefulness of the notion of a learning organisation is not that it will be striven for by management to improve organisational effectiveness – it is that it offers a theory about how therapeutic communities work, as suggested above. The central ingredient that distinguishes a learning organisation is the facilitation of communication. If communication within the organisation is facilitated, good new innovative ideas can be raised, discussed and, where suitable, implemented. The learning organisation unlocks the potential of the staff by giving them the opportunity to comment and taking their contribution seriously.

This is the same process that turns a ward of neurotic patients into a therapeutic community – structuring and facilitating the communication by the staff enables the residents to provide therapy for each other, to benefit from each other's experiences and understandings and to help each other move forward. However, this same process changes those same patients into vocal commentators on and critics of the policy and practice of the local management and, in turn, the same culture of communication and welcoming of comment changes the local management into commentators on and critics of the senior management. In theory and in practice, this culture of engagement and involvement with the decisions of senior management can only improve organisational effectiveness, because of the points made in the learning organisational literature. Involvement generates ownership by staff (and clients) of the organisation and its aims, this increasing their input into their work.

The downside is that it is much easier to wield authority behind a closed door, away from those who can construct a legitimate criticism, and away from those affected by the more difficult decisions that have to be made. Management in a therapeutic community or a true learning organisational setting is goldfish-bowl management, where every nuance can be examined, explored and critiqued. As well as being exhausting, it can be less than decisive, as it becomes more difficult to stand fast to difficult decisions in a barrage of facilitated and legitimate criticism.

Within this goldfish-bowl managerial culture caused by the learning organisation culture, a second specific factor operates, concerning the nature of the client group, and the specialist function of the organisation. With Grendon's residents, as is probably the case with most people in prison, there is a particular issue with authority, as I have already suggested. This particular issue with authority can be taken several ways. To start with, it is very common for clients to have had an experience at the hands of authority that has been abusive in some way: at its most concrete, this will have been a physically abusive father, although the abuse of authority might be via a sexually abusive carer, a violent gang leader, or even in the client's experience with the law enforcement agencies. Grendon men will almost all have bad experiences of authority. Second, and perhaps as a reaction, all Grendon men have 'issues' with authority. Commonly, the man with the violent father (Eddie, for example) will get into a cycle of contempt for the statutory authorities, school, housing, social services and police, resulting in his provocation of these in some way, followed by an authoritative response. This response will be experienced as abusive and unfair, feeding into his 'issues'. Third, most Grendon residents will have issues in relation to their own discharge of authority. Many will have gone from being bullied to being the bullies, to passing the abuse of authority down to a subsequent generation; they may have been in a position of authority with a child and abused that trust in some way or other themselves.

While one is always sceptical of overarching meta-narratives, there is a reasonably cogent argument that much personality pathology that is managed within the criminal justice frame can be understood in terms of relations with authority. Arguably, also, much of the process of engagement with the criminal justice system is about the long arm of the authority of law getting you in the end. The process of imprisonment is the concrete manifestation of the authority of the State enacting its authority by depriving the offender of his or her freedom. So authority is an absolutely central and crucial issue for those in prison.

In many prison settings, the issue of authority is put aside somewhat, left to the appeal courts or the client's solicitor to argue using State-aided legal funding. In many prison settings, the authority issue begins and ends in the officer's order; if you are told to do something, you must do it. In Grendon, there is an attempt to open up that whole debate, to dismantle the resentful obeisance to the contemptible authority, and instead to establish a conception of authority as the enforcement of what is 'for the best'.

Again this is quite exhausting managerial work, because it dismantles the notion of someone having to do something because he is told, and instead places an expectation on the authority to justify how and why the required action is indeed 'for the best'. Furthermore, managers are fallible, mistakes are made and, in retrospect, some decisions made and actions demanded have not been 'for the best'. The manager is required to account for these shortcomings and to justify the reason for continued faith in his or her authority in the future.

To some extent, the issue of authority is dealt with by the democratisation of the decision-making process. For the client group, this democratisation is explicit, with votes being taken in community meetings about various options. The authority can then truly be said to rest with the collective. Any severe critic of the authority is a critic of the whole community and of his own engagement with the process, and he has an opportunity to leave should he wish. As mentioned above, this democratic authority of the community is devolved by the staff group who represent the ultimate authority. The staff group are in a position to veto a community decision and instead to exercise their executive authority.

Within the staff group – both at the local level of the individual community and at a whole organisational level – the democratisation is implicit rather than explicit. Most of the time governance is achieved by the process of consensus building or, perhaps more accurately, establishing what the prevailing consensus is and acting on the basis of this. Managerially, the process of achieving consensus is similar to the process of arriving at a clinical decision described above – where there is an extended debate between the different disciplines (see Chapter 5), resulting in a shared negotiated plan. I have argued that this is the best process for arriving at decisions about difficult, complex and confusing clinical dilemmas over personality disordered patients. It is less clear that this is the best process for arriving at a strategic direction at an organisational level. A significant task of the management group is to establish a balance between the consensual, discursive style of decision-making that pertains in a therapeutic community clinical team, and the more incisive directorial style more common in organisational boardrooms. One of the difficulties in establishing this balance is that, with a speciality function of working with personality disordered clients, the dynamics from the factory floor can and do permeate the senior management corridor, influencing decisions. The wider debate and establishment of a consensus can act as a safeguard against the distortion that these personality dynamics can produce – but this is a function of the specialist work that will be explored further below.

Management in Grendon represents authority in a setting where much of the discourse is about the abuse of authority by the authority, in a communicative culture that results in a goldfish-bowl feel. The advantages of this setting include the development of rigour and acute accountability in the development of strategy and in decision-making. The disadvantage is the potential confusion between organisational and clinical management, with potential paralysis of the managerial executive function if subjected to the same process of debate and consensus establishment.

Operational management and clinical leadership

Grendon, when it was set up in 1960, had a clinician as its chief executive equivalent – following the normal practice at the time of hospitals to be run by a 'physician superintendent'. The overall management of a hospital by a physician superintendent, aided by a lesser cadre of 'administrators', had the advantage of having clinical issues to the fore in strategic development and planning, but it had the disadvantages of being subject to capricious administration and the risk of a 'country club' style of management, with the hospital run for the benefit of the physician superintendent's friends and colleagues, rather than in the interests of patients. How to balance effective operational administration with professional advice and leadership is a central problem in the management of health care organisations. Who is in charge of a hospital: the powerful consultants or the chief executive?

The development of 'general management' in the Health Service involved the separation of the roles of generic management and clinical leadership. In the management of health services where generic managers are in overall charge, the pursuit of good clinical practice becomes a political tool in negotiations. The managers may propose a change that will be more organisationally effective, and the clinicians may resist with the complaint that the change will have a negative impact on good clinical practice. In this debate, good clinical practice is a subjective and mysterious variable, known only to the senior members of the clinical staff. As a response, for example, the operational managers strive to devise objective measures of good clinical practice, to be able to get a handle on this powerful tool being wielded by the clinicians, and this process itself is criticised as having a negative impact on good clinical practice (form-filling rather than spending time with patients, for example).

The central problem for health service managers is that their senior professional and clinical staff are difficult to manage because the bulk of the intellectual capital of the organisation is contained within this group. More traditionally, it is expected that the main thinking ability of a company is to be found in its boardroom. In hospitals this is probably not the case; the hospital consultants' group cannot simply be 'managed' in a traditional sense. Instead a much softer approach of leadership and encouragement needs to be taken; the task of managing medical consultants has been likened to 'herding cats' – a difficult and time-consuming activity that is an art instead of a generic management competency. The partial solution to this dilemma is that the hospital chief executive is in overall charge, but he appoints a medical director as the clinical lead. As the chief executive's appointee, the medical director will be instrumental in bringing his colleagues round to the strategic view of the hospital board and, likewise, will act as a guide for the board on the advice from the senior doctors. More recently, the device of 'clinical governance' has been developed as a way of performance-managing the senior doctors via the medical director, as an attempt to make the debate bureaucratic.

In Grendon there is a similar dynamic, although the roles and functions are arguably clearer. As explored above, a prison as an organisation has a clear line of authority and accountability to the prison governor, who is in overall charge. If the prison governor decides that the situation in his prison is such that therapy is not possible, he can refuse to allow in the professionals whose job it is to do this. The clinical activity in the setting takes place with the acquiescence of the prison governor, and it is within his gift to withdraw this at any time. As mentioned, this occurs rarely, if ever; but it brings a clarity to the managerial debate not present in debates about hospital management.

The icon for the clinicians in Grendon is 'therapy'. With new management initiatives, the acid test is whether a particular decision or organisational strategy is compatible with 'therapy'. A celebrated example that recurs every so often is the centralisation of food preparation. Each Grendon community has a small food preparation area – the 'pod'. Developments over the last few years in the catering industry have increasingly moved away from localised food preparation towards centralised preparation and chilled distribution. Organisationally, the Grendon food preparation model is an anachronism that has a price tag on the bottom line. Clinically, it is imperative to maintain some form of community cooking and serving for the therapeutic communities' sense of living together. Managerially, it is financially indefensibly inefficient.

In the mid-1990s, in Grendon, a radical management change was made as a response to this debate. Whereas, formerly, in each community there had been an uneasy collaboration between the therapist and the senior officer/unit manager, it was decided that the therapist would him- or herself become the unit manager. The line manager of the community units would be the lead clinician – the therapist.

A significant contributor to this model was the notion of 'dynamic administration' in group psychotherapy. In a small psychotherapy group, the therapist not only conducts the group clinically, but also is responsible for ensuring that the room is available, bringing in new members and for the associated paperwork and so on. The importance of this idea is that the group is administered with consideration of dynamic factors. For example, a generic manager cannot have a sense of the emotional impact of a group having to be cancelled at short notice because of a room usage clash, or have a sense of the emotional flux involved in bringing in new group members. Only the therapist, the clinician, can have a sense of these things, and so it makes sense for them to have administrative responsibility. A similarity was drawn between this 'dynamic administration' of a small group and the process of management of the therapeutic community unit, so it was concluded that the therapist should be in charge managerially.

There were considerable advantages noted during the operation of the 'dynamic administration' approach. Nothing would ever happen to a resident without the therapist, and so the therapeutic team, being aware; no one would be taken into or removed from the community without the agreement of the therapist, and therefore the clinical team; there would be no changes in operational policy either enacted or mooted without the therapist and therefore the clinical team, being aware and able to assess the clinical impact in advance. The authority of the therapist benefited from the militaristic chain-of-command quality that accompanies line managerial responsibility in the Prison Service. The therapeutic community could truly be administered and held in a holistic way, because everything about every client came through the clinician – the therapist.

The criticisms of the approach on the surface were that the tasks of clinical leadership and facilitation of a therapeutic community are very different from the task of management of a 40-bed high security prison wing; there were allegations of aspects of management being forgotten, and so, with supra-organisational advice, the experiment was discontinued. These problems are disputed and other hypotheses have been raised about why the experiment collapsed, including a concern about the location of too much power in one aspect of the prison's work – the therapeutic function – with the possible consequence of neglect of other aspects – for instance, the security function – that might be disastrous. There is some ground on which the first concern is based. The theory of dynamic administration in group psychoanalysis is based on the management tasks involved in establishing a meeting of eight or so people once per week over a period of several years. It is managerial activity of pretty low intensity compared to the management of a complicated 40-bed therapeutic community with a staff complement of 20 in a high secure prison.

The second criticism derives from an account of the natural history of therapeutic communities, *Charisma and Routinisation* (Manning 1989), in which there is a central thesis that therapeutic communities require a charismatic leader to initiate them – to overcome the organisational resistance of the host service, and the cultural opposition of the new staff. Without such a strong, central, perhaps slightly omnipotent and narcissistic figure, they are unlikely to become established. Once established, however, they require a different sort of leader: someone who is more of a bureaucrat who will protect the community via the establishment of networks and alliances. Likewise, within the community, the task moves from one of the centralised manufacture of an ideology to the sort of facilitation of pluralistic debate described above. This critique would argue that the dynamic administration experiment took place at a time when there was a re-engineering of the therapeutic process taking place, with the recent appointment of the first NHS consultant psychiatrist in psychotherapy to the post, and the establishment of small group psychoanalytic type psychotherapy as the central unit of Grendon treatment. The introduction of group analytic principles into Grendon represented a cultural turnaround that required a period of resumption of charismatic management within each of the communities.

What replaced this structure formally, and what had preceded it less explicitly, was a dual managerial responsibility structure similar to the Health Service division of labour between a hospital's chief executive and its medical director. In this arrangement, the generic management of the unit is carried out by the senior prison officer at the same time as the unit is clinically led by the therapist. In this model, the argument goes, the clinical lead can concentrate on leading the clinical work without having to be sidetracked by clinically irrelevant issues, such as the career development of the officers. The advantages of this approach include a more appropriate division of tasks and a clarification of the different roles of generic and clinical management which, in turn, can be seen as a separate disciplinary contribution to the multi-disciplinary team. Also, while often denigrated, management has its own specific competencies, and management of a prison wing especially so; so the overall functioning might be expected to be better with these two tasks clarified and the most suitable person for each role responsible for them.

The disadvantage is that what is clinically relevant and what is not can only really be decided by the clinician. It is only by having sight of everything that the therapist can filter out the important things. This need for wide clinical scanning of data is amplified in psychodynamically-orientated therapies. In psychoanalysis, the therapist adopts a position of 'free-floating attention', able to notice not only the linear track of the patient's discourse, but also the manner in which the account is delivered, the patient's attire and general attitude, the order and form of the words and so on. The reason for this is to glean clues about the patient's unconscious. The patient presents his conscious stream of thought as he speaks, and by nature tries to keep hidden deeper, more hidden anxieties and conflicts. The therapist's task is to divine from mistakes, slips of the tongue and so on, what lies behind the manifest account. To get clues as to the unconscious mental contents, all aspects of the presentation need to be utilised. In a residential setting, this extends to a need to filter all the information about the patient that is generated. Furthermore, in Grendon, where the client group are practised at preparing and managing the information flow about themselves so that people only get to know that which the individual wants them to know, the need for access to all the information is further emphasised.

FRED

Following the subsiding of Fred's anxiety about his heart he had a review, at which the issue of his parachutes was discussed. The issue of his near transfer out to a drug unit was revisited, with a more detailed exploration of how Fred had managed to create such a split between different members of staff. It seemed clear that there was a part of Fred that was engaged in treatment, and wanting to make progress, as was illustrated by his progress in psychodrama. However, there seemed to be a different part that was desperately trying to get away.

One of the officers spoke up, saying that he had been talking to Fred prior to his seeing the drug counsellor, when he had said that the place was 'doing his head in'. 'Yes,' said the senior officer, 'that was why we got Dave [the drug counsellor] in to see him.' The therapist was intrigued, given that, at the time, there was apparently no knowledge of who had referred to the drug counsellor, and now it seemed the senior officer had done so. 'Well,' the senior officer said, 'I thought that it would be OK, and I think we've got to offer drug counselling to anyone who asks.' The therapist was irritated, and suggested that it might have been relevant to involve him in this decision.

In practice, the information that flows to the therapist becomes a variable, vulnerable to interference by interdisciplinary dynamics as well as splits and manipulation by the client.

Organisational dynamics

There is a tradition of exploring organisational dynamics within a psychodynamic frame (e.g. Sofer 1972). The third point to make regarding the management of a setting such as Grendon is that, while many organisations get by without having to examine their own organisational psychodynamics, an organisation with the task of treating or containing personality disordered individuals will not. The reason for this is to be found in the nature of personality disorder pathology which, as has been mentioned above, locates itself in the relationship space between two people. Organisations consist of networks of relationships – relationships between managers and subordinates, between different disciplinary workers in the same community team and between external and internal agencies – each of these relationships providing a stage on which the personality disordered person may locate his psychopathology. Indeed, the richness of the networks of relationships within the organisational setting provide the substrate for the containment and processing of the psychopathology of the personality disordered person. Because the organisational dynamics are a significant and important element of the clinical resource, there is a need to be sensitive to the psychodynamics of both the organisation as a whole and its constituent subsystems.

A good example of psychodynamic work applied in an organisational setting is some work carried out by Menzies (1988) who looked at the work carried out by student nurses on a busy surgical ward in the 1960s. She found that undue priority was given to menial and routine tasks, such as folding sheets, while patients were left alone or managed in an impersonal way. She proposed that the focus on menial and routine tasks had the function of protecting the staff from the anxiety and stress of seeing people in pain, in fear and dying – all very traumatising aspects of the work of a surgical nurse. The importance of Menzies' work was illustrated by the widespread adoption of key-working practices across not only nursing but also other casework settings. The notion that the organisation might find some way of protecting itself, might invent some form of displacement activity to protect staff from an anxiety of the work, is an example of thinking about organisations psycho-dynamically.

FRED

In the conversation between the senior officer and the therapist about Fred's referral to the drug counsellor, the senior officer was also a little irritated. Both felt that their area of authority was being challenged. 'Look,' said the senior officer, 'I've had security on my back for months about this bloke – they are sure he's at the centre of things, and they want him out; it's as simple as that. He said that Grendon was doing his head in, and he wanted out to somewhere else that he could get on with his therapy; I thought that a drug unit might be a possibility. That's it.'

The therapist remained irritated, and after the meeting met the senior officer by himself. It emerged that the senior officer had indeed been under considerable pressure and that the referral to the drug counsellor had been something he felt he could do that was clear and decisive. The therapist was sympathetic. He could understand that Fred had been testing everyone over the past few months, that it was difficult to bear and that all sorts of other options currently seemed easier than keeping him and keeping at the therapeutic work with him, which seemed the most difficult thing to do. The therapist and senior officer agreed that the therapist would discuss the situation with the governor in charge of the security department, to take some of the pressure off the senior officer who felt alone in resisting the expulsive dynamic.

A second contribution to understanding how organisations function psycho-dynamically was made by Main in his description of the 'special patient' (1989). The 'special patient' is one in a psychiatric setting who absorbs everyone's time and energy and yet who is fascinating; the patient whom people take positions over and argue about. With the special patient, the staff group take on and enact the pathology of the patient in some modified form. In his practice in the Cassel Hospital therapeutic community, Main's model was that there would be a separation between the psychosocial nursing function, and the more explicit psychodynamic psychotherapy work. A characteristic dynamic in the Cassel is when the psychotherapist and nurse have strikingly different views about the patient. Main's model was that the patient projects different parts of him- or herself onto the different people, and that in a structure of joint supervision the conflict that emerges between nurse and psychotherapist is informative of the conflict taking place in the patient's mind (James 1986).

EDDIE

Eddie had a review session where his progress through the period of his disillusionment with therapy and subsequent depression were raised. In the meeting, a difference of opinion emerged about Eddie between two of the officers. The pair not infrequently fell out over issues. On this occasion, one was angry with Eddie for threatening the staff with the judicial review. 'It was horrible when all that was going on. I don't think that he's moved at all – he is now like he's always been, that was us getting beaten up like everyone else in his life has been.'

The other officer disagreed, not so much putting the case for Eddie's defence, but rather worrying about his self-harm potential. 'He's gone right down, you know, sort of gone into himself. I feel quite hopeless about him – I don't know what we can do. I was thinking maybe it was time for him to move on because we can't do anything for him, and he might just get more down if we keep him here.' 'Rubbish,' said the other, in an aggressive tone. 'He's got you round his finger, bleeding a heart for him…' The therapist interjected, suggesting that this was a bit strong, and there was a pause, broken by someone asking the probation officer what he was smiling about. 'Sometimes,' he said, this place is amazing – you two have just become the different Eddies that we've got to deal with, one aggressive and hostile, the other collapsing into depression and hopelessness. I find myself feeling both aggressive and fed up with him, and I worry that if I stop feeling angry with him, I'll collapse into his hopelessness.'

EDDIE

Following the review, the staff fed back to Eddie their conclusions, namely that he was struggling currently, and there was an offence re-enactment in his litigiousness and demands. When he was frustrated, it seemed his rage threatened to brim over and destroy things that were valuable to him – Dan, his relationships and now his Grendon treatment. He seemed to act aggressively before thinking. His other alternative reactions to frustration seemed to be a triumphant beating of the system (with his manipulation of medication that he could then sell) or a catastrophic collapse into depression.

Eddie was angry and stormed out of the room, shouting that he didn't need this, and stomped upstairs. The staff group waited for a minute to see if he might return, then dispersed, with the senior officer sending an officer up to check he was OK. Eddie sat silent on his bed, and wouldn't respond. The observant officer saw some trays of paracetamol in his bin and asked him about them. Eddie didn't respond again, and the officer became concerned that he had taken an overdose. Various staff were consulted, and it was agreed that the most important thing was for him to be assessed in the local casualty department for a blood paracetamol level and appropriate treatment. After two days or so in hospital, he returned.

The staff group was quite traumatised by these events. It was common for residents to storm out of meetings in rage, but uncommon for them to go straight on to self-harm. While it was rather characteristic of Eddie – the grand gesture on the spur of the moment – it still left an anxiety about unpredictability. One of the officers was particularly angry, and decried the therapist to his fellow officer friends in the gym that lunchtime, saying he was mad and unprofessional, and should have discharged Eddie or given him what he wanted when he wanted to go. 'This way we are all sitting ducks – he does what he wants, and if anyone stands in his way, he's gonna top himself. How can you work with that?' Privately, he raised the same concerns with his manager. The senior officer advised him to put this view in the next sensitivity meeting, which he did, saying he was angry at the way Eddie was getting away with things, the dropping out of therapy, the medication, he even got his own way with the family day, and saying that he thought that for some reason he was the therapist's favourite, so that the therapist couldn't be objective. The therapist was a little taken aback at what he perceived as an ambush, wondering what the rest of the staff group was feeling. There was an uncomfortable silence in the room with everyone avoiding each other's eyes, that made it clear to the therapist that the officer's concerns were shared.

In the following therapists' meeting, the issue was raised. The therapist complained that the officer concerned was well-networked into a particular clique who were the 'young lions': they drank together, played football and other sports together, and at times seemed to think as one. He proposed that the antipathy to trying to continue working with Eddie was understood as part of a competitive culture between the two groups: on the one hand sporty, macho prisoners and, on the other, this group of officers with a similar value set. He spoke with a tone that presaged concern about professionalism and complaints about conduct. The other therapists were as surprised at this rather ill-tempered account as the therapist had been about the ambush in the sensitivity meeting, wondering if the therapist himself was engaging in the same sort of competitive posturing that he felt the officer was. One teased the therapist that he was just jealous he was too old and crusty to be a young lion any longer.

The perspective that this comment provided enabled the therapist to acknowledge that the accusation of favouritism had hurt because he himself had struggled with a wish to get rid of Eddie that he had had to control. The group reflected, until someone suggested that the whole episode of bilateral character assassination between the therapist and the officer was itself an enactment of the battle between Eddie and Dan in the index offence. In further discussion, it became clear that a particular form of football-oriented masculinity that was currently important for Eddie and the officer had also been important for the therapist some years ago. It might therefore be that Eddie was a bit of a favourite for the therapist, and that in some way the argument between the therapist and the officer had the same competitive Oedipal quality that Eddie had had in the index offence with Dan.

In the following sensitivity meeting, the therapist proposed this hypothesis, namely that controversy about Eddie with two sides doing each other down might be a repetition of what took place with Dan on the night of the murder. The psychologist remarked that she had been surprised at the falling out between the officer and the therapist because the two seemed to get on quite well, even despite their respective allegiances to Manchester City and United. 'As I remember, both Dan and Eddie were fond of Dawn, but ended up fighting. You two usually see eye to eye and both like kicking spherical bits of leather around a park, but want to go for each other's throats all of a sudden. Eddie must have something to do with this; it can't be a coincidence, or I suppose it could just be a man thing.'

In Grendon, the principal storage silo for projections from the residents seems to be the antipathy between the disciplines. Members of staff can generate quite angry feelings about colleague staff members of different disciplines that at times can spill over into formal complaints and investigations. For the most part, efforts are made to try to understand these inter-staff disputes and resentments with the hypothesis that, first, they are sparked by traumatising dynamics stirred up by the work and, second, they contain valuable information about the psychodynamics that they dramatise.

While superficially one might hope that a more collaborative culture might be established, such an aim is naïve in this setting. The genesis of these bad feelings about colleagues is in the clinical work that is taking place. It is much easier to fear a professional complaint from a colleague than to fear that the person you have just challenged and irritated in the group killed the last person who crossed him. People working in Grendon who engage in the transference with Grendon men with histories of considerable violence take their lives into their hands. A way of surviving this is to construct a fantasy of persecution and danger from a colleague – a sort of psychic equivalent to folding sheets for those working with the personality disordered.

FRED

The therapist returned from the meeting with the security governor surprised at the extent of information and suspicion that had been amassed about Fred. The suspicion was that some of his more regular visitors were bringing in heroin for him that he was distributing. He spent lots of time during exercise when the whole prison goes out together with an old friend from a different prison with whom he had 'worked' distributing drugs before. Enquiries were being made with the police liaison officer about some of his visitors, and nothing had been turned up yet, but it was probable that one of his contacts forming a link in the chain to the outside would be known. Part of the therapist's surprise was irritation that he had not known this before and this bit of feedback had not been passed on. The therapist had agreed with the security governor a form of words that could be used in a feedback session with Fred to make him aware of the fact that he was seriously jeopardising his position, and that there was an awareness of his activities, without compromising the information itself.

In the meeting, Fred was furious, and reminded the therapist and senior officer who were meeting him that he still had contacts, he could still get things done to people, he wouldn't be in here for ever and he was getting out one day. He knew that the therapist and the senior officer had families. Both were disturbed by these threats, even though Fred calmed down as the meeting progressed.

The therapist was angry that the situation had got this far, angry with the security department who had not kept the community staff group informed and angry with the probation officer who was the lead therapist on Fred's group for not taking up the issue earlier and more consistently in the group. As the story was recounted in the staff group, the probation officer was himself angry that the meeting had taken place at all without his being present.

In the following sensitivity meeting, the issues were addressed. The intelligence about Fred should have been passed to the staff group by the senior officer who, instead of doing this, had made an appointment for Fred to see a drug counsellor. The issue of Fred's using Grendon as a new market-place should have been taken up more consistently by the probation officer and the therapist should have divined that there was more going on than met the eye. Everyone seemed angry with each other.

Gradually a theme emerged about why things hadn't happened. Each person had felt rather insidiously intimidated by Fred. On the surface he was affable, but somehow it seemed to be an easy confident affability that might come from knowing that you have as an ally an East End gang. The senior officer hadn't wanted to 'shop' Fred to the community team by divulging the detail of the intelligence, and instead did what felt like the therapeutic thing by referring to a drug counsellor; the probation officer had felt a constant dynamic of intimidation and control of the agenda by Fred that had been noticed when Fred had been in the frame for drugs before, while the therapist had to reflect that Fred's threat had simply crystallised a deep and barely conscious fear that stalked him of this prisoner's potential for violence and that he had been happy not to know about the extent of Fred's activities.

The broad hypothesis is that in an organisation dealing with the processing of personality disorder pathology, the structures and culture of the organisation itself will be utilised to contain and process the dynamics that emerge; the client group will ferret out the splits and fissures that exist and deposit their own pathology therein. The organisation can collectively wring its hands about how awful its internal dynamics are, but trying to resolve the inter-staff tensions as issues between staff are both a waste of time and unhelpful in the overall task. The currents and storms that afflict the organisation are often symptomatic of the mental storms and conflicts in the minds of the client group. The task of the management of the organisation is to facilitate the exploration of these storms and elucidate what they mean and what they say about the clinical work that is taking place.

It is interesting that organisations that run along therapeutic community lines have a very characteristic culture, and as a practitioner with experience of working in a therapeutic community one can immediately get a sense of this on walking through the door. It is a sort of communicative easiness, of everyone talking to everyone else, of the chief executive being known to the doorman by his or her first name, not in an uncomfortable way of 'We've had a directive to refer to the CEO by her first name' but the use of a name that derives from genuine familiarity and personal acquaintance. This may be because the therapeutic community ethos that is explicitly created on the factory floor of the clinical work extends up the whole organisation, and the whole organisation acts within a culture of a flattened hierarchy, reality confrontation, permissiveness, sense of community and a shared working task.

A significant effect of this is that the location of the client group psychopathology that has been illustrated above at the level of the community team can become located in the management of the organisation itself. The fluidity of the whole organisation brought about by its communicative culture facilitates the passage of factory-floor dynamic concerns and processes into the senior team, so that in the same way as a therapeutic community staff team need to keep an eye on the pathological psychodynamic influences that might be shaping and determining their decision-making, the senior team needs to maintain a similar awareness.

For this reason, Grendon's senior management board reflects in its constitution a community team – with multidisciplinary representation. The Grendon board includes the director of therapy, the director of research (the lead forensic psychologist) and the senior probation officer, as well as the majority of governor staff, reflecting the community teams which consist of the therapist, psychologist and probation officer, as well as the majority of officers. The board, of course, has other organisational functions such as finance and personnel and these do not have a therapeutic community equivalent, reflecting the different tasks between an organisational management board and a clinical unit. In a sense the need for the multidisciplinary representation at this level is to protect the management board from stray clinical dynamics that may reach their level, enabling the board to focus on its own task, as well as being able to offer a professional brief about the core business of the organisation.

EDDIE

One of the men in Eddie's group was serving a sentence for the rape of a 14-year-old girl – his stepdaughter. By and large, Eddie's group had done well in allowing this man to be a genuine member of the group, so that he wasn't now excluded as the 'bacon', but was Sandy, who had been allowed to tell his story, had talked about his offending, both those offences for which he had been prosecuted and those for which he hadn't. His comments were welcomed as legitimate contributions and he was a valued group member. The community had been angry with Eddie for his overdose, seeing it as 'taking the piss', and this theme was being echoed in the small group. Sandy suggested that the manner in which the overdose had been taken was a bit like having a fight, or punching someone – Eddie had gone straight out of the meeting, gone upstairs and started knocking back tablets. 'Pretty extreme, wouldn't you say?' he said, to no response. 'Pretty er, pretty dramatic, eh?' he went on.

In the group, Eddie's style of flying off the handle was seen as hysterical, all a big show, and at times he was accused of being a bit of a drama queen. It was this aspect that Sandy was pushing at, and his taunt got a response. 'You pervert bastard, keep your fucking mouth shut, people like you should be fucking shot.' Sandy was angry at being traduced in this way and responded by pointing out that his offence was with a 14-year-old, and that what he had done was bad, but that Eddie had said nothing about his activities, and wasn't Dawn 13 when... He was interrupted by another group member who told the two of them to shut up – Eddie was picking fights again, as usual.

In the staff supervision following the group, the old issue of the difficulties of integrating sex offenders and violent prisoners was discussed.

It is important for the violent prisoners to have the opportunity to explore their own sexual histories vicariously, and to reflect on how a good proportion of their sexual activity encapsulates violent attitudes to women, and how much of it might be technically offending behaviour. The problem is that traditionally in prisons there is a hatred and murderousness between sex offenders and those in for other crimes, such that most prisons have a segregation system to protect the former. In Grendon, those whose offending is sexual complain that they feel intimidated in the small groups and therefore not able to explore their issues fully.

EDDIE

The usual suggestion was made that Eddie's fury might suggest some personal vendetta against paedophiles – perhaps he had been the victim, although there was no such account so far of this being the case. Following the group, privately, Sandy spoke to the group facilitator, saying he was finding it difficult, and could he transfer to G Wing – the community that specialises in those with a sex offence.

There had recently been several other incidents regarding sex offenders housed in mixed therapeutic communities, and one of the governor staff became interested. He noted that the numbers of sex offenders had increased so that, in addition to G Wing's complement of 40 or so, there were about five or six people on each community serving a sentence for a sex offence. Within the governor's group, concern grew about this, in terms of both the control problem and whether sex offenders could have proper therapy in a setting that includes killers who may have assaulted sex offenders in the past as a form of sport.

The issue was raised on the board in passing, but became a major item with strong views being expressed each way, that it was dangerous to mix the two offender groups and that it was important to do so. The civilian disciplines managed to impress on the governorial team that while it was an important issue, it was also important not to make any decisions before a fuller debate; and that it was not yet clear what the issues were. This was agreed and, after the meeting, separately, the different disciplines discussed the issue further.

There was incredulity among the therapists that the proposal had got so far that something structural needed to be done, and several understandings emerged. First, there had been an element of Eddie's dynamic; Eddie's aggressive and intimidatory attitude both in person and via his lawyer could be seen to be bullying the community staff group – and this dynamic seemed to be extending itself into the senior team. Eddie didn't think that he should have to have a sex offender in his group, and so Eddie was making his views known in his loud, intimidating and perhaps slightly dramatic way. Second, the whole prison was still struggling with the reality that the complementary cognitive Sex Offender Treatment Programme funding had been withdrawn, and that the issue of how to treat sex offenders properly and fully was a difficult strategic issue that was not being addressed. Instead the senior team was fretting about what was happening in Eddie's small group. The third dynamic was that Eddie's attitude to women, with its rather default macho denigratory tabloid flavour, was perilously close to that of some members of staff. Just as Eddie projected all his perversity into the sex offender so that he could disavow it and attack it, likewise, the therapists hypothesised, some of the middle management officers might be doing the same thing, projecting their own ambivalence about sex-offenders into Eddie and his ilk.

It was the board's task to run the organisation, not deliberate on the therapy of individual residents, which was the task of the community team. This feedback was informally circulated, and the issue receded although, in retrospect, the preoccupation of the board may have helpfully contained some of the anxiety in the community team. Eddie had become something of a special patient, who intimidated the team, and whose name was known on the management corridor.

This fluidity of psychodynamics within a therapeutic community organisation enables difficult dynamics that cannot be contained by one team to rove around the structure and be contained somewhere else, perhaps in a split between two of the disciplines, perhaps in a related item for the management board. This movement of dynamics and issues means that it is important for the management group to conceive of the whole organisation as a community: The whole staff group are the therapeutic community, and the management board is the equivalent of the therapeutic community staff team – the director of therapy is the therapist; the lead psychologist, the psychologist; and so on. As well as acting as a management board with administrative and strategic responsibilities, it is important for the board to recognise that it needs to function as a multidisciplinary therapeutic team, whose task it is to explore and understand the meaning and dynamic origins of the conundrums it is thrown as well as having an eye to devising actions to remedy them.

Managing a personality disorder service requires the incorporation of other dimensions into the usual processes of strategy and change management. The interface and relationships between individuals and subgroups within the system themselves become the stage for the struggles of the personality disordered clients, and this needs to be borne in mind as part of the managerial process. To some extent, the facilitation and maintenance of a communicative culture, understood either as a whole organisational therapeutic community or as a learning organisation, enables these client dynamics to be distinguished from the real business of the day. The downside is that this creates a goldfish-bowl type of management, with energetic criticism of decisions such that a strategic tack can be difficult to hold, and with the risk of descending into a preoccupation with infighting and paralysis. The solution, to some extent, is to attempt to be a good authority that may make mistakes, but that listens and does its best in the circumstances. In the same way as the client group will grapple with the fallibility of their clinicians and yet have to grow to accept and trust the authority that they represent, the organisation grows to have the same attitude to its managers. To some extent.

CHAPTER 8

Evidence and Audit

The history of public sector organisations over the last two decades has been one of the integration of managerialism into their functioning. In turn, the preoccupation of these new structured managerial organisations for the past decade has been with efforts to drive up quality, improve efficiency ensure effectiveness and devise performance measurements to track progress. This chapter will summarise two things in relation to Grendon's work: first, the evidence base for Grendon's effectiveness and, second, the methodology for audit that has been developed.

Straddling two government departments – the Prison Service as a Home Office agency on the one hand, and the National Health Service and the Department of Health on the other – Grendon has had to keep pace with two rather different interpretations of the quality, efficiency and effectiveness agendas. As described above, in Chapter 1, the Home Office quality assurance structures for rehabilitative programmes have been heavily influenced by the 'What Works' movement in criminology and forensic psychology, which exists alongside the prison standards audit work and the more qualitative Chief Inspector of Prison's inspections. In the Health Service, there has been more of a struggle to introduce a robust general managerial structure in the face of the powerful professional groups, in particular the doctors, so the development of quality assurance structures making different hospitals comparable is considerably behind that of the Prison Service, which is after all a disciplined service, with the advantages of being much smaller and leaner. In the UK Health Service, the coining of the term 'governance' to emphasise the accountability of public sector bodies to their statutory masters passed into the debate about making senior doctors accountable for their clinical practice – and the term 'clinical governance' was born.

Initially, clinical governance replaced the piecemeal requirement for clinical staff to demonstrate the efficacy and evidence base of their practice, to carry out ongoing audit of their clinical outcomes and to engage in continuing professional development. These were structured and rolled up into the new collective term of 'clinical governance'. Paradoxically, as the notion of clinical governance was developing in the Health Service, Grendon, as part of the Prison Service, was somewhat ahead of the game, already having clear performance, appraisal and quality assurance mechanisms in place, and with an ongoing process of assembling an evidence base and rationale for effectiveness as part of the process of applying for Home Office Accreditation as a rehabilitative programme. This chapter briefly covers these areas, describing some of the evidence base on which the Grendon treatment rests and looking at some of the audit models that have been devised to assure quality of the treatment process.

Evidence

There have been several centres producing outcome research on democratic therapeutic communities, including the Henderson, the Cassel and Grendon. For example, there was a number of papers from the Henderson Hospital in the 1970s (e.g. Whiteley 1970). In a 1984 five-year follow-up Copas *et al.* (1984) reports a 36 per cent success rate rising to 60.5 per cent for those who remained in treatment for six months or more. A study was carried out in the Cassel Hospital (Rosser *et al.* 1987), showing a similar type of treatment effect. The difficulty with all these studies is that the definition of success seems poorly operationalised compared to current norms of outcome methodological rigour, as they were largely based on clinical impressions and an arbitrary clinical judgement of degree of improvement.

In the prison sector, the longest-established therapeutic communities, Grendon and the Max Glatt Unit, both carried out treatment efficacy studies in the 1970s and 1980s. The largest study of Grendon was that by Gunn, summarised in a book (Gunn *et al.* 1978) and a series of articles, one of which included a ten-year follow-up (Gunn and Robertson 1987). Gunn's work evaluating Grendon was much more objective than the more impressionistic measures of outcome from the therapeutic communities in the 1970s, and it used the variable of the rate of reconviction as a gold standard of efficacy which has subsequently become a main outcome variable for programmes in the criminal justice sector. The two-year and then a ten-year follow-up from the data did not show an effect on reconviction, although 'to summarise the psychological and psychiatric results, it seems that there has been a reduction in neurotic features, an increase in social self-confidence, and an improvement in attitudes to authority figures' (Gunn and Robertson cited in Shine 2000, p.97). The lack of an effect on reconviction of Grendon's treatment had been seen in several previous studies (e.g. Newton 1969, 1971), although again with evidence of desirable change in other variables.

Criticism of reconviction as a measure include lack of subtlety of the measure, with driving offences standing alongside robberies, and the fact that conviction is based on so many more variables, from police vigilance to court processes. Nevertheless, there is an argument that, with large enough samples, some of these methodological flaws can be overcome, and in the 1980s, studies began to emerge that demonstrated an effect on reconviction. Following the 1984 Copas *et al.* analysis of data from the Henderson Hospital, which identified a relationship between time in treatment and outcome, Jones (1997) studied the Max Glatt Unit – a 30-bedded democratic therapeutic community in Wormwood Scrubbs prison that has now closed – and also found a significant link between time in treatment and reconviction rate. Those who left treatment before completion reconvicted at a rate of 82 per cent, whereas those who completed the programme had a reduced 55% reconviction rate. Utilising this methodology, Cullen (1994) distinguished between two groups of the Grendon treatment group – those who stayed more than 18 months, and those who stayed less than this period. The reconviction rate for the former group who did not complete treatment and stayed less than 18 months was 50 per cent, while the rate for those who completed treatment, staying more than 18 months, was down to 19 per cent (n=103 and 47 respectively).

Cullen's study had no control group, but one was included in a replication by Marshall (1997), who followed up a cohort of 700 Grendon men at four years, comparing them to a waiting-list control group of 142, who had been referred to Grendon but, for one reason or another, were not admitted. Marshall demonstrated two main things. First, compared to a comparator general prison group, Grendon referrals were of higher risk than the general prison population. Second, there was a reduction in reconviction rate of between a quarter and a fifth between the untreated waiting-list control group and the treated Grendon group who stayed more than 18 months. This would suggest that a treatment in Grendon of more than 18 months reduced the risk of re-offending by about 20–25 per cent. The same cohort of men was followed up at seven years by Taylor (2000), who replicated these findings, and identified a 60% reduction in recall for life sentence prisoners treated at Grendon compared to a risk matched group from the general prison population.

In their review of the outcome literature for therapeutic community treatments for antisocial personality disorder, Dolan and Coid (1993) complain about the difficulties in comparing outcomes from a heterogeneous group of clinical settings, the lack of the use of rigorous diagnostic criteria either for psychopathy or for other clinical variables, concluding that the evidence is 'equivocal'. In a more up-to-date review, Lees, Manning and Rawlings (1999) studied 294 therapeutic community outcome studies, 52 of which had a control group. By employing conservative criteria this number was reduced to 29, and these studies were subjected to meta-analysis that unequivocally demonstrated a statistically significant beneficial treatment effect of the therapeutic community. Clearly, this study has a different starting point, namely to identify whether a residential setting organised as a therapeutic community is effective, not to investigate the effect on a particular pathology or treatment group, such as psychopathy.

There seems to be an emerging empirical evidence base for supposing that therapeutic community treatment is effective. Likewise, there is evidence that treatment for the severe and high-risk personality disordered people who are referred to Grendon is to some degree effective. But these empirical data are much more equivocal than the clinical, subjective, qualitative evidence that emerges in the course of the work: the dynamic progress people make, the change noticed by relatives and acquaintances and so on, the richness, texture and understanding of his story and offending that the inmate develops during treatment. These impressionistic data are much more powerful and persuasive evidence of the efficacy of the process, but are usually only accessible to those engaged in the treatment process as clinician, client or intimate third party.

The power of the emerging psychodynamic process and its persuasiveness may explain why the investigation of empirical measures of outcome is not a central preoccupation of those engaged in exploratory psychodynamic treatments. At the clinical coal-face, one can see the process working in real time, and all one's energies are taken up with the single case-study methodology and trying to understand this, rather than other issues. More congruent with a psychodynamic perspective is being clear about the parameters and boundaries of the setting, which is closer to the rubric of audit.

Psychopathy

Something like 50 per cent of Grendon's population score 25 or more on the revised Hare Psychopathy Checklist (PCLR) (Hare 1991) denoting them to be psychopathic. About 25 per cent score above 30, denoting them to be severely psychopathic and very high risk. Because of this, and a culture in forensic settings that claims highly psychopathic people are untreatable, issues of Grendon's treatment efficacy are closely related to whether it has any impact on this group specifically. A second driver to address the psychopathy issue is that, as will be explored in more detail below, the Dangerous and Severe Personality Disorder (DSPD) debate in the UK and the variety of dangerous offender legislation in other jurisdictions is all about what to do with psychopaths who score highly on the PCLR.

The development of Cleckley's clinical (1941) description of a psychopath into an empirically respected measure has created an extremely powerful risk measurement tool (Hare 1991). Less fortunately, this has led to a fast-growing mindset within the criminological field that, because of their duplicitousness and charm, this group is untreatable (Thornton 1998). Interestingly, one of the oft-quoted studies in support of the untreatability of this group was from an avowed therapeutic community at Oak Ridge Canada – the Pentanguishine Unit, which demonstrated a reduction in reconviction rates for those in treatment who were not PCLR psychopaths, but an increase in recidivism for those who were PCLR psychopaths (Rice, Harris and Cormier 1992). In the therapeutic community field, this study has been much criticised, in particular because the therapeutic community treatment was compulsory, and therefore potentially very damaging, and because other aspects seriously undermined the notion that this was a therapeutic community in the UK understanding. Nevertheless, there is an increasing literature confirming that high PCLR scorers are refractory to the cognitive didactic programmes that have shown themselves to be so effective with other offenders.

On top of this empirical evidence about the difficulty of treatment of high PCLR scorers, elements of folk law have grown in the fertile soil of fear and hatred that this group creates. For example, there is a theory that, not only are they untreatable, but worse, they use the psychological and social skills that they learn on the psychological treatment programmes in which they partake to become more effective offenders, or more efficient psychopaths, so increasing their risk profile rather than reducing it. The result is to propose that there is a significant minority of the serious offending population for whom, at the current state of knowledge, nothing can be done, and for whom any attempt treatment will make them worse. To some extent, via the variety of programme elements that are being developed for DSPD and other similar efforts in different countries that are described below, the issue is being tackled head on, but for many years Grendon has had to make a case for continuing to offer treatment to people in this group who were suitable.

There are two criticisms that can be levelled at this position that psychopaths are untreatable and that no attempt should be made to treat them. The first criticism is epistemological: it is an unscientific position. In his criticism of psychoanalysis and Marxism, Popper argued that these two disciplines could not be considered as sciences because they were irrefutable (1962). Popper proposed that the essence of the scientific method was the creation, testing and refutation of scientific hypotheses. If you disagree with your psychoanalyst she may understand this as your resistance; if you disagree with a radical Marxist interpretation of your exploitation, this will be interpreted as a 'false consciousness' inculcated by the power of the owners of the means of production. There is no way out of the tautology. Whatever your interpretation of your opinion is, it can be countered by a further interpretation from the same theory.

This sort of dilemma seems to be common to the interpretive disciplines, where the process of interpreting a situation according to a particular perspective can be flexible to incorporate new material. So, according to this tautology, a glib and deceitful psychopath who says that he really wants to change and look at the harm that he has caused is being glib and deceitful, and there is no way that he can be anything other than glib and deceitful. The problem is similar to the philosophical language trick of asking someone if he is a liar – whatever he says cannot be believed.

The difficulty with the PCLR psychopathy issue is that although the scoring of psychopathy on the basis of the Hare checklist is an empirical scientific process and therefore carries the weight, power and reliability of empirical science, nevertheless the implication that psychopaths are untreatable because of a high PCLR score is an interpretation, and an irrefutable interpretation at that. The protestations of the individual at the unfairness of the influence of the PCLR score can be interpreted as psychopathic behaviour, further evidence of the interpretation. The effort legally to challenge rehabilitation or release decisions based on the PCLR score will be further interpreted as evidence of psychopathy. The effort to get to grips with the literature by the individual or his representative is prevented and will be further interpreted as psychopathic.

The score may be scientific, but the interpretation is not scientific. The score is objective and refutable. The methodology of the test, its inter-rater reliability and its relation to actual risk are all refutable, and therefore scientific. The application of the findings to a particular individual or to a group of individuals is an interpretation. As an interpretation, it is potentially irrefutable, and therefore mere opinion, not scientific evidential fact. The interpretation of the test score to support a hypothesis of untreatability is not scientific because it is not refutable. The problem is that the interpretation is mistaken as being as scientific as the score itself and that, as a generality – and for a huge cohort of people – the interpretation is mistaken as a scientific reason to exclude from treatment, and so to exclude from an opportunity for rehabilitation and release.

A more clinical approach sees the PCLR score as a contribution to a clinical picture, rather than the only determinant of it. This more holistic clinical approach is the one taken in Grendon, and the one that will be taken in the DSPD programme. The PCLR will make an important contribution to overall assessment, along with other risk and personality disorder diagnostic instruments, clinical opinion, previous history, mental state, observed behaviour, and so on.

The second criticism of the PCLR industry and associated folklore is psychodynamic. Working with offenders and perpetrators is a difficult business. Sometimes these people have done hateful things, and it can be difficult to manage one's own personal sense of disgust and revulsion. One way of doing this is to split the perpetrator population into a group who can be helped and who are worthy of attention, and into another group who are purely hateful, and to be despised and feared. Constructing a 'truly despicable' group can be helpful and valuable as a tool to be able to work with other slightly less despicable people. The high PCLR scorers fulfil this function very well; the rhetoric in reports and the literature about this group seems to be a litany of the evil that men can do and be, applied to an individual seemingly unrelated to the client who is being referred to. The phenomenon of the group of untreatable psychopaths is an illustration of organisational splitting and projection (described above), which may be helpful in the short term, but which damages the whole in the longer term.

A psychodynamic approach to psychopathy starts from a different position and might go something like this. During development, the individual needs to find ways of managing frustration, anxiety and rage, and different people will develop different defensive styles. Psychopathy is an example of a defensive constellation that includes a disavowal of vulnerability, attachment and empathy which can be quite extreme. There is an assumption that the more extreme and rigid the defensive structure, the more fragile and fragmented the ego that is being defended. The therapeutic task is to explore the nature of the defensive structure, and then the reasons for the ego fragility, so that some change can be brought about. The strength and rigidity of the psychopathic defensive structure reflects the need of a weak fragile ego that has to erect a vast and frightening outer shell to protect it. The task of the therapist is simply to get down beneath the defensive shell and begin a dialogue with the part of the client that is the weak fragile ego. Clinically, this is the experience: that in a psychodynamic setting of sufficient intensity the biggest and baddest psychopaths can be reached, even if fleetingly.

One of the features of psychopaths that makes cognitively-orientated psychotherapists wary of them is their propensity to lie and be deceitful. In particular, there is anxiety that the psychopath may feign progress while actually not engaging in treatment. Cognitive therapeutic treatments need to assume a positive motivation for change in the individual who approaches the programme; they need to assume that homework will be done and they have to take at face value the client's claims. Such features are not of concern to a psychodynamic treatment, which works under the assumption that duplicitousness, impulsivity, manipulativeness, grandiosity, lying, poor accountability and lack of empathy are characteristic of all personalities, including that of the therapist. These traits are assumed to be present in anyone, to a greater or lesser degree, and the therapy is designed to get underneath these superficial defensive processes. Psychodynamic therapy assumes that it is the human condition for a person to be lying to him- or herself all the time, so tackling these factors in a psychopathic client, whatever his or her presenting symptoms, is the everyday work of the psychodynamic method. The psychodynamic distinction between manifest content (what is said) and latent content (what is meant) provides a theoretical underpinning to the culture of trying to get underneath the surface statements, and not taking them at face value.

A second factor is the dismantling of the 'bogey man' dynamic. From a psychodynamic perspective, the contents of a psychopath's rap-sheet are similar to the contents of a normal person's unconscious fantasy life. A psychodynamic model of the psyche involves terrible and dark forces and violent and perverse fantasies that are expunged from consciousness by a variety of processes; so both the psychopath and the therapist are guilty of the despicable, be it in fantasy or reality. The task is to understand why, for the psychopath, the fantasy has to be enacted or why the usual empathetic channels that normally act as a barrier to cruelty have had to be dismantled. The ego-defence theory of psychopathy (Meloy 1988) conceptualises the symptomatology as a reaction to an attachment disorder, in turn a result of extreme early trauma. If an individual is subjected to extreme trauma, an adaptive response might be simply to shut down feeling – to stop having feelings at all. Without feelings, a conception of one's own feelings or a conception that the victim has feelings, the usual constraints on ill-treatment of others are collapsed. Little boys pull the legs off spiders; psychopaths can do this to people, as if they are not sentient beings. Both the trauma and the attachment disorder can be explored and to some extent mitigated by an attachment to a therapeutic process.

This discussion responds to the question of whether Grendon is effective with high PCLR scorers by undermining the legitimacy of the question, by asking why this group should be any different from any other group. It articulates the ways that psychodynamic treatment identifies and treats psychopathy in more normal personalities, and just carries on this work with those psychopaths empirically at high risk. Empirically, the question is much more difficult. There is evidence that those who drop out of treatment in the first six months are more psychopathic, and that Grendon's efficacy data summarised above might be for a less psychopathic group. There is anecdotal evidence both ways, of high scorers who have returned to Grendon, been struggled with for a few more years, and precipitated an incident in exactly the same way as they did previously, implying little progress. The collective clinical view is that some do progress and, even if they struggle to progress in terms of their behaviour, they are nevertheless reached: this makes a psychological difference. These are small steps.

Auditing a therapeutic community

One of the paradoxes of the psychoanalytic setting is the combination of rigidity and fluidity. Sessions will take place quite rigidly at a fixed time with a fixed duration, and with a consistent task – for the patient to free-associate while the analyst listens with free-floating attention, and for both to try to understand the material. However, the spoken content of this rigid setting may be wholly anarchic and chaotic, and very different from session to session, from patient to patient and from analyst to analyst. Therapeutic community practice has a similar paradox between the structured and the free, with a regular structure of community meetings and small groups on the one hand, and unpredictability and diversity of content and culture on the other. As Grendon is in the criminal justice system, accreditation with the Home Officer Joint Accreditation Panel is as I mentioned earlier the major vehicle of clinical governance, and this has required the twin tasks of describing the programme and structuring an audit process. The main difficulty with this process has been the nigh impossible task of defining the model of therapy of the therapeutic community, as this represents a central and live problem in the work. Compared to this, the process of developing an audit structure has been relatively straightforward, to the extent that it has been about capturing the structure of the treatment rather than what happens in it.

On behalf of the Association of Therapeutic Communities (ATC), Kennard and Lees (2001) devised an audit checklist that identifies required structures and draws conclusions about culture, thus giving a score for the therapeutic community. For example: All members (staff and clients) can question managerial issues, psychological processes, group and institutional dynamics; for example, client members can question why staff members are grumpy, why a staff member is leaving, why a meeting is cancelled, etc… Solutions to problems are discussed and understood in the community before action is taken… This basic structure has been used to form the backbone of both the Home Office Accreditation Panel audit structure for democratic therapeutic communities, as well as forming a large part of the ATC's audit process in the Health Service. In order to explore this further, some background will be necessary to introduce the different context of audit in the different fields.

A Home Office Accredited programme usually has its audit structure broken up into four areas, which are co-incident with the four distinct managerial functions that are involved in the running of a psychological therapy programme in an organisational setting. The first of these concerns 'programme management', and consists of the generic managerial tasks that a psychological treatment structure would require – an undisturbed room; administrative support; staff to be released and prisoners to be freed up to be able to be brought to the sessions and so on. These management tasks are framed in terms of quantifiable deliverables – How often was a group understaffed? Does the room have a flip chart? – and together comprise the programme management section of the audit. Because this represents generic management, in a prison setting, the 'programme manager' is likely to be a governor. The second segment concerns 'treatment management', consisting of the more professional standards aspects of the programme. These might include ensuring that all staff are appropriately qualified; that requisite training courses have been attended; that the treatment materials are available; that staff attend the supervision sessions that are required, and so on. Again, these parameters are framed in measurable terms and given scores. Because many of these issues are professional variables, the treatment manager is often the psychologist. The third is 'quality management' – with the more nebulous and subjective focus on the quality of the treatment delivered. Some of this can be measured – each session is taped and a proportion reviewed by auditing staff to gauge adherence to the programme. Other sources of evidence about quality include written reports and the accounts of staff and clients. These more evanescent criteria are in the realm of professional and subjective expert opinion rather than being operationalised, and scores are given in the judgement of the panel – [expert audit or accreditation panel]. The fourth is more straightforward, consisting of 'through-care management' – auditing the processes of linking up with external agencies, sending copies of reports and co-ordinating case conferences – which tasks are usually carried out by the probation officer. Again, these are framed in terms of numerically measurable performance indices. For therapeutic communities such as Grendon, many of these parameters are the same as would be required for a cognitive-didactic offending behaviour programme in a prison context. Programme management contains targets for the provision of staff, rooms, goods and services required to run the programme. Treatment management contains required actions and targets for staff training, component disciplines, treatment structures and so on; and the fourth element, through-care, has requirements for external liaison.

For therapeutic communities, the debate takes place in the realm of quality – how to ensure this. In the cognitive programmes, each session is videotaped, with the video pointing at the facilitator. These tapes are sampled and scored on various parameters by auditors when they visit. The argument has been made that it would be inappropriate for small group and community settings to be videoed for later audit scrutiny, because this would have a materially detrimental effect on the therapeutic process. Furthermore, a video quality audit process would generate more than 30 hours of video footage per week per community – prohibitively time-consuming to process. So, the mainstay of the quality audit process of the Home Office programmes – the ability to be able to go back and look at the video of the session – is deemed not possible in a therapeutic community setting. Thus the task has been to devise an alternative, and this has evolved into a bilateral process. The first side is that the panel needs to be sure that there is a quality therapeutic community process taking place. To achieve this, the external ATC auditors can apply the Kennard Lees Audit Checklist (KLAC), described above. This will produce a score relating to the general level of functioning of the therapeutic community considered as a whole. The problem is that, from a criminological perspective, this is not enough; there is a need to demonstrate specifically that criminogenic factors are being effectively tackled.

In the different descriptions of models of therapy described above, three broad models were proposed. Model 1 was that the therapeutic community treats personality disorder in general, and antisocial personality disorder in particular; Model 2 proposed that the therapeutic community specifically targeted criminogenic need and Model 3 suggested that the therapeutic community was itself a mutative treatment environment, that individuals liable to offend can be immersed in a therapeutic community environment and will emerge changed and different – less dangerous and risky if the starting problem is antisocial behaviour. If this third model of therapy holds sway, then the only necessary quality measure is that of the quality of the therapeutic community process. If this is good, then people immersed in it will improve. A good score on the KLAC is the only necessary quality requirement. The critique of this view from the criminologists is that this is insufficiently detailed. More detail of the actual treatment process is required to be audited in terms of quality. Effectively, it is insufficient to demonstrate the quality of therapeutic community practice; it is also necessary to produce evidence of the quality of the process of targeting criminogenic need and to audit it. The task was to find a way of demonstrating that targeting this need was taking place to an external observer.

So a new model of therapy needed to be developed: one that explained the treatment process in terms of criminogenic need and identified clear points at which criminogenic need was identified and tackled, and could itself be rated in terms of how effective it was. As mentioned above, the crucial features that were identified were the recognition of offence re-enactments taking place during community life; the lateral linkage between aspects of daily community life, so that things happening in one sphere would be relayed and then explored in different settings; the iterative process of enrichment of understanding the offence and responsibility for it that can be seen to be developing over time and the communication and awareness of offending profiles for community members across staff and client groups.

With this alternative model of therapy, audit trials could be established for each of the parameters. Offence re-enactments would be recorded as incidents, and in the group and community write-ups there would be a record of the linkage of this with the index offence. A offence re-enactment taking place in education could be tracked back across the minutes of the different meetings – the community meeting, the small group, the staff meeting – to demonstrate this lateral linkage element. By selecting several residents to review in detail, the auditor might become familiar with the criminogenic profiles of several inmates, then follow the course of the evolution of understanding of their offending by interviewing staff and inmates and following the exploration of the individual criminogenic factors through the sequence of small group write-ups. Staff and residents' levels of awareness of their fellow community members could be assessed via semi-structured group interviews, asking staff and inmates about the residents who have been chosen to be reviewed in depth. In effect, the criminogenic audit is a qualitative study on the extent to which a given therapeutic community setting is impacting criminogenic factors, exploring the validity of the different elements in the model of change.

The therapeutic community quality network

In the Health Service, the temperament and flavour of the quality initiatives have been different from and softer than those of the criminal justice or Home Office public sector. In the ATC there was a recognition that there was a need to develop some form of quality assurance structure, and initially plans were laid to develop an accreditation model similar to that which operated in the Prison Service. There was a concern, however, that this model was over-centralist and paternalist, and that the notion of an expert panel sitting in judgement on the clinical practice of members of the community of communities was congruent neither with therapeutic community culture nor with the broader Health Service professional and clinical managerial culture.

A model that fitted much better was that of the 'quality network' – which involves a facilitated peer review process. Such a quality network involves three stages. The first is the development of a set of standards of current good practice that can be used as an audit benchmark. This has now been developed and consulted and is in regular use, with a structure of review and updating. The items in the audit can be summarised as 'KLAC plus' – i.e. they comprise the backbone of the Kennard Lees Audit Checklist with other parameters and dimensions added on that are pertinent to the delivery of an actual residential service.

Developing these standards is itself an iterative process with members of the network. The second step involves setting up a peer review and audit structure. In the case of therapeutic communities, staff and residents from one community visit other communities and assess their performance against the standards that had been developed and by reference to their own experience of practice. The purpose of the audit visit is to feed back to the client community suggestions and comments on their practice. These suggestions and comments would be to inform, enlighten and perhaps challenge the client community rather than to be scrutinised in public or by a third party.

The third element is to gather together members of the quality network to feed back and share in general the results and recommendations for good practice that are emerging in the audit process, thus facilitating a process of continuous improvement and innovation in standards of practice. These yearly 'network conferences' become a central focus, and complete the audit loop in the yearly audit cycle.

The content of the ATC's standards document has been largely derived from the KLAC document developed from the Home Office, and described above, along with other more general quality patient care and residential practice guidelines. At the time of writing, the first cycle of the process is taking place, with standards agreed, and cross-community audit visits taking place.

CHAPTER 9

Looking Forwards and DSPD

The Dangerous and Severe Personality Disorder (DSPD) initiative is the British version of a development that is taking place in a number of jurisdictions to address the problem of people who remain so dangerous at the end of their custodial sentences that there is a high level concern about their being released. Currently, when very dangerous people are released, all that can be done is for the police to be informed of the concern and for society to hope that they are picked up for a minor misdemeanour that can legitimise a further period of incarceration rather than a further murder or other major offence.

Current practice is that, as a very dangerous person approaches release from a sentence, and where there is a sense of a clear personality disorder or mental illness making the individual refractory to any risk reduction rehabilitative programme, that person is referred to forensic psychiatry. The question raised is whether detention under the Mental Health Act can be justified, with transfer to a high security hospital where the person can remain until there is some evidence of a reduction of the risk that he or she presents, rather than being released at the ending of an arbitrary length of time determined when sentenced. The problem with this approach is that in part it offends against natural justice. The individual serves his sentence as *lex talionis* for his crime then, just at the end, the goal posts are moved several miles and he finds himself facing an indefinite length of time incarcerated, albeit in a different environment.

The other difficulty with this approach is that, as mentioned above in Chapter 1, the pathology of personality disorder fits uneasily into a mental health frame, and this has resulted in the last decade in a steady reduction in services available for personality disordered people in the public sector, reflected perhaps most notably in a reduction in transfers of personality disordered people from prison to hospital settings in the forensic field. This reduction may be for many reasons, including a strong policy focus in the 1990s on concentrating mental health services on the 'severely mentally ill' –

meaning those with Axis 1 disorders – psychosis, schizophrenia and depression.

Perhaps more important are the cultural sequelae of the 'care programme approach' which firmly ensconce the medical model of mental disorder, with the patient conceived as helpless and the carer given all the responsibility for the patient's continued welfare. For more classically medical mental illnesses, such as schizophrenia, where there is a clear link between personal welfare and regular compliance with an anti-psychotic drug regimen, it is important for the responsibility for the outcome to lie with the carer. Personality disorders are by their nature unpredictable and thus the effects of treatment will also be unpredictable. The chaotic complexity of personality, its pathological aspects, and the relation of these to external events are something that no carer can predict or control. The only person who can begin to do so is the person him- or herself. Personality disorder does not sit easily in a frame of carer responsibility, and the refusal of forensic psychiatrists to take on care responsibility and to treat this group, reflected in the falling rates of transfer for this diagnosis, confirms this.

With personality disordered people, unpredictability is a foundational aspect of the pathology and, as mentioned above, the establishment, re-establishment or re-emphasis of the individual's responsibility for his or her own actions and responsibility for his or her own predicament is a central treatment focus and goal. In the current culture of adverse incident inquiry and (arguably) blame when things go wrong, both the attribution of responsibility and the unpredictability of the pathology weigh against clinicians agreeing to take responsibility for the care of personality disordered patients. Perhaps one of the few predictable things about working with the personality disordered is that there are sure to be adverse incidents with a Grendon-type client group, often quite severe.

In this setting some form of DSPD or dangerous offender legislation provides a conceptual bridge between normal criminals who can be detained during a sentence and released at the end in the reasonable hope that they will not return to prison on the one hand and, on the other, people who by virtue of a mental illness can be detained under mental health legislation until an improvement in their clear mental illness means there is a reduction in their level of risk to others. An example is the difference between a man of formerly good character serving a sentence for manslaughter having killed a fellow driver in an accident while driving home drunk one evening and a man with schizophrenia driven to kill prostitutes by his hallucinatory voices when psychotic, but who is quite normal when adequately medicated so that the voices are gone.

I have suggested above in Chapter 1 that a significant contributor to the momentum that established Grendon was the development of the first modern Mental Health Act in 1959. In the same way, a significant impetus to the development of the DSPD treatment in England has been the process of overhaul of the Mental Health Act that has been in the formative stages over the late 1990s (Henderson 1999). The process of developing legislation to encompass the interface between the law and mind or mental illness throws up a huge dilemma about what to do about those people who are not mad in the psychiatric sense, but are mad in every other – those with severe personality disorder. Arguably, in the 1950s, the solution was Grendon; in the 1990s it is DSPD.

A second impetus has been some of the difficulties that have been experienced by the personality disorder units in the special hospitals. In the late 1990s, there were the Daggett allegations about the Personality Disorder Unit in Ashworth Hospital in Liverpool – an aggrieved patient alleged the distribution of pornography and the grooming of children by paedophiles in the Unit – the children being brought in as visitors. In fact, given the severity of disturbance that is contained by the UK High Secure Personality Disorder Units, the number of disasters have been few; but those that there have been have become high profile, with a series of investigations and recommendations. Indeed, there is a sense that each decade there will be a high profile problem and a response. Sequentially, the recommendations of one set of investigations will advocate a more austere and structured regime, creating allegations of brutality. When these allegations are investigated, a more therapeutic and relaxed regime is recommended. Almost inevitably, this more therapeutic regime is then perverted, leading to a problem (such as the Daggett issues) and the pendulum swings again to advocating more structure and authoritative austerity.

During the Ashworth inquiry (Fallon *et al.* 1999), the team extended their remit to looking at other models of care. This included the TBS (Terbeschikkingstelling) system in the Netherlands, where there is a clear division of offenders into three distinct streams: those with mental illness in hospitals, those with personality disorder in the TBS system, and normal prisoners. This survey also included Grendon, which was another model – the development of a specialist treatment facility within the prison structure itself. Gradually a consensus emerged that the answer was to develop a specialist system for those with personality disorder, subsequently termed DSPD, and the debate turned from this to how it would be structured.

The third impetus seems to be taken by many as the prime mover, namely the Stone case. In brief, this was the horrible murder of a mother and one of her daughters, with a second daughter left barely alive. The case gripped the nation's attention. It emerged that the perpetrator, Michael Stone, had been around psychiatric services and, indeed, had received a personality disorder diagnosis, but had either defaulted from care or had not had care provided for him. In short, he was one of thousands of disturbed and dangerous people who fell between the two stools of health and criminal justice. From a health perspective, he was a difficult and dangerous man, with psychological disturbance as an ancillary part of the picture. He could be put into the catch-all diagnosis of personality disorder, but was not primarily ill enough to warrant detention under the Mental Health Act. He had not been convicted of an offence at the time, so could not access the custodial rehabilitative sector. Around this case a debate took place between the then Home Secretary and the president of the Royal College of Psychiatrists about who should have been responsible. The Home Secretary and a section of policy-making opinion concluded that it indeed was the responsibility of the clinicians. Apparently, the proposals for the DSPD third service were a response to this failure. An alternative hypothesis is that the thinking had been in train for some time and that the Stone case was a useful illustration of the issue to which the DSPD developments were designed to respond. Something had to be done, there seemed to be a national mandate, and so plans were drawn up.

The clinical context

The 1990s in the UK saw a considerable contraction of services for those with personality disorder. Over the years, many of the large psychiatric hospitals had identified the issue of how to treat in-patients with primarily personality disorder. Because this client group can be quite self-destructive and disturbed, they can be difficult to rehabilitate and discharge, seem refractory to treatment and often require a more psychological treatment environment than was present in most large psychiatric asylum wards. Consequently, in many services a psychiatrist or clinician with a flair for or an interest in the treatment of this group would set up a specialist unit in the hospital, which would perforce have some strong therapeutic community cultural elements. As the large hospitals were closed, these units became unviable and were often also closed. This was not part of a strategy: the whole ethos of in-patient psychiatric care changed to a small number of beds for high dependency, acutely ill patients, rather than the notion of longer-stay beds for larger numbers of people, some of which could easily be earmarked for specialist personality disorder treatment use.

At the same time, as psychiatric care resources were instead placed in the community, there seems to have been a reasonable concern that the community psychiatric teams might get clogged up with providing counselling and psychological support for the 'worried well' – or 'neurotic patients' – or, more probably, those with personality disorder. In some ways, there is a temptation to try to struggle creatively and psychologically with a psychologically troubled or traumatised individual rather than simply to plough through depot medication clinics or chase reluctant mentally ill patients in remission to ensure compliance with medication. Consequently, the policy focus on the severely mentally ill being treated by the community psychiatric services was a way of ensuring that the chronic psychotic population who had been re-established in the community by virtue of the efficacy of long-term anti-psychotic medication did not fall through community services, default on their treatment, and so end up back in hospital.

Part of the rigour with which this policy was applied must be related to the fact that personality disordered people are often difficult and unrewarding to treat, so that there is a large constituency in the psychiatric field for whom their exclusion from services is emotionally congruent. And so, over the period of implementation of psychiatric community care, those with chronic and enduring psychological treatment needs from their personality disorder had to be contained by GP surgeries (leading perhaps to the explosion in the number of GP counsellors) or by other voluntary counselling agencies such as the Samaritans.

There were some personality disorder services available. Small services consisting of a part-time medical consultant psychiatrist in psychotherapy with a largely educative remit to train junior psychiatrists, and two or three specialist inpatient units, namely the Cassel Hospital, Francis Dixon Lodge and the Henderson, existed. Indeed, Henderson Hospital successfully argued a case for being the provider of a national specialist service and became, in the late 1990s, the national provider of personality disorder services, with funding to build two new Henderson Hospital clones in the Midlands; but, again, this illustrated the move of personality disorder services away from being part of local psychiatric services.

For personality disorder services to survive in the years of the internal market in the Health Service, they had to argue that they were offering a specialised service. The term 'Severe Personality Disorder' was coined by the Henderson and the Cassel hospitals to distinguish between two different groups. One group was people with personality disorder who could just melt away to be treated by cognitive therapists, GP counsellors and the voluntary sector. The other group remained a headache for the psychiatric catchment area services. This second group would be those who posed a severe self-harm risk, who would end up detained under the Mental Health Act and would self-harm because they had been detained; who would then be discharged from the Mental Health Act, and would harm themselves because they had been discharged from the provisions of the Mental Health Act. Patients who would self harm as any plans towards discharge from hospital were made; patients who would be admitted on a 'revolving door' – in and out every few weeks as their intense engagements in a sequence of relationships or activities would collapse. These sorts of patients mobilised psychiatrists to lobby for the expensive specialist services offered by the Cassell and Henderson, and the term Severe Personality Disorder oiled the wheels of funding committee deliberations.

It was clear that the personalities identified in the criminal justice sector were very similar, but with an externally aggressive symptom cluster rather than a self-damaging one. Health Service severe personality disordered patients cut themselves; criminal justice severe personality disordered people cut other people. The aetiology of identity disorder and confusion is similar, the expressed symptom cluster is different. The distinction between the people with severe personality disorders in the Health Service and those who concerned the Home Office was that the latter were dangerous to others – so the term 'Dangerous and Severe Personality Disorder' was born.

In the secure sector, the issue of personality disorder treatment had not been dismantled because each of the special hospitals had a proportion of their patients detained under the Mental Health Act with a diagnosis of personality disorder. Each of the three special hospitals had personality disorder units with some, such as Woodstock Ward in Broadmoor, being identified as centres of excellence, but there was concern that, on the one hand, these units seemed to be accident-prone, as mentioned above; and, second, that it was difficult to identify an objective threshold which warranted admission. Perhaps because the Mental Health Act requires the personality disordered individual to have a degree of treatability to justify detention, the judgement of how treatable an individual is is rather subjective; investigating the Daggett allegations, Fallon et al. (1999) described the process as a 'treatment lottery'.

While the Prison Service had its problems, it seemed to be a safer pair of hands in terms of the containment and management of personality disordered individuals than the special hospitals. The Grendon unit, with its 230 beds, seemed less accident-prone than some of the special hospital units (at least it did prior to the three escapes in 2001), in spite of very much more in the way of resources being ploughed into the latter, and Grendon's being very much larger as a discrete unit. A view emerged that the best option might be a 'third service' – ideally with the clinical acumen of the forensic health service and with the structural and procedural solidity and safety of the Prison Service. The initial White Paper identified the options of placement in the Prison Service, the Health Service or an entirely distinct and new third service.

The evolving DSPD project

The response to the White Paper was a flurry of anxiety about the human rights aspect, with well people who at some point had been told they had a personality disorder fretting in front of the TV news cameras about whether they were going to be locked up indefinitely. This centre of public debate was misguided for two reasons. First, out of the 75,000 or so people in prison or secure psychiatric care in England and Wales, the DSPD group had been identified (by combining statistics on prevalence of antisocial personality disorder with indices of risk pretty similar to aspects of the Hare Psychopathy Checklist) as 2000 or so people who were effectively the most dangerous people in the country. The clear sense was that the detention order was for those who were extremely dangerous. For this group, the proposed order was indeed tough, with unlimited detention until there was evidence of improvement sufficient to allow rehabilitation.

Second, the panic that people might be locked up for ever without having committed a crime seemed odd to psychiatrists who, under the Mental Health Act, quite regularly lock up people who have not offended. The legislation would indeed be tough, but the threshold would be very high so those detained would have long criminal histories of both prosecuted and unprosecuted crimes.

There was a recognition that the questions to which the development team had to find answers were rather large; for example, defining DSPD. The strategy adopted was to get the ball rolling by trialling pilot sites and treatments in different settings. A prison and a health service unit were selected for pilot units and are currently in the process of establishment. At the same time, work was being done about conceptualising the notion of DSPD, in part driven by the task of putting together an assessment programme that would indeed distinguish those with severe personality disorder who presented a high risk from others who either had just a severe personality disorder or were a high risk but didn't have a personality disorder.

The European Declaration on Human Rights states that people can only be deprived of their liberty as part of a criminal justice punishment process or in order to be treated. The DSPD legislation would retain people for the latter rather than the former reason, so it becomes clear that the emphasis would have to be on treatment. As a result, the policy thinking veered over to the health side rather than the prison, a move that was amplified by the use of the new Mental Health Act as the vehicle by which the new legislation would be introduced. People being specifically detained for treatment cannot be housed in prison settings, so the DSPD pilots being built in prisons would have to have a discrete entrance or be separate in some way. The new draft Mental Health Act had two parts, the first for normal psychiatric practice and the second for DSPD. This precipitated a storm of protest from the psychiatric profession who objected to being conceived of as agents of public control; but the vision for DSPD underwritten by a comprehensive Mental Health Act was coherent, if professionally unpopular.

In the meantime, plans were afoot to identify resources in the community that could be accessed for DSPD people in the later stages of their treatment. It became clear that there was little in the way of structured treatment programmes because of the policy of withdrawing services for this group in the 1990s. In response, an expert panel was convened to develop a national strategy for the treatment of personality disorder, which published its deliberations and proposals in 2003, *Personality Disorder: No Longer a Diagnosis of Exclusion (NIMH 2003)*. In brief, this document required each NHS trust to have an identifiable lead service for the treatment of personality disorder, a necessary first step to establish a foundation on which DSPD community services can be developed.

The Department of Health's previous foray into services for those with severe personality disorder had been to commission the two new Henderson Hospital clones in the Midlands, and it seemed as though an alternative model had been identified as more cost-effective – therapeutic community Henderson-type work carried out in a day hospital setting, enabling patients to be engaged in an intensive psychological treatment for a fraction of the cost of an in-patient programme. This seems to be the vision of the future, that each major mental health provider will have some form of personality disorder treatment facility, ideally in some form of day hospital therapeutic community format, contributed to by the various psychological therapy resources available locally. This facility in time will treat personality disordered clients irrespective of whether their symptom expression is centred round self- or other harm – whether they would traditionally be known as generic or forensic.

A fairly clear definition of what a DSPD person is and the broad structure of the treatment were developed within the frame of the draft Mental Health Act. A DSPD person would have a greater than 50 per cent chance of serious re-offending, which would be identified by a battery of actuarial tests. This person would also have either very severe psychopathy (identified by scoring 30 or more on the PCLR, or more than one personality disorder evident, the personality disorders being diagnosed clinically and also via actuarial testing. If the person has both these attributes, making him or her of very high risk and with personality disorder, the task is to identify whether there is a link between the aspects of the personality disorder and the offending.

If, for example the individual is a paedophile, and has a schitzotypal personality disorder, living in a world of heavy and detailed fantasy, then the question for the Mental Health Tribunal (a quasi-judicial body who will determine suitability for detention under the Mental Health Act) would have been to determine whether there is a link between the personality disorder characteristics and the risk of offending. If the person's detailed fantasy is about Star Trek and learning Klingon, and his offences are opportunistic, when looking after children, for example, then the link will not be made. The risk is not related to the identified personality disorder. If the content of the detailed fantasy life in which the individual lives is about sadistic sexual treatment of children, then it may be.

The programme would have been structured as follows. Referral sources would have been from the multi-agency public protection panels in the community, from prisons or from secure health settings. Those who passed an initial triage process would have been admitted to an assessment unit where they would have spent three months taking actuarial tests and being clinically interviewed. Following this, the evidence gathered was to be presented to the Mental Health Tribunal, and the determination of DSPD status made. Those who were detained as DSPD would be transferred to a treatment setting with the opportunity to engage in the treatment programme. It is recognised that not everyone would wish to engage in treatment and, because the patient's consent is required to administer psychological treatments, he or she would have the opportunity of being looked after while refusing treatment. Because of the framing of the process under the Mental Health Act, these units were most likely to be like current high secure hospital provision, and the levels of cost per year are envisaged to be closer to high secure Health Service costs than prison or Grendon costs.

The treatment regime itself, its culture and ideology, is likely to be locally determined, although there are some influential models that are floating around. One influential model is the Dialectic Behaviour Therapeutic approach, a combination of an Eastern philosophical attitude with a monitoring and control of the disorganised emotional states that can accompany personality disorder (see Linehan et al. 1994). A second approach has been emerging simultaneously in several different centres, for example Hare's Psychopathy Programme (Hare 1991) and Wong's Violence Reduction Programme (2003). In brief, these models propose that the particular issue for psychopaths is that of their responsivity to the programme. If they want to engage in it genuinely, rather than duping the programme leaders that they do, and that they are making progress; if they take it seriously, then they might benefit. The task is to get them to take it seriously, and this can be achieved (according to the programme) by debate and negotiation.

The second major element of the psychopathy programmes is a behavioural focus on the main antisocial symptom, namely violence, and its treatment. Wong's approach, in his assessment tool, the violence risk scale, and the programme, helpfully dissolves the 'tombstone' feel of PCLR-type definition of psychopathy, where assessment of risk is largely based upon 'static risk factors' – previous offence history, which cannot be changed. The Wong programme distinguishes these from 'dynamic risk factors' – things that contributed to the offences (such as mental health problems, etc.) that can be mitigated, reducing risk – and focuses on tackling these (Wong 2003; Wong and Hare in press).

Once the DSPD person is making progress, he descends from high secure care to medium secure: again with the Health Service model firmly in mind, to equivalents of Regional Secure Units, and again with several pilots in the process of being developed. Following this there will be a stage of hostel or minimal supervision accommodation in the community, with a requirement that the individual continues to attend some form of personality disorder treatment programme in the community. The nature and shape of these services has yet to be determined, but day hospital type therapeutic community combined with a more standard type of out-patient care seems a strong possibility.

At the time of writing, there seems to have been a change in the vision, such that the overarching structure of Part Two of the Mental Health Act driving the DSPD service will probably not have the central role that had been envisaged. Instead, the old criterion of 'treatability' will be removed from the Mental Health Act. Personality disordered people can only be detained under the 1983 act if deemed 'treatable'. This will allow people to be detained by virtue of their risk, rather than solely in relation to treatment of their psychopathology.

The success of the pilot sites in their respective prison and high secure health settings seem to have become the main drivers, and it seems that the DSPD co-ordination function at the centre has become strategic rather than executive or managerial. The DSPD project is a strategy for dealing with DSPD people in different settings, prison and health, rather than being a discrete and integrated centrally driven programme. It would appear that people with DSPD may be detained under the Mental Health Act within high secure health settings, or they may be transferred to prison units operating DSPD programmes if they are already serving prisoners. As such, the two groups of DSPD people will be treated in parallel, and rehabilitative programmes from the health and criminal justice sectors will be used in parallel and developed by the central strategy group to meet the needs of this difficult population.

Grendon and DSPD

The initial estimate of the number of people with DSPD being about 2500 in England and Wales was made on the basis of combining data from the recent survey of psychiatric morbidity (Office of National Statistics 1998) with centralised data of offending nationally, expressed as static risk factors. Using the same methodology, Grendon's population was surveyed, and it was found that between 110 and 160 of this 2500 were currently in Grendon. Between 50 per cent and 75 per cent of Grendon's men would be defined as DSPD (Henderson 1999). This figure raised a paradox because, clinically, few Grendon men could be put into the DSPD category; it is probable that if they were sent to an assessment centre, few of them would get over the threshold. This seems to be related to two factors. First, people who come to Grendon have, to some degree at least, recognised that they have a problem and that they need some help to do something about it. There is, in Grendon men, a degree of recognition of personal responsibility for the problems that they have caused to others and to themselves. Of course, this is not complete nor necessarily entirely sincere – but it is present in some form. This acknowledgement of a degree of agency in his difficulties and the request for help in itself is a significant step that reduces the risk that the person represents. Conceived in psychiatric terms, it represents a degree of insight into the problem of the personality disorder that he has.

The second way of looking at the paradox is that Grendon men in their earlier years probably would have passed the assessment centre threshold. Had the diagnosis of DSPD been in existence ten or twenty years before, between 50 and 75 per cent of Grendon's population would have a DSPD order. The difference is that they are now five or ten or twenty years on, and they have mellowed with age, or been softened by experience with the criminal justice system or, with life experience, they have got more of a grip on what is going on. Whatever the cause, the Grendon men of today are the DSPD people of five or ten years ago. The first cohort of DSPD people will seem refractory, impossible and very dangerous now, but after five or ten years of stretching the system to breaking point, they will look more like Grendon men and begin to be interested in reflecting on what has happened in their lives, and why they are where they are.

The big difference between those men who come to Grendon and those who would be judged by the Mental Health Tribunal as suitable for a DSPD order is that Grendon men are motivated to receive treatment. In the discussion above about assessment and about the way that treatment works, a theme running through the whole fabric is that of motivation for treatment. The assessment process is assessing motivation for treatment as the most important variable that is present. It may be fledgling, and it may be hidden behind a bravado of wanting to come to Grendon for 'easy bird' on the one hand, or hidden behind a simpering wish to make 'no more victims' on the other. Irrespectively, the assessment process tests motivation for treatment as does every subsequent aspect of treatment. If a resident transgresses the rules, the only stick that there is to encourage him to look at the meaning of what he's done is that, if he does not, he will be discharged. The only stick that there is to encourage people to come to groups and community meetings at all is that if they do not, this will be questioned by the community, and they risk being discharged. So in a therapeutic community context, motivation for treatment is a sort of glue that holds the whole process together. This motivation is likely to be absent in most of those newly diagnosed as having DSPD, so a Grendon-type treatment for DSPD people would not be appropriate. The hope is that gradually, for DSPD people, the recognition of the need for treatment and the motivation to engage in treatment will grow during the detention – perhaps fuelled by a realisation that there will effectively be no way out until there is a real reduction in the risk that they present, and that the only way to achieve this will be engagement in such treatments.

So it may be that at the point of moving on from high secure to medium secure treatment, DSPD people may become more interested in and open to a Grendon-type approach, delivered perhaps in Grendon or the new Dovegate Prison for those with DSPD in the prison sector, or in some form within the health sector for those detained under the Mental Health Act. Such step-down rehabilitation is likely to remain the minority of Grendon's work for the foreseeable future, so Grendon will continue in its work with sentenced prisoners, providing a service to them and to the Prison Service who find them difficult to manage, in parallel with the developing personality services in the health sector under the Mental Health Act.

Prison therapeutic communities

In the late 1990s, following the publication of the Marshall study demonstrating Grendon's effectiveness (Marshall 1997), the English Prison Service Board committed itself to building and opening two new therapeutic community prison units. In November 2001 the first of these, a 200-bed unit in Dovegate Prison near Burton-on-Trent, was opened, and it is now in the process of building a culture and history. The therapeutic community, which consists of four discrete community units and an assessment and special treatment unit, sits in a larger more normal prison setting run by a private contractor. The therapeutic community section of the prison is based very much on the Grendon template, but run entirely separately. The Dovegate communities differ from Grendon in a number of respects. In the managerial structure, the community therapists are the overall line managers of the units, and the director of therapy is effectively the governorial lead of that section of the prison. This is rather different from Grendon's more matrix managerial structure, with unit management distinguished from clinical leadership, following the Health Service model of clinical organisational management.

There is a cultural difference also: the ideology of the Dovegate communities seems to be more based in a criminology/forensic psychology frame than the clinical/psychiatric/medical one that's Grendon's. Perhaps as a consequence, Grendon's culture is much more 'therapeutic community as an application of psychoanalysis', following the tradition of medical psychotherapy. Dovegate has more of a 'therapeutic community as an application of cognitive psychotherapy' flavour – as might be anticipated from a criminological frame. This change of emphasis is structured in the staffing arrangements, with a multidisciplinary team comprising a lead therapist (most often a forensic psychologist), a probation officer and the custodial 'care officers'. The distinction in Grendon between what was originally the medic/psychiatrist and psychologist, but which subsequently became the psychodynamic psychotherapist and forensic psychologist described in Chapter 5, is not replicated in the Dovegate model. I have argued above that this disciplinary complementarity, with its clear identification of different and at times adversarial ideological approaches, hones the quality of the debate about the patient, and the lack of these added dimensions to the clinical work probably impacts on the work in a way that would be interesting to explore.

A second significant difference between the two units, Grendon and Dovegate, is that in the latter it has been decided not to attempt to treat psychopaths who score above 25 on the PCLR. Again, this reflects a more forensic psychology/criminology perspective than Grendon's broader clinical outlook. This will have a major difference in the functioning of the two units, because it is clear that the higher PCLR scorers are the more trouble-some clients, and Grendon has about half of its residents scoring 25 or above. The decision not to treat this more difficult group, while ostensibly made on the basis of good empirical evidence about its treatability, may actually be more related to the discussion above about the level of disciplinary diversity in each staff team. Grendon has three full-time professional staff per community, a psychotherapist, a psychologist and a probation officer; the Dovegate communities have only two, with the psychotherapist/clinician being the discipline that is not present. Grendon's extra clinical resource and dimension probably enables it to tolerate and work with the extra dimension of disturbance that accompanies the highly psychopathic residents. Dovegate might struggle to contain the more psychopathic individuals that Grendon can because Grendon has more professional input. Similarly Grendon struggles to contain patients with a mixture of personality disorder and mental illness that the high secure hospital personality disorder units can, again because of their increased input of professional expertise.

The second new therapeutic community that has now opened and is in the process of establishing a culture of practice is a unit for women in Winchester Prison. The project plan has been to change the current 90-bedded female part of the prison into some form of therapeutic complex, to include a therapeutic community. This development fills a very large gap in the provision for women. Possibly the commonest question asked by Grendon visitors is whether there is a similar facility to Grendon available for women; well now there is.

The unfortunate closure of the Max Glatt Unit in March 2002 in large part was a result of it being out of kilter with the rest of the prison in which it was housed. Wormwood Scrubbs is now a large local prison, meaning it has a transitory population either on remand and awaiting court proceedings, on short sentences or awaiting transfer to a longer-term facility. The Max Glatt Unit was a treatment facility for longer-term prisoners and in spite of it being the oldest prison therapeutic community was out of place. The two other small therapeutic community units are alive and well, however. A 15-bed unit in Aylesbury Prison caters for youth offenders, and a 30-bed unit in Gartree Prison that caters specifically for life-sentence prisoners in the early stages of their life sentence has a specific niche to cater for.

For almost half a century, Grendon has been quietly helping difficult and disturbed men out of their difficulties and has quietly been an inspiration for staff, demonstrating what is possible, both in terms of humane secure containment and in terms of the treatment of antisocial personality disorder. Most of all Grendon has been quietly showing its residents what is possible for them.

References

American Psychiatric Association (1994) *Diagnostic and Statistical Manual of Mental Disorders Fourth Edition* (DSM-IV). Washington, DC: American Psychiatric Association.

Andrews, D. and Bonta, J. (1994) *The Psychology of Criminal Conduct.* Cincinnati, OH: Anderson.

Barton, W. (1959) *Institutional Neurosis.* Bristol: Wright.

Boyers, R., Orril, R. and Specials, S. (1972) *Laing and Anti-psychiatry.* Harmondsworth: Penguin.

Bion, W.R. (1961) *Experiences in Groups.* London: Tavistock Publications.

Cleckley, T. (1941) *The Mask of Sanity.* St Louis, MO: C.V. Mosby Co.

Copas, J.B., O'Brien, M., Roberts, J. and Whiteley, J.S. (1984) 'Treatment outcome in personality disorder: The effect of social, psychological and behavioural variables.' *Personality and Individual Differences 5,* 565–573.

Cullen, E. (1994) 'Grendon: The therapeutic prison that works.' *Journal of Therapeutic Communities,* 15, 4, 301–310.

Dale, M. (1994) 'Learning organisations.' In C. Mabey and P. Iles (eds) *Managing Learning.* London: Thomson Business Press.

Dolan, B. and Coid, J. (1993) *Psychopathic and Antisocial Personality Disorders, Treatment and Research Issues.* London: Gaskell.

East, W.N. and Hubert, W.H. de B. (1939) *The Psychological Treatment of Crime.* London: Her Majesty's Stationery Office.

Fallon, P., Blueglass, R., Edwards, B. and Daniels, B. (1999) *Report of the Committee of Enquiry into the Personality Disorder Unit, Ashworth Special Hospital.* London: Her Majesty's Stationery Office.

Foucault, M. (1965) *Madness and Civilization: A History of Insanity in the Age of Reason.* London: Tavistock Publications.

Freud, A. (1936) *The Ego and the Mechanisms of Defence.* Revised edn. 1966. London: The Hogarth Press.

Freud, S. (1900) *The Interpretation of Dreams.* Collected Works, Standard Edition, Vols. 4 and 5. London: The Hogarth Press.

Freud, S. (1905) *Three Essays on Sexuality.* Collected Works, Standard Edition, Vol. 7. London: The Hogarth Press.

Freud, S. (1923) *The Ego and the Id.* Collected Works, Standard Edition, Vol. 19. London: The Hogarth Press.

Genders, E. and Player, E. (1995) *Grendon: A Study of a Therapeutic Prison.* Oxford: Clarendon Press.

Goffman, I. (1961) *Asylums: Essays on the Social Situation of Mental Patients and Other Inmates.* New York: Doubleday.

Gunn, J. and Robertson, G. (1987) 'A ten-year follow-up of men discharged from Grendon prison.' *British Journal of Psychiatry 151*, 674–678.

Gunn, J., Robertson, G., Dell, S. and Way, C. (1978) *Psychiatric Aspects of Imprisonment.* London. Academic Press.

Haigh, R. (1999) 'The quintessence of a therapeutic environment.' In P. Campling and R. Haigh (eds) *Therapeutic Communities: Past, Present and Future.* London: Jessica Kingsley Publishers.

Hare, R.D. (1991) *Manual for the Hare Psychopathy Checklist – Revised.* Toronto, Canada: Multi-Health Systems.

Harrison, T. (1999) 'A momentous experiment. Strange meetings at Northfield.' In P. Campling and R. Haigh (eds) *Therapeutic Communities: Past, Present and Future.* London: Jessica Kingsley Publishers.

Henderson, A. (1999) 'DSPD prevalence in Grendon: A survey.' Grendon Internal Paper. Unpublished.

James, O. (1986) 'The role of the nurse/therapist relationship in the therapeutic community.' In R. Kennedy, A. Heyman and L. Tischler (eds) *The Family as Inpatient.* London: Free Association Books.

Jones, L. (1997) 'Developing models for managing treatment integrity and efficacy in a prison-based TC: The Max Glatt Centre.' In E. Cullen, L. Jones and R. Woodward (eds) *Therapeutic Communities for Offenders.* Chichester: John Wiley.

Kennard, D. and Lees, J. (2001) 'Checklist for Democratic Therapeutic Communities.' *Therapeutic Communities 22*, 2, 143–151.

Kennedy, H. (2001) 'Reply to Estella Weldon.' Edward Glover Lecture, Portman Clinic, London.

Kreeger, L. (1994) *The Large Group: Dynamics and Therapy.* London: Karnac.

Lewis, P. (1997) 'Context for change (whilst consigned and confined): A challenge for systematic thinking.' In E. Cullen, L. Jones and R. Woodward (eds) *Therapeutic Communities for Offenders.* Oxford: Clarendon Press.

Laing, R. (1959) *The Divided Self.* London: Tavistock.

Lees, J., Manning, N. and Rawlings, B. (1999) 'Therapeutic community effectiveness.' High Security Psychiatric Services Commissioning Board Briefing Paper.

Linehan, M., Tutek, D., Heard, H. and Armstrong, H. (1994) 'Interpersonal outcome of cognitive behavioral treatment for chronically suicidal borderline patients.' *American Journal of Psychiatry 151*, 1771–6.

Main, T. (1983) 'The concept of the therapeutic community: Variations and Vicissitudes.' In M. Pines (ed) *The Evolution of Group Analysis.* London: Routledge.

Main, T. (1989) *The Ailment and Other Psychoanalytic Essays.* J. Johns (ed) London: Free Association Books.

Manning, N. (1989) *The Therapeutic Community Movement: Charisma and Routinisation.* London: Routledge.

Marshall, P. (1997) *Reduction in Reconviction of Prisoners at HMP Grendon.* Home Office Research Bulletins 61.

Martindale, B., Mörner, M., Rodriguez, M. and Vidit, J. (1997) *Supervision and its Vicissitudes.* London: Karnac.

Martinson, R. (1974) 'What Works? Questions and answers about prison reform.' *The Public Interest 10*, 22–54.

McGuire, J. and Priestley, P. (1995) 'Reviewing "What Works": Past, present and future.' In J. McGuire (ed) *What Works: Reducing Reoffending. Guidelines from Research and Practice.* Chichester: John Wiley and Sons.

Meloy, J. (1988) 'The psychopathic mind: Origins, dynamics and treatment.' Northvale, NJ: Jason Aronson Inc.

Menzies, I. (1988) 'Social systems and defence against anxiety.' In *Containing Anxieties in Institutions. Selected Essays* Vol. 1. London: Free Association Books.

NIMH (National Institute for Mental Health) (2003) *Personality Disorder. No Longer a Diagnosis of Exclusion.* London: HMSO.

Newell, T. (1999) 'Prisons and personality disorder.' Conference presentation. Unpublished.

Newton, M. (1971) 'Reconviction after treatment in Grendon.' Chief Psychologist Report Series B1. In J. Shine (ed) *A Compilation of Grendon Research.* Gloucester: Leyhill Press.

Norton, K. (1992) 'A culture of enquiry: Its preservation or loss.' *International Journal of Therapeutic Communities 13*, 3–25.

Office of National Statistics (1998) *Psychiatric Morbidity Among Prisoners.* London: Government Statistical Service.

Popper, K. (1962) *Conjectures and Refutations.* New York: Basic Books.

Rapoport, R. (1960) *Community as Doctor.* London: Tavistock.

Rice, M., Harris, G. and Cormier, C. (1992) 'An evaluation of a maximum security therapeutic community for psychopaths and other mentally disordered offenders.' *Law and Human Behaviour 16*, 4.

Rogers, C. (1967) *A Therapist's View of Psychotherapy. On Becoming a Person.* London: Constable.

Rosser, R., Birch, S., Bond, H., Denford, J. and Schachter, J. (1987) 'Five year follow-up of patients treated with inpatient psychotherapy at the Cassel Hospital for Nervous Diseases.' *Journal of the Royal Society of Medicine 80*, 9, 549–55.

Segal, H. (1973) *Introduction to the Work of Melanie Klein.* London: The Hogarth Press.

Sereny, G. (1999) *Cries Unheard. The Story of Mary Bell.* London: Pan MacMillan.

Shine, J. (ed) (2000) *A Compilation of Grendon Research.* Gloucester: Lethill Press.

Shine, J. and Morris, M. (1999) *Regulating Anarchy. The Grendon Programme.* Aylesbury: Springhill Press.

Shine, J. and Newton, M. (2000) 'Damaged, disturbed and dangerous: A profile of receptions to Grendon therapeutic prison.' In J. Shine (ed) *A Compilation of Grendon Research.* Gloucester: Leyhill Press.

Skinner, B.F. (1938) *The Behaviour of Organisms.* New York: Appleton-Century-Crofts.

Smartt, U. (2000) *Grendon Tales – Stories from a Therapeutic Community.* Winchester: Waterside Press.

Sofer, C. (1972) *Organisations in Theory and Practice.* London. Heinemann.

Taylor, R. (2000) 'A seven year reconviction study of HMP Grendon therapeutic community.' In J. Shine (ed) *A Compilation of Grendon Research.* Gloucester: Leyhill Press.

Thornton, D. (1998) 'Psychopathic traits and response to different forms of treatment.' Seminar presentation. Unpublished.

Weber, M. (1946) *From Max Weber: Essays in Sociology.* Gerth, H.H. and Wright Mills, C. (eds) London: Routledge.

Whiteley, J.S. (1970) 'The response of psychopaths to a therapeutic community.' *British Journal of Psychiatry 116*, 517–529.

Wong, S. (2003) 'The Violence Reduction Programme.' Unpublished draft.

Wong, S. and Hare, R. (in press) *Program Guidelines for the Institutional Treatment of Violent Psychopathic Offenders.* New York: Multi-Health Systems.

Woolf, H. and Tumin, S. (1991) 'Prison Disturbances', April 1990, Cmd. 1456. London: HMSO.

Yalom, I.D. (1985) *Theory and Practice of Group Psychotherapy* (Third Edition). New York: Basic Book

Subject Index

Author Index